Entrepreneurial Systems for the 1990s

Recent Titles from Quorum Books

Entrepreneurial Systems for the 1990s

THEIR CREATION, STRUCTURE, AND MANAGEMENT

John E. Tropman

&

Gersh Morningstar

Foreword by
SAM ZELL

Q

QUORUM BOOKS

New York • Westport, Connecticut • London

658.42
T856e

Library of Congress Cataloging-in-Publication Data

Tropman, John E.
    Entrepreneurial systems for the 1990s : their creation, structure,
and management / John E. Tropman and Gersh Morningstar ; foreword by
Sam Zell.
        p.   cm.
    Bibliography: p.
    Includes index.
    ISBN 0–89930–288–2 (lib. bdg. : alk. paper)
    1. New business enterprises.   2. Entrepreneurship—United States.
I. Morningstar, Gersh.   II. Title.
HD62.5.T76   1989
658.4′2—dc19   88–15424

British Library Cataloguing in Publication Data is available.

Library of Congress Catalog Card Number: 88–15424
ISBN: 0–89930–288–2

First published in 1989 by Quorum Books

Greenwood Press, Inc.
88 Post Road West, Westport, Connecticut 06881

Printed in the United States of America

The paper used in this book complies with the
Permanent Paper Standard issued by the National
Information Standards Organization (Z39.48–1984).

10 9 8 7 6 5 4 3 2 1

Contents

Figures and Tables

FIGURES

TABLES

Foreword

Professor John E. Tropman was the winner of the Bernard Zell/Leonard W. Lurie Prize Competition in the Teaching of Entrepreneurship for 1986. This competition was created to foster interest in entrepreneurship among students and others. It is designed to create an interest and develop an approach that would lead more individuals to be entrepreneurial regardless of their career. A winner is chosen by selecting the course program that most successfully suggests such an approach. The winner receives a cash award and a one-year appointment at the School of Business Administration at the University of Michigan. During this year, the recipient will devote their time to the development, teaching, and evaluation of their prize-winning program.

Entrepreneural Systems for the 1990s evolved from the intense interest and attention that Professor Tropman directed toward the area of entrepreneurship during his one year tenure at the University of Michigan as the winner of the 1986 prize. As a result of this relationship, Professor Tropman has not only become a significant contributor in this area, but has joined the Awards Committee as a judge assisting us in selecting future recipients.

The subject of entrepreneurship represents an arena with much heat and relatively little light. The successful enterpreneur is much needed and in short supply. Society could gain much by supporting the entrepreneurial impluse.

The effort and attention given this subject reflects the attractiveness of the entrepreneur's performance while at same time continues to puzzle the observer as to how these characteristics are encouraged and perpetuated. Nothing generates economic growth and job creation like an entrepreneurial orientation. Hopefully this book and the continuing activities of an individual like Professor Tropman will help all of us better understand the subject

matter and maybe even find a way to recognize and encourage more entrepreneurial spirit and effort in America.

Sam Zell

THE ENTREPRENEURIAL IMPULSE

In an important sense American society can be called the Entrepreneurial Society. We were founded, after all, by Entrepreneurs—at least of a sort. To be sure, the Pilgrims were not necessarily looking to market a new product; but they were looking to introduce a new service—in their particular case, a religious service. They struck out on their own and against rather staggering odds to make their imprint. They had many of the characteristics we would associate with Entrepreneurs: tolerance of risk and of ambiguity, a certain confidence in their own rightness, and a willingness to give up a good deal to prove the validity of their collective vision to the world and to each other. In that specific sense, it is fair to say they were ambitious. In short, then, they had the Characteristics of Entrepreneurs. They had the Competencies required to launch their venture, and the Conditions and Context were favorable to make it work.[1]

These founding characteristics, as Stinchcombe (1965) points out, are fundamental for all organizations, whether they are clubs, firms, or states and nations. The United States didn't *become* a land of opportunity. It was *born* as a land of opportunity. The very structure and culture of its founding character were entrepreneurial in nature. It is this deep structure that we call the *Entrepreneurial Impulse.*

This Entrepreneurial Impulse has continued to manifest itself throughout our history. The initial Entrepreneurs of religion and salvation quickly fell out; and the process of decentralization, so common among entrepreneurial enterprises began. Route 128 around Boston is lined with all manner of the small firms that have spun off from various high-tech developments in the area. These small firms are merely repeating a historic New England process of community spin-offs, with new communities forming almost as soon as the original is established.

After the initial settling and resettling, agricultural Entrepreneurs and others seeking a better life began the move west. We call them "Pioneers." We can think of them as "lifestyle" Entrepreneurs, pushing for a better and more open setting within which they could conduct their own affairs.

Both the Pilgrims and the Pioneers needed to move away from existing structures that they found inhospitable to their ideas, orientations, and wishes. They found it necessary to establish new structures that in turn were inimical to those who later followed them. Those divestitures, then, removed organizational supports and created a climate in which invention and self-reliance were necessary. In a land of very few people, great distances, and limited overall bureaucratic structure, self-reliance was more than a moral virtue. It was simple necessity. Inventiveness had to be as common as doing the dishes.

In a structured society, both physical and political institutions create conditions favoring these developments. The lack of well-developed and entrenched governments for the Pioneers moving west meant that few rules existed to prohibit or to direct any particular kind of activity. Ready solutions to problems weren't there, so they had to be developed.

As the country became more populated, more structured, more bureaucratic, opportunities for physical mobility as a vehicle for entrepreneurial expression declined, at least in their historical form characterized by Pilgrims and Pioneers. California seems to provide an exception to this general decline. There, cultural entrepreneurship exemplifies the continuation of the Entrepreneurial Impulse. Gevirtz (1985) notes this effect in the following passage:

Hank Riggs, professor of industrial engineering at Stanford, former vice president of Memorex Corporation, and now a member of the board of directors of six small high tech firms, observes: "The single biggest piece of folklore is that Stanford created Silicon Valley. It was really the atmosphere, the cultural climate that did it. Most of the high tech companies didn't come out of Stanford. . . . Silicon Valley is really a social and cultural phenomenon. It has to do with risk taking, acceptance of failure, and change being at the core of that culture. That's why it happened here and not in Cleveland. It's the lack of societal pressure, nobody caring what they think at the country club." (P. 58)

Lest you think it is only California, ingenuity has also been a hallmark of another part of our country. Indeed, *Yankee Magazine* in a special commemorative issue (September 1986) published a special celebration of this history called, "The Genius of New England: Unforgettable Examples of Yankee Ingenuity in All Its Curious Glory." As mentioned, Boston's Route 128 also owes something to this cultural tradition.

In many of its expressions, however, the Entrepreneurial Impulse has become choked and blunted in the contemporary American scene, especially in recent years. We no longer seem to be characterized by the kind of innovation that was once such a strong part of our past. Many large American business firms have come perilously close to failure. Some have failed altogether. All too often these failures occurred because the business leadership was unable to mobilize the necessary new approaches and fresh ideas and to transform these into new products and services that the failed businesses might have offered. A business-as-usual approach continued during a time when business-as-usual meant business failure. It is not surprising, then, that Richard Darman would describe big corporations as "bloated, risk-averse, inefficient, and unimaginative" (Blaustein, 1986).

There is, nevertheless, no decline in the willingness to undertake entrepreneurial adventures in our society. We see examples of it on every hand. It is especially obvious in classes on entrepreneurship that are offered by many of the nation's great universities. Rarely, indeed, is there a student in such classes who has not had some personal entrepreneurial experience. Sam Zell, principal of Equity Financial Management and an eminently practical businessman, believes that there is talent around in quantities that would stagger the imagination if it could be catalogued. We just have to use that talent.

Although the Entrepreneurial Impulse is still to be found in American society, it appears more covert at the moment, more suppressed than it should be for both individuals and society. And therein lies a substantial threat to our future, for in the complex world of the last years of the twentieth century, new ideas, new approaches, new products, and new services all represent the essential ingredients that will permit things to go well. If we fail to supply an appropriate level of innovation, the problems surrounding us nationally and internationally will be overwhelming. James B. Quinn (1979) outlines some of those problems:

1. Feed a new population as large as the world's entire population in 1940 but with less use of chemical fertilizers and pesticides.

2. Develop and deliver as much new energy as has been produced in all history to date—with each increment harder to find and to develop—and yet eliminate acid rain like those which have reached pH_3 levels in Sweden and New England.

3. Meet additional demands for foods, raw materials, and products 100% greater than today with land resources ever more marginal and safe ways of disposal ever more difficult.

4. Generate new capital at an annual rate at least as high as today's, despite the government's preemption of capital for social redistribution.

5. Genuinely improve the living, working, education, urban and environmental habitats in both industrialized and developing countries.

6. Simultaneously increase each nation's health standards, shift from disease cure to

morbidity prevention systems and restrain population growth within reasonable bounds.

7. Employ thirty to fifty percent more people, many in service industries while increasing productivity enough to halt inflation.

8. Accomplish all this without fatally disturbing natural equilibrium or creating resource crises that lead to war. (P. 19)

These are the challenges for the Pilgrims and the Pioneers of today and of the future. Accomplishing objectives like these is what Robert Reich (1983) calls the "next American frontier." Because of our abundance of natural and human resources and because of our special heritage, the United States has special responsibilities to unlock available entrepreneurial talent and to permit it, once again, to be the central hallmark of our society. The Entrepreneurial Impulse is there. The talent is most assuredly there. Indeed, on the American scene at this very moment there is a coterie of potential entrepreneurial performers of unlimited skill and promise. But they are like members of a premiere symphony orchestra without a conductor and without suitable orchestrations—the plan for blending and interlinking of their talents and instruments—that will permit them to create the sublime music of which they are capable. A conductor and the right orchestration: it is toward acquiring these that this book is directed. It is toward the effective interlinking and blending of entrepreneurial elements that we now turn our attention.

I

The Entrepreneurial Matrix: Personal Qualities and the Entrepreneurial Manager

"Look. It's real simple. When Newton discovered much of what we call modern physics way back in the seventeenth century, he said it all. 'I can see things because I stand on the shoulders of giants.' "

"You mean, he was using the work of a lot of other scientists."

"Exactly. You see, most people in life just don't get this: they think life's a solo kind of thing. You got to prove yourself. You got to start from scratch, like Horatio Alger or something. Bullshit. All you have to do is to fill in a few gaps between the huge amount of knowledge available. Geniuses [ed. Entrepreneurs!] are simply people who use all available data and structure their observations on that [sic] data in logical fashion."

"People who see patterns..."

"Precisely....And those patterns are theories...."

—From *The Manhattan Project,* by David Bischoff

INTRODUCTION

What is an Entrepreneur? There have been hundreds of definitions in dozens of books; but, basically, it comes down to a few, simple observations. The Entrepreneur is a combination of the thinker and the doer. The Entrepreneur sees an opportunity for a new product or service, a new approach, a new policy, or a new way of solving an historic problem. But the Entrepreneur also *does* something about what is seen. The Entrepreneur seeks to have an impact on the system with her or his idea, product, or service. It is this thinking-doing combination that gives entrepreneurial efforts their special appeal.

COMPETING THEORIES OF ENTREPRENEURSHIP

Many think of the Entrepreneur as one who engages in small business. Sometimes that is true; sometimes it is not. For a small business to be considered an entrepreneurial effort, it must be characterized by the introduction of a new product or a new service, or there must be something different, inventive, or innovative about the business or venture.

Others see growth as a central feature of entrepreneurial activity. Again, growth alone is not sufficient. Simply expanding the size of one's business by buying another business, for example, is not necessarily imaginative, different, or innovative. In fact, Reich (1983) suggests that it may even be destructive.

Still others see risk and its association with business as essential to the entrepreneurial activity. Again, although risk is certainly a component of the introduction of new ideas, products, and services, risk is neither a necessary nor a sufficient condition. It is a new approach not the risk that characterizes an Entrepreneur.

Psychological Approaches

Considering the Entrepreneur as combination of Thinker and Doer is enough as a start to our discussion. It contains a flaw, however, that is the primary subject of this book. Using the word *entrepreneur* suggests that the Entrepreneurial Impulse is located within the person. Such an explanation articulates well with the penchant in American society to individualize and personalize all activities. Is something wrong in a large corporation? It must be one person's fault—perhaps the fault of several persons—but in either case the solution is simple: Find the rascals and turn them out. The industrial insight of interchangeable parts becomes transformed into a perspective of interchangeable people. If the part is wrong replace it. If the person is wrong replace the person. Less attention is paid to the *system* of interactions of which we are all a part, that is so important for the entrepreneurial function to flourish.

The literature in the psychology of organizations has the Entrepreneur full of *traits*—sometimes *qualities*. The term *natural* often comes into play, as in "this individual is a natural athlete" (For one study, see Begley and Boyd, 1987).

There are several problems with this line of thinking. It suggests that ascribed characteristics are more important than achieved characteristics. In effect, those who talk about Natural Entrepreneurs are also saying, "There's nothing I can do to develop entrepreneurial activity—it's natural." There is nothing you can do—"either you got it or you ain't." This is what Wolfe (1984) calls "The Right Stuff" theory of entrepreneurship. For some, these phrases ring bells and cause heads to nod. It is probably no accident that

The Natural and *The Right Stuff* have appeared as titles of major American motion pictures in the 1980s. There are, indeed, a number of traits that many people (some very knowledgeable) think are associated with entrepreneurship. Among these are:

1. *Risk taking.* The Entrepreneur is an individual who takes risks—who is characterized by risk-taking behavior. The Entrepreneur is, therefore, one in a new business, operating outside of established organizations.

2. *Independence.* The Entrepreneur is an independent individual who does not like to work for others, who would rather work for himself or herself.

3. *"Internal locus of control."* This concept, developed by psychologist Julian Rotter (1966), differentiates people along the dimension of how they perceive life's events to be controlled. Those who believe they have a great influence on what happens to them are characterized as having internal locus of control. Those who believe that what happens to them is the result of luck, fate, chance, or forces "out there" have an external locus of control. People who begin new ventures are more likely to be internally rather than externally oriented.

4. *Thriving on excitement.* Although some individuals seek the tranquil life, others are excitement and action oriented. Entrepreneurs fit the latter category for they like the excitement of the new and the different.

5. *Self-starting.* Entrepreneurs begin things on their own authority, using their own ideas and energy as justification. "If you wait around for new ideas to be introduced, you often have a long wait."

6. *Self-confidence.* Entrepreneurs have abundant self-confidence, a strong belief that the new product, service, idea, or approach they're proposing has merit. This confidence is necessary because others are less likely to be supportive of new ideas. Hence, one not only needs to believe in the new idea but must have sufficient self-belief to overcome hostility and criticism.

7. *Flexibility.* Entrepreneurs are flexible. Markets and systems change. Businesses must change with them. One's own ideas may need to be adjusted either over time or overnight.

8. *Persistence.* Entrepreneurs are persistent. They're individuals who can keep at things in spite of setbacks. Sometimes persistence may be the opposite of flexibility and indeed, one may be flexible in change when one should be persistent and persist when it's time to flex. How does one know?

9. *Ambiguity.* Entrepreneurs can tolerate the ambiguity of choice that confronts them. Some individuals find uncertain situations difficult to deal with, threatening, and psychologically problematic. Not so, the Entrepreneur. Entrepreneurs are not only less affected by ambiguity, but are capable of exploiting it and turning it to their own advantage. Indeed, ambiguity may enhance their excitement.

10. *Pattern recognition.* Entrepreneurs are capable of resolving conflicts through pattern recognition. They are capable of seeing how everything fits together, catching a glimpse of the forest while others are struggling with the trees.

11. *Low need for support.* This is closely related to self-confidence, but Entrepreneurs

are more than confident. They have a low *need* for the support of others. This low need for support allows them to take action that others might consider risky. With new ideas, however, the validation from others is low. Because of this laconae, one not only needs confidence in ideas but one also needs the ability to proceed without lots of encouragement and backing.

12. *The right stuff.* This is Wolfe's phrase (1984), and it sums up the psychological view of entrepreneurship. One needs to have these traits, these characteristics, if one is to be an Entrepreneur. A bit of circular reasoning is involved here, for Entrepreneurs are usually studied first and then pronounced to have some or all of these characteristics.

COMPARATIVE THEORIES OF ENTREPRENEURSHIP

The psychological perspective on entrepreneurship is deficient in two important respects. First, it tends to be passive rather than active with respect to the Entrepreneur. It tends to assume that you either have the right stuff or you don't, and it is generally silent on whether you can develop characteristics asserted to be important. Furthermore, it is short on a discussion of competencies, quite aside from the issue of whether or not you have particular psychological characteristics. Are there skills you could hone in order to be better? We believe there are, on both counts. You can develop and enhance certain psychological orientations if such orientations prove to be necessary. Regarding them as traits simply fixes a particular orientation for all time. As in any enterprise, whatever your native propensities, and however you hone those propensities, there are always tricks, skills, hints, techniques, even proprietary knowledge that can be developed. Part of the purpose of this volume is to suggest what some of those are.

A second failure of the contemporary theory, however, is its tendency to ignore the external environment. Are there conditions or contexts in which the Entrepreneur operates? Most certainly there are. The structure of the firm. The structure of the local community. The support that particular Entrepreneurs get from their families, psychologically and materially, all make a significant difference in whether or not any particular Entrepreneur will emerge successfully.

The environment, also, is subject to manipulation and influence. It may not be as easy to have a significant impact on the larger scale or macroenvironment as it is on the smaller scale or microenvironment, but both are open to change. In her book *The Change Masters* (1983), Rosabeth Kanter points out that many macrochanges are a result of the accumulation of microchanges acting on the work setting around the immediate area. These in turn stimulate larger changes at other points within the organization. The possibility of changing the meeting structure and committee behavior within the whole organization as a result of a small conspiracy of individuals de-

Table 1.1
Comparative Theories of Entrepreneurship

	ENVIRONMENT	
	PASSIVE	ACTIVE
INDIVIDUAL:		
PASSIVE	You Have the Right Stuff Theory: "Personality Is What Counts"	Necessity Theory: "Times Make the Person"
ACTIVE	The Great Person Theory: "Person Makes the Times"	Ensemble Theory: "The Orchestration of People Is What Counts"

termined to improve the quality of decision making in their company is a theme we developed in another book, *Meetings: How To Make Them Work For You* (1984). The overall point is a crucial one: The environment is not simply passive and "out there"; it is amenable to change that may reshape it, resculpt it, re-form it, just as the individual's own traits and competencies can (though just not as much). The chart above (Table 1.1) helps to illustrate what we mean.

The typical theory of entrepreneurship, which we call the "You Have the Right Stuff Theory," is generally—and surprisingly—passive in nature. You have traits; the world exists. If you happen to have the right traits at the right place and time in the world, entrepreneurship may be the result. When looked at in this light, it is not a terribly appealing theory. It suggests that too much is given and too little created. Modifications of that theory are either the *Great Person Theory* or the *Necessity Theory*. Both, of course, have their adherents.

The Great Person Theory suggests that Entrepreneurs have such charisma and personal magnetism that they wind up shaping and structuring the times in which they live. In this case it doesn't matter too much whether the world is ready for fried chicken or home delivered pizza or Big Macs. Colonel Sanders, Tom Monahan (Domino's Pizza), or Ray Kroc's (McDonald's) people will make us want it. Some of the most celebrated Entrepreneurs fall into this category—Henry Ford, Thomas Edison, William Lear, Howard Hughes—insisting that things *can* be done, fighting (to use another movie title metaphor) "Against All Odds." And, of course, there are individuals like this. That's not the issue. The question, rather, is of a different sort: Does this kind of theory represent an adequate description of the *full* range of the entrepreneurial function? We think not.

Others argue the converse of the Great Person Theory. We call it the Necessity Theory, which we derive from "Necessity is the mother of invention." This approach suggests that, for the most part, everyone is ordinary until extraordinary conditions come along and squeeze ability and creativity, talent and leadership out of those who never dreamed or believed they had it.

The Ensemble Approach

A more appealing theory, it seems to us, is one we call the "Ensemble Approach to Entrepreneurship." This theory suggests that both the individual *and* the environment are important aspects of the entrepreneurial function. It is virtually impossible to understand the development and flourishing of entrepreneurship without understanding both dimensions. Moreover this perspective contains both active and passive elements. Some aspects of our personalities are, to some extent, given. Let us emphasize, however, that passive does not mean rigid. It means only somewhat less amenable to influence but still able to be influenced. Certain aspects of the environment—large-scale demographic structures, for example—are also less susceptible to modification. Other aspects of the environment can be readily modified. We call this perspective "The Four C's Theory Of Entrepreneurship."

THE FOUR C's THEORY OF ENTREPRENEURSHIP

The Four C's Theory of Entrepreneurship can be understood through four basic concepts: *Characteristics*, *Competencies*, *Conditions*, and *Context*. This perspective incorporates psychological traits through the concept of *Characteristics*, but it also adds an individual level to such traits. The concept of *Competence* suggests that there are certain Skills behaviors that can be learned and must be practiced. It also suggests that there are certain *Conditions*—within the family, within the Firm, within the community—that are favorable to the development of new ideas and to the introduction of new products and new services. These are given in part, but they can also be sculpted. Finally, there are certain *Contexts*—larger scale, macroenvironmental forces—that can be similarly favorably disposed toward entrepreneurial functions. Though less amenable to influence, these can also be shaped; and aspects of them can be used and exploited.

Each of these elements can favor entrepreneurial development, but they can also work against it. Some individuals may not have the requisite Characteristics or enough of them. Or, they may have the right Characteristics but not the Competence. Or, the Context or the Conditions may be negative. You need to look, therefore, not only at the presence of each of these four components, but at their simultaneous interaction. Entrepreneurial activity will be at its highest when each of these four elements is in the positive column. Such activity will be at its lowest when each is in the negative column. For the most part, entrepreneurial activity is a mixture. Thus, the orchestration of Characteristics, Competencies, Conditions, and Context is of the utmost importance.

Many Entrepreneurs fail. In part, that failure is due to a lack of attention to Characteristics, Competencies, Conditions, and Context, and to a failure to orchestrate these appropriately within a given situation. Many times, even though a new idea has been introduced, a new product or service offered, its possibilities remain largely undeveloped because the Conditions were wrong or the Context inappropriate. Similarly, business persons, managers, or leaders may not get from their employees the kinds of creativity and imagination that are needed. This may have nothing to do with any specific deficiencies on the part of the employees. Instead, it may result when the business persons, managers, or leaders themselves do not know how to structure work Conditions and Context to generate the required productivity. We focus, therefore, on the structure, creation, and management of entrepreneurial systems and the importance of the concept of *Entrepreneurial Management*; the ability to manage innovation and new ideas creatively.

Consider a typical Entrepreneur who thinks up a new idea or observes a new opportunity for a product or service. That is the Thinker part of the Thinker-Doer approach. But that Entrepreneur also needs to be able to put together a structure that will enhance the idea, remove problematic parts from it, and make it better. The Entrepreneur needs to put together a structure that will assemble the requisite information, people, and resources to make the venture go. In short, the entrepreneurial function is not only an idea generating function; it is also a *doing* function. We call this "doing Entrepreneurial Management."

The old definition of entrepreneurship—"finding a need and filling it"—is too superficial and too passive for our purposes. It conceals more than it reveals. The Four C's approach—Characteristics, Competencies, Conditions, and Contexts—goes considerably deeper into the broad requisites of entrepreneurship. Table 1.2 outlines some of these requisites.

Table 1.2 suggests some of the Competencies, Conditions, and Context important to Entrepreneurs.

Characteristics

We've already discussed some of the Characteristics that are reputed to be (and are, in many instances) associated with the entrepreneurial person. The most important thing to remember about Characteristics is that they are changeable and adaptable. To be sure, in the mystery of the acquisition of certain psychological traits and conditions some people seem to wind up with "risk take-ability" and others among us do not. However, in the list given earlier in this chapter, there is no Characteristic that cannot be honed, no tendency that cannot be augmented and improved, and no allegedly negative character trait that cannot be modified if that is what a person is

Table I.2
The Four C's/Ten S Theory of Entrepreneurship

Individual/Personal		Environmental/Social/Cultural	
Characteristics	Competencies	Conditions	Contexts

Individual/Personal

Characteristics — Self (Ch.1)
1. Risk
2. Locus of Control
3. Independence
4. Excitement
5. Self-starting
6. Self-confidence
7. Flexibility
8. Persistence
9. Ambiguity
10. Pattern Recognition
11. Low support need
12. The right stuff

Competencies — Skills (Ch.12)
1. Introducing New Ideas
2. Intellectual
3. Interpersonal
4. Mixed
5. Organizational

Style (Ch.11)
1. Personal Style
2. organizational Style

Environmental/Social/Cultural

Conditions — Staff (Ch.10)
1. The Need for Others
2. Recognizing Relevant Conditions
3. Rewarding
4. Inspiriting
5. Rewarding
6. Advancing
7. Training
8. Evaluating

Subculture (Ch.6)
1. Managing Organizational Culture
2. Matrix of Corporate Values
3. Cultural Mixing and Phasing
4. The Firm Logo and Motto

Strategy (Ch.7)
1. Strategic Dicta
2. Strategic Techniques

Structure (Ch.8)
1. The Jerry-Built Structure
2. Macro-Structure
3. Meso-Structure
4. Micro-Structure
5. Linking Structures
6. Evaluation Structures
7. Unusual Organizational Topologies

System (Ch.9)
1. Three System Properties: Flows,Exchange,Transformation
2. Establishing Entrepreneurial Systems
3. Establishing Idea Processing Systems
4. Establishing Intelligence Systems
5. Enhancing System Functioning
6. Establishing Informal Systems
7. Reward and Motivational Systems

Contexts — Superordinate Culture (Ch.5)
1. Values
2. Attitudes

Superordinate Structure[1] (Ch.5)
1. Population
2. Organization
3. Environment
4. Technology

---

1. This system is an adaptation of the Peters/Waterman (1982, p.101) "7S System." As they originally wrote about it, it contains superordinate values, strategy, structure, system, staff, skill, and style. We've modified it to a ten category system that includes self, structure, subculture, superordinate culture, and superordinate structure.

interested in doing. That point is an important one for the potential Entrepreneur to keep in mind.

More importantly, perhaps, there are three other realms of great importance that need attention before of an entrepreneurial venture has a high
probability of success: Competencies, Conditions, and Contexts. Therefore,
we caution you against relying too heavily on Characteristics as a high pre-
dictor of success. Part of the problem here is that many studies of Entrepreneurs pick the successful ones, look and see what "traits" they possess,
and erroneously argue that it was these traits that led to success. In fact, a
more carefully controlled and scientifically rigorous study would look at both
failures and successes. But little information is available on this point. Therefore, even though change in personal orientations, motivations, tendencies,
and so on can and may be accomplished, we caution our readers not to take
these accomplishments as tantamount to success in the entrepreneurial
world. Increasingly, there is recognition that sociological, economic, and
political factors need to come together with psychological factors in order
for success to occur. The penchant in American society for individualizing
everything encourages us ("forces us" might be a better phrase) to over-
attribute both success and failure to the efforts of individuals. This mode
of analysis tips us away from attention to Competencies or, to the extent it
takes Competencies into consideration, reinterprets them as givens and,
thus, places them erroneously in the Characteristics box. The main attention,
therefore, needs to be on Competencies, Conditions, and Contexts. In this
chapter, greatest attention is placed on Competencies because, generally
speaking, those are the elements within our greatest control.

Competencies

To be a successful Entrepreneur, you need to have certain Competencies.
By this we mean that you need to be able to do certain things and to do
them reasonably well. Simply being tolerant of ambiguity does not, in itself,
produce much. Nor does the ability, alone, to take risks produce wealth and
commercial success. Flexibility, persistence, pattern recognition—in fact,
none of the Characteristics mentioned before can generate, in and of themselves, entrepreneurial well-being. A set of specific Competencies needs to
be linked to all of the Characteristics already discussed. The total list of
Competencies in that set could go on for many pages, but they can generally
be divided into two major groups: *Skills* and *Style*.

Think of Skills as acquired performance modalities in a range of areas
from writing and speaking to specific business experience and the ability to
undertake self and failure analyses. Reasonable people may differ with respect to the degree to which risk take-ability can be enhanced, but there is
virtually no debate about the fact that business experience can be garnered,
that the ability to prepare effective reports and business plans can be learned

and improved, that the ability to communicate orally improves with practice, and that there are things about each of the other Competencies that can be learned. In fact, it's probably true (though a firm conclusion on this point awaits further research) that individuals use Competencies to substitute or compensate for gaps or weakness in certain Characteristics. Maybe a particular Entrepreneur is not the world's greatest risk taker; but the lack of that personality feature may be compensated for by in-depth business experience and the ability to evaluate opportunities. Individuals with only the Characteristics may be among those who fail early, because they do not have the Competencies to carry out the activities to which their "nature" impels them.

Style is the second half of the two Competency groups. Knowing what to do is certainly important, but doing it within a certain Context, and fitting and adjusting your talents and abilities into the extant organizational structure—be it society or firm—is also crucial. It is essentially Style that McCormack (1986) talked about in his famous book, *What They Don't Teach You at the Harvard Business School.* There are, of course, many different Styles; and most Entrepreneurs need to have a Style or role repertoire of available presentations of Self in order to handle the range of Conditions in which they are likely to find themselves.

An understanding of both Skills and Style is crucial. For that reason we have devoted a full chapter to each of the Concepts later in this book. By way of introduction, however, we present a general overview of each concept.

The *Skills* successful Entrepreneurs and Entrepreneurial Managers must ultimately develop fall into five major categories: introducing ideas, intellectual skills, interpersonal skills, organizational skills, and mixed skills (the nature of which will become clear in a moment). It is important to understand that all five categories are needed for the overall achievement and success of an entrepreneurial venture.

Skills in introducing new ideas is a summary concept for the whole entrepreneurial impulse. It refers to the need for a combination of intellectual skills, interpersonal skills, organizational skills, and mixed skills to accomplish the total purpose of new idea introduction.

Intellectual Skills are those that involve essentially cognitive elements; that is, knowledge or awareness of things. These include such skills as technical business knowledge, for example, and awareness of idea stages and developmental sequences, failure analysis, self-analysis, and so on.

Other Skills are essentially interpersonal in nature; they involve the heart rather than the mind. Interpersonal Skills require the ability to deal primarily with people and with the affect, rather than the ideas, that people present. Listening, Modelling, Bargaining, and Coaching all fall into this category.

Additionally, there are the Skills that represent a mixture of Intellectual and Interpersonal Skills. Group Management is a good example because it involves both a knowledge of the group decision process (an Intellectual Skill) and an ability to be aware of group dynamics (an Interpersonal Skill).

Other examples include Oral Communication, Network Building, and Orchestration of People and Ideas.

Organizational Skills involve creating organizational forms. These are forms that foster entrepreneurial activity.

Style is a second major Competency group you will require in your entrepreneurial efforts. Style is the way you go about performing the intellectual or interpersonal tasks. That's the personal aspect; *Personal Style*. The way the organization goes about creating and carrying out its mission is the *Organizational Style*. Both are important.

Conditions

Characteristics and Competencies are essentially individual and personal in nature; they are psychological features or learned skills, or interpersonal techniques that are in the possession of the individual person. Conditions and Contexts move us away from the individual person into the milieu or immediate environment surrounding the individual person. It is that milieu into which the Entrepreneur must fit (and in the use of the word *fit* we do not mean *conform*) and from which the Entepreneur must draw resources, and to which the Entrepreneur's products must be distributed.

Conditions refer to the organizational or interorganizational matrix within which the Entrepreneur carries out his or her daily activities. Context is the macroenvironment—the society, the world, the attitudes and structures of the society, that influence the Conditions, Competencies, and Characteristics. Conditions can be thought of as a kind of intermediate level between the microlevel of Characteristics and Competencies and the macrolevel of Context.

There are five major areas of Conditions with which the Entrepreneur needs to be concerned: Staff, Subculture, Strategy, Structure, and System. These are subjects discussed in chapters later in this book, so only a brief introduction is necessary now.

Staff. *Staff* is one of the "soft" "S" categories identified by Peters and Waterman (1982). It refers to the overall configuration of talents, abilities, interests, and commitments of the individuals who are hired members of the organization or others whose livelihood is inextricably linked to the organization. Although typically not considered as Staff, these latter represent an important people resource that should not be ignored. To elaborate on this a bit, hiring and firing—who should be brought on and who should be let go—are certainly important concerns with respect to Staff. It is also important, however, to understand that a similar range of concerns focuses upon the client-customer-patient ring. Although they are technically not Staff, they are individuals who either supply themselves or their products to the organization or who purchase products from the organization. Thus, they represent the other major people resource with which the Entrepreneur needs to be concerned.

There are eight major areas that the Entrepreneur needs to attend to when thinking about Staff. The first of these is *recognizing the need for others*; others are needed for the accomplishment of entrepreneurial effort and are central to entrepreneurial success.

The second is *recognizing relevant Staff conditions*. Such recognition involves taking an assessment of current Staff, finding out where the venture or enterprise is at with respect to Staff strength, Staff weaknesses, Staff needs, and Staff potentials.

The third is *recruiting high quality Staff*. Without a constant influx of new, qualified people—both to expand the enterprise and to replace those who have already left—the entrepreneurial activity is likely to be doomed.

The fourth major area is *inspiriting the current Staff*. This inspiriting is crucial. One of the jobs of the Entrepreneur is to motivate and excite the Staff who are working right now.

The fifth area is *recognizing the need for appropriate rewards*. Rewarding Staff is likewise crucial. Not only is there a recognition of the need for appropriate rewards, but some emphasis on the term *appropriate* is important. Money is a key reward. But other kinds of rewards may also be effective from time to time. Such things as compensatory time, special office locations, flexibility of work hours, or special parking places are among the things you can consider as possible rewards.

The sixth area is *advancement potential*. Most of us like the sense and hope of getting ahead. When someone begins a job, that individual, in almost every instance, holds the hope that in time a new job will materialize with more money and, perhaps, with a bigger title. Facilitating the upward mobility aspiration of Staff is an important job of the Entrepreneurial Manager. Their advance will help the firm or division advance.

The seventh area is *training Staff*, which is closely related to the idea of advancement. Jobs are learning experiences. We all recognize that. Many Firms, however, especially the smaller ones, leave that learning up to the Staff person. With a little organization and planning, educational and training programs—sometimes on a stand-alone basis, sometimes in combination with other organizations or departments—can be started and carried through. Many individuals regard the availability of such training opportunities as a very important form of compensation. But whether it is or not, from the Entrepreneurial Manager's point of view it is a way to direct, possibly inspirit, and suggest the kinds of activities and the kinds of competencies that are needed.

The eighth major area is *evaluating Staff*. All too often evaluations occur *post hoc*, after something has gone wrong and evaluation is undertaken and blame is assessed. Unfortunately, such reactive evaluation systems do very little except divert blame from the boss. Proactive systems that set the goals to be met well in advance are far more desirable.

Subculture. In fairly recent times, organizational *Subculture* has achieved an ascendency of attention that is almost inverse to the avoidance of it in bygone years. Typically, the term *organizational culture* rather than organizational *Subculture* is used. We've selected the word *Subculture*, however, in order to emphasize the fact that, whatever culture the organization develops, it is a Subculture within the larger American culture. There is an IBM Subculture or a Hewlitt-Packard Subculture or a 3M Subculture, but these Subcultures, like ethnic and religious Subcultures, must coexist and articulate with the larger Superordinate Culture.

This terminological correction does not tell us much about Subculture. The following definition does: Subculture refers to the norms and values, the attitudes and beliefs that characterize the organization over time and space. This characterization transcends the careers of any particular members of the organization. It is through Subculture that one important aspect of organizational compensation ("psychic income") is provided.

The Entrepreneurial Manager needs to attend to four specific areas of the Subculture. These areas are managing organizational culture, the matrix of values, cultural mixing and phasing, and the Firm logo and motto.

Managing organizational culture refers to the simple idea that culture, norms, and values can and should be managed. Cultural systems influence the work place. It does not make much sense to let them arise all by themselves. Instead, the kinds of norms and values that you need for your success can be introduced into the enterprise. This will aid both in the Staff selection process and in providing appropriate modelling.

The problem with organizational values, like any values, is that they are often in conflict. Managers need to realize that there is not *a* set of values that is to be introduced. Rather, there is a conflicting, contrasting set of values. Part of cultural management involves attending to these conflicts—recognizing them and dealing with their ebb and flow.

Cultural mixing and phasing refers specifically to this ebb and flow. The conflict between *excellence* and *satisfaction* in organizational life provides a useful example. Organizations are committed to excellence, but they are also committed to satisfaction. This is probably true of all of us. We like excellence and are, in all probability, excellent in some areas. None of us is, however— nor is any organization—excellent in every aspect. One of the jobs of the Entrepreneurial Manager, with the help of others, therefore, is to select certain areas for excellence and other areas for satisfaction. These areas may change over time, but balancing the excellence-satisfaction commitments is an important dimension of Entrepreneurial Management.

Finally, as an Entrepreneurial Manager, you may want to pay attention to firm logo and motto. You can think of these as snapshot representations of the organization's mission and purpose. The logo and motto are minute embodiments of the organizational culture. Discussions about what the logo and motto should be are often among the most productive organizational discussions because they force organizational members in a sentence or picture to explain their view of the organization. Often this allows for latent conflicts to surface and begins the process of accommodation to the various forces that are likely to be present.

Strategy. Organizational *Strategy* is an important organizational condition that encompasses the organization's answer to Naisbitt's (1983) question: "What business are we in?" It is the formal statement of the mission or goal of the organization within its market and within the larger Superordinate Structure and culture. It is the codified package of organizational decision with respect to its market and its position in its market (first to market, second to market, etc.). It is the set of organizational documents, perceptions, edicts, and so on that both serve as the link between Subculture and Substructure and inform Structure.

There are two strategic aspects—*strategic dicta* and *strategic techniques*—that Entrepreneurial Managers should master. Strategic dicta refer to a set of formal rules that is useful to know or consider when forming strategy. Strategic techniques provide some ways to do this.

Structure. *Structure* represents the "hard" aspects of the organization with respect to its parts and shape. Think of the organization Structure as being like the design of a house. Each house has a certain number of square feet, but the ways those square feet can be organized are open to lots of variation: one large room, many small rooms, upstairs-downstairs, and so on. With organizations in particular, a range of familiar structures presents itself to the Entrepreneur: a tall structure or a flat one or a round one; one that is centralized or one that is decentralized; it is possible to focus on the input, throughput, and output aspects of structure.

Organizations can be further divided into analytic structures; such as, financial structures or personnel structures. It is important for you to think very hard about the organizational structure you wish to adopt and the way in which that organizational structure may change over time. Whatever the structure winds up being, the entrepreneurial craftsman should remember that Structure follows Strategy; the organizational structure is the *servant* of organizational orientations, goals, missions and roles; *not* their dictator. When structure becomes the boss, then it's akin to looking under a street light for a needle that you lost a block away in a dark alley because it's easier to see under the light. The problem with structural dominance may sound silly when presented in that form, but that form represents an honest, fairly straightforward picture of the problems many organizations experience.

A number of structural areas require your attention. Important among them is the "jerry-built" structural problem. This is the problem that occurs when organizational pieces are added helter-skelter without any thought to their relationship to the overall strategy. The result is what might be called the "Rube Goldberg Organization." One of the reasons people look under the street light is that they actually believe that's where they should be looking. In a complex organizational design it's not infrequent that people don't know where to go. All of us have had that befuddling experience in hospitals, trying to follow the colored tape marks on the floor to our destinations. It is rumored that from time to time some individuals set off along a given path and never reach their destination, spending the rest of their natural days wandering around and around, looking for the exit.

Three particular aspects of Structure deserve attention: the Macro-Structure, the MesoStructure, and the MicroStructure. The MacroStructure refers to that part of the organization that links to the outside—macro—environment. The MesoStructure is that we call (or often think of as) the *organizational chart*. It's the organization with which we are familiar. The MicroStructure refers to the work station or daily work area. Each of these needs attention. Each can be improved.

Linking Structures and Evaluation Structures are also important organizational elements. Given even a fair number of organizational parts (divisions, sections, subsections, etc.), you will need to be concerned over the ways in which those subparts link each to the other. Evaluation Structures refer to that set of activities and locales that review organizational performance. Linking Structures and Evaluation Structures are the special responsibility of central administration. All organizations have these structures, even small ones; and the Entrepreneurial Manager needs to be aware of the problems and potentials of each.

Finally, you might want to experiment with unusual organizational typologies. We're all familiar with the organizational chart. Suppose you were to bend that into a circle so that you have a kind of organizational wheel instead of a chart. The CEO is not at the top now—"over" others—but in the center with radii extending out to intermediate points and to the edges. This organizational concept is fun to play with because it realigns the organizational architecture and, thus, has the potential for realigning organizational thinking, as well.

System. The parts of the organization must be linked by flows of some sort or another. The rooms of a house are linked by flows of electric power through the electrical System and by flows of water through the plumbing System. Individuals are guided and directed through the rooms of a house by the flow of traffic.

Of particular importance to organizations are flows of power, money, and information. (Some argue that both power and money reduce themselves to information and are, in fact, modes through which information is communicated.) Paper flow can be charted in an organization. So, too, can telephone flow or formal and informal interactions. A dynamic picture of an organization or venture would show the organization as a moving entity, much like blood flows through the body connecting bodily parts.

In addition to flows, exchanges and transformations occur within systems. Exchanges are those system operations in which one set of goods and services is exchanged for another. Transformation occurs when organizational processes actually change that which is exchanged—just as plants transform sunlight into energy.

Attention to organization Systems is generally an underdeveloped area in entrepreneurial activity or organizational and firm activity. Everyone is familiar with organizational Structure, and everyone knows what we mean when we say we are going to reorganize. Very few people, however, talk about changing the Systems of an organization to accommodate new changes in organizational formats and designs. It may be *assumed* that Systems change automatically, but that assumption is all too frequently honored in the breach. Entrepreneurial Managers need to establish and attend to organizational Systems and especially establish entrepreneurial Systems because they are unlikely to grow up by themselves. In addition, Entrepreneurial Managers need to establish idea Systems and intelligence Systems, develop and support informal Systems, and augment and enrich the reward and motivational Systems, which are currently in existence. Finally, Entrepreneurial Managers need to enhance current system functioning through processes of assessment and review.

The story is told, and purported to be true, of a large manufacturing firm that had a significant manufacturing problem that it could not solve without developing a special, unique process. It spent an enormous amount of money and a great deal of time developing that process. Finally, the company achieved the development and immediately set about to patent its new process, laying out another considerable amount of money in that effort. The company discovered to its chagrin and consternation that the device had already been patented many years before, but it was one of those many solutions for which, at the time, there was no problem. Worse, the company found that the original inventor of this particular solution was one of their own employees and that they, the company, already owned the patent for the process they had invested so much of the company resources to re-invent (Green, 1986). The system of communication within this organization was especially poor. Information present within the System was unable to be retrieved before large sums of money had been wastefully expended.

Contexts

If Conditions of entrepreneurial life focus heavily on the entrepreneurial organization, itself, and its Staffs, Subculture, Strategy, Structure, and System, then one remaining arena of entrepreneurial attention remains to be explored: the Context. The Context is the macrocircle within which the entrepreneurial organization lives. Sometimes, as in the case of firms nationalized in a revolution, the Context makes itself felt with devastating and impoverishing suddenness. It is not likely that an individual Entrepreneur can influence the Context to any great extent—although there have been instances where it has happened. It is more likely the case that the Entrepreneur finds a niche opened up by particular changes within the environment or particular areas within the environment. Two major environmental sectors required attention: Superordinate Culture and Superordinate Structure.

Superordinate Culture focuses upon the prevailing values and attitudes, the belief System of a particular community or a nation. Ideas for new products and services are not pursued frequently because the world is not ready for an X or a Y. Thus, ventures are sometimes ahead of their time. Alternatively, Entrepreneurs stick with old ideas, even as the Context is changing. The refusal of American automobile manufacturers to recognize attitudinal changes in favor of smaller, more economical cars and cars of higher quality was an important factor in their significant loss of market share to the manufacturers of other nations. Some of those other manufacturers not only captured that aspect of the market but were aware that the polyglot market still contains that element that the American manufacturers thought was the total market; that is, a wish for upscale, more luxurious products. A splendid example of that adaptability is the Honda. Its early models were, roughly speaking, indistinguishable from a lawn mower. It was impossible to tell whether the driver was cutting the grass or going to the market. How different those early models are from the present day luxury lines. That kind of adaptability is an important aspect of success.

Superordinate Structure refers to the large-scale societal conditions in which ventures succeed or fail. The ten macrochanges John Naisbitt (1983) identified in his book as megatrends fall into this category. Entrepreneurial attention to them allows for repositioning and redevelopment of strategies. Needing particular emphasis are four superordinate structural elements: (1) population structures, trends, and developments; (2) changes in the organization, work, family life, and community; (3) environmental changes, especially changes related to natural resources and waste disposal; and (4) technological changes, especially those involving energy conversion and information storage and retrieval (these four elements will be referred to as POET).

The Four C's—Characteristics, Competencies, Conditions, and Contexts—are singly very important. When all are in the positive column, as we have previously indicated, entrepreneurial success is likely to be assured. Unhappily, both Entrepreneurs in new ventures and bureaucrats in old ventures tend to forget one aspect or another of the Four C's. As a result—some early, some later—they fall on hard times. An intensive analysis into entrepreneurial and bureaucratic failure, we are convinced, would reveal differential patterns of deficit among these Four C's. It is as yet too early to tell whether certain types of ventures are more likely to have deficits in certain types of areas. As we shall see in upcoming chapters, for example, Entrepreneurs are particularly adept at spotting gaps and niches in the societal

Context. They are also likely to have some of the necessary Characteristics. The problems seem to occur in the areas of Competency and Condition. Many Entrepreneurs suffer from incredibly rapid growth and are unable to configure an organization appropriate to that particular difficulty. Other organizations do not experience growth and are not able to cope with that problem. It is important, therefore, that all four work together in concert; and it is to a discussion of a concert of the components that we now turn with preliminary special attention to relationship of change to the Four C's.

THE RELATIONSHIP OF CHANGE TO THE FOUR C's

Change is so closely intertwined with Characteristics, Competencies, Conditions, and Context that it may almost be considered a fifth C in its own right. Change may be of many sorts. In the case of Characteristics and Competencies, we are *creating change* by adjusting, adapting, and modifying our own personal repertoire, approaches, and skills to meet different opportunities available in the environment.

In the case of the Conditions we are far more likely to be *controlling change* than creating it. The Conditions in the work place and in the organization are always changing. The difficulty, as we have observed with many of America's large companies, is that the direction of change is frequently negative. Bureaucracy increases. Communication channels and Systems become clogged. The process of innovation declines. What is needed, therefore, with respect to Conditions is averting negative change directions and developing positive ones.

Finally, with respect to Context, it is certainly possible to capitalize on change. Capitalizing on change means adjusting the Conditions of your organization; changing your Competencies or (to the extent possible) your Characteristics to align them with the ever-changing Context in which your organization works and in which you live. Such adjustment will prevent failure and may enhance success. Such adjustment involves the perception of the environment, which is always changing. Firms and businesses die. In part, they do so because they are unaware of changes in the Context, changes to which they need to adjust. Tichy and Devanna (1986) talk about this phenomenon as "the boiled frog effect." They point out that if you place a frog in a pan of water over a Bunsen burner and let the temperature of the water rise extremely slowly, ultimately the frog will boil to death. This example is not a pleasant one, but the message is powerful. Slow changes in the environment are just as real as rapid ones. The fact that we can't recognize them as changes at any particular point in time does not mean that change is not occurring. In fact, it is for this reason, Tichy and Devanna argue, that whole sectors of industry, living in what they call "cultural cocoons" —steel, motorcycles, and consumer electronics are a few—experience the boiled frog effect because they did not recognize the changes in their own business environments.

But capitalizing on change can involve other aspects, as well. The large number of women in the wage labor force has created a boom for the restaurant and prepared food industries. The increasing number of chronologically gifted Americans (those over 65) remains to be exploited by merchants catering to the needs of that particular age group.

These examples can be multiplied many times over. However, the point is that as awareness of Context becomes sharpened, opportunities for products and services become clearer. Unexplored niches develop where none existed before. But before new ideas for products and services can be addressed to these evolving markets, their potential must be recognized. It is the recognition of the reconfigurations of Context created by change that allows you to capitalize on it. A structure that permits such capitalization is the Four C's Conference.

THE FOUR C's CONFERENCE

One way to proceed to engage in the change process within a big or small organization, at the beginning or at the end of the development cycle, is through the Four C's Conference. A Four C's Conference involves all members of the organization, broken down into the appropriate subsets. The Conference is geared to a collective, group oriented process, designed to provide information on each of the Four C's—Characteristics, Competencies, Conditions, and Context. It also encourages questions about the ways in which change can be created, controlled, or capitalized on with respect to a particular firm or venture.

Individuals are assigned and are responsible for one of the Four C's. All individuals prepare a *Characteristics Assay*. This is a report on their own Characteristics and on the kinds of improvements and changes in these Characteristics that they can consider making. All individuals prepare a *Competencies Assay*. In this they outline the Skills that they have developed and suggest areas in which they would like to learn more. The same is done with Style. Teams of individuals are assigned to report on the organizational Skills Structure, the Strategy, the System, and the Structure and Subculture of the organization. This is called the *Organizational* or *Conditions Assay*. Finally, teams are assigned to assay the Context from an environmental scan, a *Context Assay*. One group focuses on the environmental structure and the kinds of changes and developments in it that are most noticeable. Another group is assigned to the environmental culture where the beliefs, values, attitudes, and opinions are most prominent (or most characteristic) of a contemporary time.

All of this work is done *before* the Conference. The Conference, itself, always follows the same three-step process in the same order. At each step each of the Four C's is examined, focusing first on facts, second on problems, and third on opportunities. Ideally, although it can be done in less time, the Conference is organized to take place over a three-day period—as little as a day if all details are carefully attended to in advance. For the purposes of this discussion, we assume that you have scheduled it over a three-day period—which really works best.

The Conference begins with Day One dedicated to reviewing the Contextual facts, Conditional facts, Competency facts, and Characteristic facts, as reported by the assays. Groups and individuals share their particular views of the factual situation. Discussions are limited to the factual situation. Regardless of whether individuals perceive those particular facts as relevant or not, helpful or not, useful or not in subsequent discussions, it is important to begin at that point.

Day Two focuses on problems. These will be problems either with respect to the facts or with respect to gaps in communication and other missing pieces that seemed to have caused organizational problems in the past.

Day Three focuses on opportunities. These may come in any of three areas: (1) the needs, as represented by environmental changes; (2) the Competencies and Characteristics, as represented by the Self reports; or (3) the Conditions of the organization, as represented by the Conditions Assay. Given any of these three, it is then possible to reconfigure and reposition the organization to create necessary change at the Characteristics and Competencies level, to control change at the organizational level, or to capitalize on change in the Context.

Usually, the Four C's Conference will end with a set of plotted new directions for the organization over the next eighteen to twenty-four months. Sometimes, as in very high speed, high development industries—computers and computer related electronic products, for example—a Four C's Conference might be held as often as every six months because the relevant changes, Competencies, Conditions, and Contexts are in that much flux. In other organizational settings a longer time frame could be developed.

Key Elements of the Four C's Conference

There are many kinds of elements that a Four C's Conference[2] might involve. Nine are especially worth mentioning here:

1. *Mind Frame.* A Four C's Conference requires a different frame of mind from "business as usual" or any other kind of group problem-solving process. In particular, openness to new ideas is imperative. So, too, is the willingness to deal simultaneously (and perhaps sloppily) with all of the ills of the organization at the same time and with all the people present.

2. *Commitment.* A Four C's Conference requires a willingness to commit time. It doesn't fit into the business as usual mold. A time commitment of several days

is usually involved. Provision might be made, therefore, for temporary organizational help to perform the essential services while most members of the organization are at the conference. The procedure we have outlined fills three days and works very well. A shorter or a longer program can also be used.

3. *Mind Float.* A Four C's Conference requires members to set aside their usual search for "quick fix solutions" or "adequate enough answers." These represent the vein of most organizations. It satisfies us most of the time, and usefully so. Those methods are not sufficient, however, for long-term organizational reconfiguration and repositioning.

4. *Nice, Neutral Facts.* The Four C's Conference needs individuals to set aside perceptions, explanations, justifications, history, reasons, understandings, lore, and all of the organization's mental activities that explain why the current situation is the best possible. Rather, there needs to be a focus on nice, neutral facts—and *facts* alone! Judgment must be suspended as to whether these facts are right or wrong, good or bad, brilliant or dumb. Furthermore, one starts by talking about problems *not* solutions. In fact early discussion of solutions is *prohibited*. All too frequently, leaping from a limited array of facts to a solution forecloses adequate discussion of problems.

5. *Options.* A Four C's Conference requires commitment to the discussion process at least long enough to come up with two or three better ideas about what is being done or how it's being done as a result of current practice and policy. If nothing emerges, you can always return to business as usual or decide that business as usual *is*, in fact, the preferred choice. But if this is true, it must be a conscious, proactive selection, not something that occurs just because one didn't spend the time to think up anything different.

6. *Suspension of Negative Judgments.* In many organizations (and in families and small groups, for that matter), the power of a negative is strong. Negative comments on an idea often generate defensive reactions. This can cause the scenario of overcommitment and collapse. In the Four C's Conference, therefore, negative judgments are suspended as much as possible. Such suspension is necessary because negativism breeds defensiveness. Instead, a positive climate is fostered. In a positive atmosphere, ways in which ideas can be used rather than what's wrong with them can be explored. The energies of the participants are focused automatically on solutions rather than on problems. Negativism is a line of least resistance—a virtual passive process—that often generates a destructive outcome. Little thought or involvement is required to engage in condemnation. Positivism requires special effort—a virtual active process—that is dedicated to the generation of constructive outcomes. Much thought and considerable involvement are required to cast circumstances in a positive mode.

7. *Ambiguity.* A Four C's Conference requires a willingness to live with ambiguity and uneasiness. These are the inevitable results of standing back, looking at what we do, and questioning it. Particular uneasiness comes from the discomfort of a question rather than the comfort of an answer.[3] Our natural tendency is to take *any* answer as *the* answer, thereby bringing an end to the examination of further alternatives. Not having an answer, even for a short time, is very discomforting for most people. When we have an answer, we don't have to live

with the discomfort of having a problem. "Quick fix," short-term solutions may be stimulated in part less by bottom line concerns then by the psychological pressure to reduce ambiguity and to come up with a decision—*any decision*—that appears to solve the problem or resolve the issue. To avoid this, individuals have to be convinced to live with ambiguity. That's not easy. There is no really good way. A step in the right direction, however, is to tell people in advance that (a) the situation will be ambiguous and (b) that such ambiguity is o.k. Indeed, because one person's ambiguity is another person's excitement, you can try to refocus the group's processes on the positive aspects of ambiguity: the openness that it implies and requires and the fun that it can generate.

8. *Presence of Confidence.* The problem with asking questions is that one may not know the answers. It is often better, therefore, to follow the sage advice "don't ask." Unfortunately, such a Strategy contains a dangerous precedent. If we don't ask, if we don't inquire, we will never be stimulated to think of things that are different or better—things that are improvements on what we have. Some managers never ask questions unless they already know the answers. Such managers lack confidence in the group's ability to generate possible answers. In situations of uncertainty and ambiguity, you *must* have confidence that answers will emerge to the questions. A particular answer may not be *the* answer, but at least it will be a good one.

9. *The Natural Superiority of Groups.* In addition to confidence in the answers the questioning process generates, you must have confidence in *the natural superiority of groups.* You need the conviction that groups, working together, challenging questions, debating, constructively disputing, can emerge with higher quality perspectives and decisions than individuals can by themselves.

10. *Challenge Existing Assumptions and Presuppositions.* Most organizations are full of lore about why things happen, what the organizational or societal forces are that make that an absolute certainty, and why nothing can ever be changed anyway. In the process of consulting for organizations, we have often been impressed with the positive certainty with which organizational lore is shared. The fact that it is lore seems to escape the individuals who are sharing it. Rather, what they believe they are telling us are unshakeable, incontrovertible facts. And, indeed, in the facts section, you will need to be careful that what you *don't* come away with is a collection of company folklore. Even in this day of number crunching and hard data bases, the range and scope of factual inaccuracies about their own organization that individuals present is impressive—sales, for example, return on investment, and other aspects of organizational life that one might think were absolutely clear. Consider the following phrase:

> The Friendly Fellows, men and women of distinction and of great competence filed scientific reports frequently and faithfully.

Scan that sentence for ten seconds. Count the number of times the letter "F" appears as either a capital or small letter. Scan it again and check your work. The answer is in note four.[4] Only a small minority of individuals get the correct number of F's in this little exercise, and it becomes a metaphor for organizational statements. So, the next time somebody says such-and-such "is true about our organization," challenge them in a diplomatic way: "Is that information right?"

"Where did you get it?" "How do you know that's so?" Challenge to existing assumptions, presumptions, preconceptions, and facts in many ways represents the heart of the Four C's Conference. It definitely should not be a place where everyone gets together to tell how great they are and what everyone else already knows. It should be a place, instead, for honest, sincere, and in-depth examination of the organization, its missions and purposes, and the business it is in. Without these kinds of challenges, the organization will not be able to change.[5]

Potential Benefits of a Four C's Conference

Going through this process on a regular basis has a number of potential benefits. The following are seven of them:

1. *A Broad Picture.* A broader picture of what the organization is doing emerges from the Four C's Conference than can be obtained by the usual "one at a time" assessments that go on in most businesses—where one issue is examined independent of or different from the whole.

2. *Common Perception.* Because everyone is in a room together, the Four C's Conference opens up the factual base for assessment and presents the challenge to everyone. All too frequently organizations fall down because one individual knows some subset of facts and another individual knows another subset. Still other individuals may even know other sets of facts. There is no real opportunity for everyone to come together and push those sets of facts up against each other to see what the result might be. Moreover, those subsets of facts tend to represent predetermined positions on the part of certain individuals. Thus, they can be considered not only subsets but preselected subsets, and the challenge that comes from confronting other subsets is not present.

3. *Sharing Identification.* Everyone in a room together creates a sharing atmosphere that allows for common problem identification, that generates common practical suggestions, and that focuses on the kinds of immediate action necessary to take steps toward organizational change.

4. *New Resources.* From this common problem focus the need for additional resources often surfaces. This is especially true for Characteristics and Competencies; discovering that certain Characteristics are not present, or are present and problematic. Needed changes become more readily apparent. Additionally, certain Competencies may be present that need to be improved. Outside resources and network resources can be mobilized to assist.

5. *Specificity.* Another positive result of the Four C's Conference is the development of specific, measurable ways to assess results. There are often many ways in which this specificity can be achieved. Thus, short-term and long-term trade offs can be explored, or quick profit versus market share approaches can be considered.

6. *A Range of Options.* An additional important benefit of the Four C's Conference is that a range of options is developed. Although ultimately one is selected, the provision of a range insures the greater likelihood that the ultimate decision is a good one. Furthermore, the unselected options may be useful at a later date or

for other units in the organization, or they can be called in when the environment changes. Consequently, the Four C's Conference generates a veritable stable of ideas and approaches.

7. *Team Building.* Bringing people together creates a sense of team building, what Akio Morita called " a family feeling" among the Staff in his book *Made In Japan* (1986). This sense of common commitment to a shared purpose will pay off well in terms of the accomplishment of any tasks that are later decided on and any goals that are to be developed and implemented.

To sum up, then, the Four C's Conference has some requisites and some benefits. Sometimes a facilitator—a guide who knows the Four C's ropes— is useful in order to help put this whole package together. Other times, regular Staff can be involved. We believe the Four C's Conference provides an exceptionally valuable total look at what a business is doing, where it might go, and what problems it might be having. It is this look that is the essential feature and virtue of the Four C's Conference. It permits a combined look, focusing on facts and all of the components of the organizational matrix, not just the consideration of one or another set of ideas. From this point of view you should not be hesitant to undertake such a conference without facilitation. What matters is that the time is set aside, preparation is undertaken, and people have a frank and open discussion using the three-step method. There is no way that it can fail.

THE CONCERT OF COMPONENTS

Overemphasis on Characteristics leads to ignoring the other elements in the Four C's scheme. This in turn leads to a limited and blunted perspective of what is needed for entrepreneurial success. The Entrepreneurial Manager not only needs to develop the elements in each of the vectors but to develop them simultaneously so that each articulates with the other. It does little good to develop specific business Strategy plans, for example, when the Context is changing rapidly in the area in question. A more flexible Strategy is needed. All the Competencies in the world will not help if the Conditions of work are not developed and structured in such a way as to make innovation productive.

Of the Four C's, two—Characteristics and Context—are less able to be influenced than others. Even with these, however, there are ways you can be proactive. With respect to Characteristics, you can seek to inventory your Characteristics.[6] There are books and programs that can help you think more creatively, tolerate ambiguity a bit more, and so on. Similarly, there are ways to take advantage of, if not change, the Context. Unfortunately, books on entrepreneurship tend to fall into either the personal category (Characteristics) or the Conditions category (*How to Make a Billion in Real Estate in 60 Days and Lose Weight at the Same Time!*). Little attention is paid to the need for bringing all these components together in concert. There are certainly ways to make this happen. One of the most effective is the Concert of Components Conference.

THE CONCERT OF COMPONENTS CONFERENCE

In this conference, Entrepreneurs schedule a day or a half day for themselves and their Staffs (and here we mean *all* Staff, not just professional Staff) to review their ventures in the light of the Four C's Conference decisions. Staff are assigned to review progress (one each if there are four Staff members) and asked to research and to present the area. Others challenge. The day is spent looking at Characteristics, Competencies, Conditions, and Contexts with respect to the particular firm in question. The norms or rules of the game for the conference are that problems and positives are brought up, both to continue the positives and to learn from the problems (or failures). You may think of this conference as a kind of "mid-course" correction conference. It supplements the Four C's Conference in that it looks at progress and integration while retaining a proactive (rather than a reactive) posture.

In preparation for this conference, staff members are asked to make suggestions at any point throughout the Four C plan period. One Staff member has the job of Four C's Coordinator.[7] That individual receives suggestions and comments and helps in the specific planning of the conference. This assures that ideas and topics that people think about throughout the year are not lost. They are kept and organized by the Coordinator who distributes packages of assignments and issues to the individual Staff members or Staff groups as the time for the conference nears.

How it is actually organized is of less importance then the fact that at least every six months—and once a quarter in turbulent, high-growth sectors—time is spent in proactive assessment. That investment will pay off well, not only in profits but in satisfaction and pride in the organization itself. All too often Entrepreneurs become successful and then fail to see the problems lying in their path. In the December 12, 1986 issue of the *Wall Street Journal*, Allen Michaels comments on the prelude to the failure of his Firm, Convergent Technologies, Inc.:

Yes, it was heady. In retrospect I can see what was happening; a guy who always questioned what he did, who wanted to sleep on decisions suddenly began to believe that all his decisions were right—because they were his. The normal apprehension that goes with decision making gave way to the dangerous conviction that we were always right. In fact, invincible. (P. 26)

Although there is no guarantee that the Four C's Conference and the Concert of Components Conference will prevent things like this from happening, they most assuredly give the firm a better chance than the usual ways.

CONCLUSION

One of two perspectives is usually associated with entrepreneurship. The first emphasizes the individual personality (*Five Traits That Lead to Success*). The second emphasizes environment (*Anyone Can Make Money in Real Estate*). Neither takes in the kinds of Competencies and Conditions that Entrepreneurs need to make a venture successful. Neither deals with ways existing firms can become more entrepreneurial.

We have suggested to you that the Four C's perspective takes in all variables that need attention. These are: (1) Characteristics of you, the Entrepreneur; (2) Competencies of you, the Entrepreneurial Manager; (3) Conditions of the organization you develop; and (4) Context in which you and the organization live and work.

Each of these elements—the *Entrepreneurial Quartet*—needs to be in place and attended to if you are to achieve success. You may not fail right away if any of the Four C's are ignored, but the weakness of inattention builds up. Problems appear. The balanced (and successful) Entrepreneurial Leader keeps an eye at all times on each of the Four C's. He or she will move among them, always working on the one that is least developed at any moment in time.

The Four C's Conference is the key to monitoring the strength and weakness of each part of the Firm. The purpose of the Conference is threefold:

1. To insure attention to the Four C's on a regular basis;

2. To involve the whole organization in those considerations (because it is the whole organization that must work together to make the adjustments that are necessary to keep current); and

3. To create an articulation of components such that all are considered together, at the same place and time, by the relevant people. Otherwise there will not be the kind of commonality needed to effect change.

In addition to the Four C's Conference, the Concert of Components Conference is an extremely valuable tool for achieving balance among the components.

The focus of this book is on the Four C's perspective. Certainly we give some attention to Self and environment, as most books on entrepreneurship do; but we consider these only in relation to balance (or the lack of it) among the Characteristics, Competencies, Conditions, and Contexts. The rest of Part I outlines other essential elements that need to be considered initially.

Chapter 2, "The Energy of Thought," outlines the importance of thinking in general about new products and services, and procedures and policies. Strange as it may seem, within our tradition of newness as a country, we appear to be at a plateau of innovation. The defining characteristic of American business appears to be stability and sameness rather than newness and novelty. For us to be successful worldwide, as Derek Bok (1986), President of Harvard University says, we will need again to live by and through our wit. The status quo can only be translated as "the mess we're in."

Chapter 3, "The Mountain Man Versus the Wagon Train," emphasizes the need for collective effort—the cooperation rather than competition. Competition is needed, to be sure, but not of the zero sum—"I win, you lose"—variety.

This point leads into Chapter 4, "The Entrepreneurial Staircase." Ideas and firms go through stages. It is imperative to know those stages and to adjust your behavior to them. Your Skills may be more appropriate for one stage than another. This knowledge can work to your advantage.

NOTES

1. There is even stronger evidence that this was an entrepreneurial venture in every sense of the word. The Pilgrims—and most of the others for the next 100 years—came to North America under charters granted by the English crown. Those charters were granted with the view to turning the colonies into profitable enterprises, with a substantial portion of that profit being returned to the crown. Thus, colonization of North America was a high risk venture for which the English crown provided the capital, the colonists, and the labor.

2. This section and the next on potential benefits are derived from materials developed by the United Way of Canada to which we provide grateful acknowledgment.

3. Man has always looked for the comfort of answers. In his book, *Magic, Science and Religion* (1954), the famous anthropologist B. Malinowski pointed out that these three institutions are answer-providing ones, each substituting in certain cases for the other. Within an office context something a little bit more mundane often provides answers; i.e., office gossip. Gossip is always evaluative. It tries to understand role violating behavior in a context of current rules because there are often many rules available to interpret and explain in a given behavioral action. People need a chance to talk about what colleagues did and to understand. This is why gossip is so entertaining and so powerful.

4. The *F*riendly *F*ellows, men and women o*F* great distinction and o*F* great competence, *F*iled Scienti*F*ic reports *F*requently and *F*aith*F*ully. There are nine Fs. Seven sound like "F" and two are "ofs". If you didn't get it right, don't worry. The accuracy rate on this little quiz runs about 20% in groups we have worked with.

5. Elements of this assessment/requirements list come from Robert Myers, president of The United Way of Canada. He has developed an intensive, challenging approach to assessing how local United Way organizations are operating, called the "On Site Process." It is one of the best organizational analysis approaches available today.

6. See, for example, Charlotte Taylor (1985), "Do You Have What It Takes to be an Entrepreneur?" or a popular booklet on entrepreneurial assessments, Hawkins and Turla, *Test Your Entrepreneurial I.Q.*, 1986.

7. In some respects, the CEO is the Four C's Coordinator, of course; but there

is a lot of material in coordinating the components that the CEO cannot do. Thus, a coordinator of components can work on the implementation of the plan and be involved in some of the detail work that might be left unattended if the "boss" tried to "do it all."

2

The Energy of Thought: The Importance of Entrepreneurship

Tropman: This book is about introducing new ideas into organizations.

Gould: Great, but that's only the half of it.

Tropman: What do you mean?

Gould: The other part is getting rid of the old ideas. They're hard to throw away. You think you've got rid of them, and you come back from lunch, and there they are again, sitting at the desk causing trouble.

Tropman: Sort of like a boomerang.

Gould: Yeah. We could call it the "Boomerang Theory of Organizational Development."

—From a conversation with John P. Gould, Dean, Graduate School of Business, University of Chicago, July 1986

INTRODUCTION

If the human species is distinguished by anything, it is the ability to learn from experience—to codify, to organize, and to transmit in a variety of forms experienced from one generation to the next.[1] And new ideas change things.

THE ENERGY OF THOUGHT

Our ancestors, the Neanderthals, learned things slowly, but they were able to accumulate and transmit their knowledge. This gave our species an incredible advantage. Think for a moment about the difference between sewn clothing and the simple use of skins unattached to one another. Consider, too, what is required to sew clothing; namely, a needle and thread.

The needle is a commonplace item in our daily lives now, but that has not always been the case. Sometimes concepts are most readily understood when presented in their simplest form, so we ask you to suspend disbelief for a moment and travel back with us to a time without needles.

It is winter. Before us is one of our Neanderthal great uncles—call him "Zung." He has just enjoyed a nourishing breakfast of spit-roasted bird and tree bark and is now picking his teeth with the short side of a wish bone. Soon, he must venture out into the cold to hunt lunch, and he ponders the pile of animal skins that he will have to tie to various parts of his body in hope of keeping away some of the icy blasts of the north wind. An idea is about to be born.

If he could figure out a way to tie the the small pelts all together into one super-pelt, he realizes that he would be able to cover more of his body more efficiently. His problem is how to do that. He might glue them, but adhesives are still several thousand years away. Then it occurs to him that a long, thin piece of sinew would do the trick nicely. All he needs is a bunch of small holes in each pelt.

In one of the pelts is the hole from the spear that brought the animal down. It is a large hole. He looks at his spear. It has a large spear point. He knows about things with sharp points. That technology developed very early with the need to kill animals for food. But the idea of a very thin, sliverlike point so far has not made its way into the culture.

Still, a hole is a hole; and he gets an insight. If the big spear head makes a big hole, then a tiny spear head would make a tiny hole. He looks about him for a sharp stone that will be small enough to make the size of the hole he needs. He finds nothing. He tries shaping a piece of flint by pounding on it with another piece of flint. No good. He only succeeds in smashing his fingers as it approaches the required size.

He sits back and picks his teeth some more. So wrapped in thought is he, that he inadvertently stabs himself with the piece of bone. He lets out a small squeal of pain, and stares at the bone sliver. From that exercise in dental hygiene something is about to emerge that will change the course of human history.

Zung picks up one of the pelts and pokes it with the bone. It takes some doing, but he finally manages to make a nice small hole. Using a rough stone, he sharpens the end of the bone still further. It doesn't take nearly the effort to make the second hole. He makes holes in the edge of a second pelt. Now comes the hard part—getting the sinew through the holes. It's tough going until it occurs to him that, if he cuts a small notch in the other end of the bone with his flint knife, he can tie the sinew there and pull it through the pelt as he makes the hole. He becomes so excited at the possibilities for sewing the pelts together that he forgets to go out to hunt for lunch, his wife gets mad at him, the neighbors in the next cave start clucking their tongues, and he is hauled before the council of elders.

Well, you can imagine how that scene is played out. Zung, very excited, says, "Hey, have I come up with a great idea. We take a tiny piece of bone, see, and we put a little notch in one end, and we attach a long piece of sinew to that piece of bone. Then we pass the pointy needle from one skin through to another and in that way fasten each skin to a different skin. We can make whole blankets."

Ung, another of our Neanderthal uncles—and indeed the rest of the council—respond as they would, no doubt, today. "The gods don't like it. If God wanted to make a tiny point with a notch in the end attached to sinew, he would have done so."

Bung adds, "And it is unnatural to join the skins of one animal to another."

Then Mung chimes in. "Besides, such a tiny spear would break."

The chorus of complaints, comments, and criticisms goes on around the fire for hours. Zung's face betrays his rising sense of discouragement as elder after elder speaks against his idea.

Zung, the Entrepreneur, tries to change their thinking. "But we could trade these super-pelts for things we need from other tribes."

The chorus of derision grows even louder. "Who would want them?" "It would be too complicated." "We tried gluing them together and that didn't work. What makes you think that your idea is any better?"

So much for poor Zung. But down the years the response to entrepreneurial concepts and suggestions has probably changed little. There is always some god that will be offended by the new idea. Of course, as a general rule, gods always tend to disapprove of new things (at least that's what their interpreters have told us over the years).

Still, these same new ideas—from a needle with a sinew attached, to the domesticating of animals, to writing and alphabets, to horseshoes—demonstrate clearly that the energy of thought is one of the most powerful forces that exist. Entrepreneurs are major developers and users of that energy. They harness it, structure it, and take the initiative in forcing us to confront the validity and integrity of new ideas, products, services, plans, and policies. This was true of our ancient relatives sitting around their camp fires in the middle of a freezing European winter. And it is true for those who develop Post-Its® for the 3M Company who must try to convince a company that has made most of its money by creating and marketing products that stick that there is money to be made and a service to be performed in providing products that don't stick very well.

Harnessing the energy of thought is amply demonstrated by a principle developed by the inventor of the modern machine gun, Sir Hiram Stevens Maxim, the ex-patriot American inventor and fixer (Slade, 1986). He was perhaps a classic in at least two regards. He conceived a number of important inventions—inventing an electric light at the same time as Edison (and later losing out in a patent fight with Edison)—and he was unable to carry through on many of his inventions. Although he had the idea of the light, for example,

Edison had the idea of the light *and* the system of power to generate the light. This gave Edison the edge.[2] (Maxim also experimented with a steam powered airplane that actually lifted off the ground, ten years *before* the Wright brothers.) But it is in the development of the modern machine gun that Maxim provides the perfect metaphor for the energy of thought.

For many years individuals had known that guns recoiled when fired. No one had been able to harness that energy. In his design, Maxim was able to capture the energy from the gun's recoil and, using a spring, transfer that energy to the performance of another function: loading the next shell and cocking the gun preparatory to firing.

Although it is not our intention to extol the virtues of the machine gun, the principle that Maxim used is one that we can all learn from. Maxim thought of the problem as one of energy transfer, or saving of wasted energy. In his book, *High Output Management* (1983), Andrew Grove calls a similar process *leveraging*. Whatever the process is called, it involves capturing the available energy of a system and using it to expand and enhance the system's activities. Ideas do this job for us quite well. It is ideas, in fact, that give the organizational system its zest—whether that system is the place where we work, or a family, clubs, lodges, or other places where we spend our time. The kinds of Systems that we find exciting are those where new things are happening. The paradox is that, while we enjoy the excitement of the new mixed with the tradition of the old, we tend at the same time to be resistant to the new. Consequently, we need help in overcoming these conservative tendencies.

New ideas are structured by two main sources. They are either *needs* driven or *means* driven. The needs driven idea is something that comes from a pressing requirement or problem for which there is no existing solution. Such a solution is called an *invention*. A new vaccine, a completely new product, or a new service can be considered in this category.

Alternatively, there are means driven developments or innovations. These arise as a current product or service is offered, perhaps with only minor modifications, perhaps with none at all, to a new market or market segment, or is assigned to a new function that it has not yet played before in the system—the use of dried corn cobs as a fuel, for example. Nothing is invented, but the application is new.

Entrepreneurial Managers are people who energize systems. They either develop them or revitalize them. They harness the energy of thought. Engaging in the harnassing process essentially involves the management of three tasks simultaneously: (1) doing your regular job, (2) understanding the problems of negative energy within an organization and finding ways to diminish its impact, and (3) introducing positive energy within the organization. Sometimes this introduction occurs by transforming negative to positive energy, as Maxim did with his machine gun. Sometimes totally new sources of energy must be introduced. Ideas are energizing elements. They can be negative or positive. Much of the success of entrepreneurial effort comes from harnessing and directing the energy of thought. The ability to introduce innovations successfully within an organization is a similar process.

In thinking about this harnessing or redirecting process, you can't simply wait for some "big idea" to come along—or the right job, or the right position. Rather, you must make energy harnessing activities a normal part of your every day routine in your home and family, in the small microenvironment of your work area and work station, and in the larger macroenvironment of the organization as a whole.

In summary, then, when any of the signs of low levels of activity arise in the home, office, or the Firm, change becomes necessary in order to keep current, in order to keep alive, in order to keep things fun, in order to keep things moving. Change comes from new ideas and new approaches. Resistance to change comes from old ideas and old approaches. The first task of the Entrepreneurial Manager is to eliminate the negative; the second is to introduce the positive.

SOURCES OF RESISTANCE TO CHANGE

In thinking over a strategy of change, the late Ron Lippitt (with Watson and Wesley, 1958) talked about change forces and resistance forces—those that promote and support new products and services and those that caution and sometimes rage against the introduction of the new and the different. Resistance forces are legion. Galbraith (1982) writes:

New ideas are never neutral. Innovative ideas are destructive; they destroy investments in capital equipment and peoples' careers. The management of ideas is a political process. The problem is that the political struggle is biased toward those in the establishment who have authority and control of resources. (P.11)

Tom Fitzgerald (1987), an organizational consultant and former GM manager, summarized what some of them can be:

1. inability to plug into the change system;
2. vested interests;
3. protection from the need to change;
4. self-comforting pattern in organizations;
5. control as a key value;
6. the difficulty of linking microactions to macrogoals;
7. self-cloning techniques in organizations;
8. social distance of management over worker;
9. lack of understanding about the true and important mechanisms of change.

To these, as related but independent factors, we add:

10. lack of conceptual energy; and
11. the inertia of institutions.

Some reinterpretive comments show what Fitzgerald means by all of these.

In many organizations employees at all levels of the Firm's hierarchy are job-oriented rather than work-oriented. They tend to identify their tasks with some version of the job description, usually the more specific and concrete aspects of that job description. As a result, they are not alert for things that need doing, whatever those things might be (picking someone up from the airport, for example, or making the coffee). Often the things that need doing are neither pleasant nor easy. If they had been, they most likely would have been done. It is never difficult to get people to travel to Florida in the winter for business meetings. It is often difficult to get them to travel to Halifax. Many organizational employees simply do not see themselves as related to the total organization in any useful way. Instead, they have a narrow, worm's eye view of their activities. Innovations, new approaches, new products, new services, are viewed (from their reference point) not as things interesting and exciting, but as more trouble than they are worth.

This leads us to vested interests. Almost all of us have such interests. Most of us fail to see the extent of our own involvements. We mask actions that advance our own personal interests, justifying them as being necessary in some larger, impersonal sense. These kinds of justifications are made for the very high salaries of corporate executives by those who will receive the salaries. Thus our own ability to deny that our interests are self-serving further compounds the problem. As Robert Myers, president of The United Way of Canada, said, "Nobody goes in to be fired who doesn't believe she or he is being promoted." Arguments against a new product of service, therefore, are likely to be couched in terms that make it *seem* as if it is wise and sound for the organization to avoid investments and risks in these areas. The fact that such investments and risks may have profound negative consequences for the individual making the argument is set aside as an incidental grace note. In this way, individuals are protected from the need to change.

For many persons, organizational structure serves much the same function as the shell does for the turtle: it protects the individual from the slings and arrows of outrageous fortune. In part, at least, this protection is to the good. If you are living on adrenaline's edge all the time, the likelihood of making innovative and imaginative new contributions is surely lessened. On the other hand, overprotection is as much of a danger as underprotection. In both cases you fail to experience sufficient outside stimulation to motivate change, adaptation, and advancement as an organization grows in size. Self-confirming styles emerge, fueled by the self-fulfilling prophecy.

The self-fulfilling prophecy—one self-comforting organizational pattern—begins with a statement or belief about the condition of the world, which at the time it is made is neither true nor false. Statements such as "we can never penetrate that market," "I can never stop smoking," or "I can't do anthing with my teenage son" are typical examples. The person who utters such statements then begins to act *as if* the statements were true. Because market penetration "cannot" be established, no efforts are made to do so. Because the drinking or smoking behavior "cannot" be stopped, no efforts are made to stop it. Because truculent, recalcitrant sons "cannot" be handled, they are not handled. Indeed, it is not unusual for efforts of a contrary nature to be taken: "I wash my hands of the whole affair." Often the result of these activities is the very event that was feared in the first place. In other words, although nothing was necessarily true at the beginning of this intellectual scenario, as the individual begins to believe that a certain thing is true, she or he acts as if it were true. This in turn creates the reality, and the last step in the self-fulfilling prophecy takes place. The market penetration has not been achieved, drinking and smoking have not been controlled, the offspring's behavior has not been altered; the observer uses these results as proof that her or his original suppositions were correct.

In a nut shell, the self-fulfilling prophecy is a reality creating and confirming procedure. With it we create those things we believe to be true and use that creation as proof that we were right in the first place. Members of organizations engage in this behavior both in their personal lives and in their organizational lives. But entire organizations can engage in self-fulfilling prophecy. No one wants small cars. Therefore, small cars aren't made. The few that are introduced do not sell well. Based on the assumption that no one really wants them anyway, they're badly manufactured and poorly appointed. After people take a look at them, no one *does* want them. Those who predicted that result in the first place are self-comforted and self-confirmed.

Change is also resisted because control is such a deep value in American society. Control is important because it represents the other side of freedom. In a society that is as open as the American society, in a society that has as many opportunities as American society has, there are a number of problematic aspects that go along with that openness. DeVries (1985) wrote a piece called "The Dark Side of Entrepreneurship." In a sense, control may be thought of as the dark side of freedom. All of the openness and opportunity in American society generates anxiety. It creates uncertainty. That's probably why "The Gong Show" is so quintessentially American: There's always opportunity to go up, to improve, but there's also opportunity to go down, to fail; at any moment you might be "gonged." It follows, therefore, that the antidote to uncertainty and anxiety is control. The social structure of our society makes change in organizations difficult, because having once established a certain amount of control, some amount of certainty within their life space, individuals are loath to reject it.

Change is additionally resisted because it is hard to link microactions to big goals. Rosabeth Kanter (1983) makes the point that this link is important. Macrochanges frequently come from accumulated microinterventions and, from a social science and organizational science point of view, certainly, the truth in these relationships is easily seen. Nevertheless, when you are actually *in* the situation, attempting to develop organizational change, these relationships may seem much more tenuous and less connected than they do to the outside observer. The same old actions are likely to be taken as the appropriate ones. They are the ones that have been associated historically with organizational goals. To do something different is to introduce uncertainty and, possibly, disorganization into the firm.

Organizations tend to reproduce themselves. Armies are always preparing for the "last" war. Units and subunits are set up like the parent unit. Field offices are structured in a similar way. It is often thought that what has worked in one setting, in one instance, in one time period, for one problem, or with one kind of employee mix, will work again in other sites, with other employees and so on. Hence, new ideas, as introduced through new organizational forms, tend to be rejected by organizations and firms.

Despite the fact that management and workers need to cooperate in the achievement of more successful products and services, social distance between workers and management creates problems in achieving this goal. In American society we receive status by association. That's why we "dress up" when we go to work.[3] Interacting across social boundaries has a number of special problems associated with it when one is talking about organizational change and the introduction of new ideas. The new operation or procedure carries with it a social baggage. If a worker suggests something to a manager, the social structure of that communication makes it less likely that the manager will accept it. Similarly, communication going the other way carries the negatives of authority and office with them. Workers are, as a result, more inclined to reject managers' suggestions.

Organizations also miss the true and important mechanisms of change. Simply put, these are people. People at all levels of the organization have ideas and, if the structure is right, will contribute that wisdom. When the structure is not right, organizations fail to use that inherent creativity.

Many firms have a lack of conceptual energy, or the excitement and fun of new ideas flowing around, being considered, being tried, being improved, being rejected, and so on. The climate and culture of the organization, therefore, becomes a problem for the introduction of new ideas simply because of what might be called "the inertia of institutions." This inertia is both structural and intellectual in nature. Old structures, old ways of doing things, and old equipment all represent one aspect of organizational inertia.

A second and, perhaps, less obvious form of inertia is embodied by old ideas, old assumptions, and old precepts captured in concrete in some organizational lore. Overcoming this inertia is one of the more important tasks of the Entrepreneur. This is true whether the Entrepreneur is already in an organization and seeking to change it, or seeking to change an interorganizational member on which he or she must depend for supplies, equipment, capital, personnel, and so on, in order to do business.

APPROACHES TO REDUCING CHANGE RESISTANCE

Whether one is talking about introducing change into an already existing firm or beginning the development of a new Firm, all of these problems need to be addressed. They are among the reasons why Firms become rigid, fail to adapt to the changes in the external environment, and eventually go bankrupt or die.

Entrepreneurial Managers need to develop strategies and tactics that can counter these negative forces. Ways to plug employees into the total mission of the organization through job rotation and broader work assignments, for example, might be developed. This same activity could decrease vested interests in particular areas and create an interest in the total mission of the firm, whether that firm is big or small.

Compensation patterns for all employees that relate both to their own and group performances and to the total organizational performance can be developed. All employees need to be exposed to the risk and the rewards attendant to the introduction of new ideas. A cash bonus for a good suggestion is one technique that has been tried in a number of places, and it has apparently enjoyed modest success. But you might consider going further, making the *expectation* of contributions to innovation, new techniques, and new ideas for products and services a part of every employee's job description.

Antidotes to self-fulfilling prophecies need to be explored. There's a sign we've seen in many Firms that reads "the difficult we do immediately; the impossible takes a little longer." This motto, borrowed from the Seabees of World War II, serves as a very mundane example of the way some firms have tried to introduce more of a "can do"—as opposed to a "can't do"—mentality into their organization. A "can't do" mentality is expressed by the poster that is also to be seen in a number of offices. It shows a cartoon figure convulsed in laughter and the caption reads, "You want it *WHEN???*" Admittedly this poster may be a gentle reminder from clerical staff to thoughtless bosses to do a little more planning in terms of getting material to them for work. The mentality it suggests, however, is negative and unsupportive. Ideas are not likely to flourish in that kind of climate.

Entrepreneurial Managers are not going to change the structure of American society. Control will remain a deep value. Social distance between workers and management will still be present. There are ways, however, that the penalties for the lack of control can be reduced through some legitimization of risk and failure in the organization and through the creation of organizational celebrations that transcend social boundaries at least within the work space. Attempts can be made to flatten and make the organizational structure more democratic. This is a point that Rosabeth Kanter (1983) repeatedly emphasizes.

If the Entrepreneurial Manager begins to take some of these actions, the inertia of institutions will be less powerful. Negative energy will be less dominant. Individuals within the organization will begin to say, "Hey, let's try it this way" or "Wow, what about this?" The manager will have liberated important change and improvement forces within the organization and decreased resistant forces.

THE INTRODUCTION SCENARIO

Don't infer from anything said to this point that all new ideas are good, that all new procedures, products, services are naturally beneficial. Such an assumption is wrong. Many new ideas are flawed and have many problems. Many more are simply rotten and should be rejected out of hand. Most of us know of at least one new idea that was either silly (the electric fork) or actually disastrous (the "New" Coke). Such knowledge tends to support a "do it the same old way" philosophy. It becomes imperative, then, to distinguish good ideas from bad ones and to look carefully at all new ideas with an eye toward improving them. There are a number of problems in this process that Entrepreneurial Managers need to recognize.

No Good Way to Assess New Ideas

It's fairly common practice among employees in firms that use the "suggestion box" to espouse the belief that the box is mounted firmly atop a chute leading directly to the furnace (paper shredder, waste basket). Never mind the truth behind such suspicions, the new idea is actually a bountiful commodity. The real problem is that we don't have any good way in most organizations for taking a look at possible new products or services. In fact, it is the intransigence of most existing Firms to new ideas that leads to the celebration of the Entrepreneur in the first place. It is for this reason writers talk of the need for product or organizational champions who follow up new ideas and approaches personally (Daft and Bradshaw, 1980).

Organizational Ghosts

New ideas clash with old ideas. This problem is part of the vested interest difficulty that Galbraith (1982) noted and Fitzgerald (1987) mentioned in a somewhat different guise. The new approach, the new product, the new service not only displaces old products and services, it displaces old ideas about what the company is, what the organization is about, and what its mission and purpose has been historically. The organizational priests tend to oppose new ideas, not on grounds that those ideas will not be productive or profitable but that they are somehow in violation of the rules and rituals of "what we are."

Old ideas represent the "ghost in the machine," ready to haunt those who strive to introduce something new. They trap us in ways we don't even understand in the same way that old routines imprison us.

The Polarization Problem

Because effective mechanisms do not exist in most organizations for assessing new ideas, and because some form of vested interests resists their introduction, new ideas often get polarized into a "them or us" mode within the organizational structure. It is this either/or dilemma that Fisher and Ury warn against in their book, *Getting to Yes* (1981). Although John Naisbitt (1983) sees us moving from an "either/or society to a multiple option society," polarization is still a major difficulty.

A typical scenario involves the Entrepreneur introducing a new idea into a hostile environment. There are several features of new ideas that make them vulnerable initially. To begin with, they're fledgling and incomplete with parts missing. Because they are new, new ideas do not have thoroughly worked out answers to all the problems that individuals reviewing them may see. This leaves them more open to attack than standard operating procedures.

New ideas are often working in uncharted territory. It is for this reason that market research is not always the best guide. Indeed, at any given moment in time a market may not exist for a particular product or service and won't until the product or service is introduced.

Because individual workers and managers do not know how to respond to these problems, they tend to adopt traditional modes, images, and methods of assessment—comfortable postures and conventional comparisons. In a new idea conference, the flaws and vulnerabilities of a new idea are used as a point of attack by opponents.

Attempts to deal with these attacks may lead to exaggerated claims by the entrepreneur because, for a new product or service, the Entrepreneur cannot prove that all of the concerns raised by opponents are invalid. Some may be viewed as correct. Counter assertions tend to be made; and, once this scenario has begun to develop, a spiral of attack and response is difficult to stop. Each phase contains more exaggeration: "the proposed product is awful" versus "the proposed product is great."

Clever opponents of new ideas exploit these exaggerated claims as a next step and propose tests or assessments based particularly on them. The *exaggerated* claims are now likely to prove false, which in turn may lead to the whole idea being rejected erroneously. Keep in mind that the failure of the claims for innovation does not necessarily mean that the idea is wrong—any more than their acceptance proves that an idea was right.

The Politics of Acceptance or Rejection

In general, ideas for new products and services are either inappropriate or appropriate, wrong or right. Their quality of correctness or their merit, however, does *not* necessarily insure their appropriate rejection or acceptance. Politics play a part. In the best of all possible worlds poor ideas are always rejected and good ones are always accepted. In the world we live in that is not always the case. Instead, acceptance or rejection is often controlled by one of two pernicious errors that cloud the business mind—and that Entrepreneurial Managers must seek mightily to avoid. These errors are (and this should come as no surprise) the *Acceptance Error*, as a result of which ideas are accepted for reasons other than merit, and the *Rejection Error*, as a result of which ideas are rejected for reasons other than merit.

Although these errors are endemic to both established and new enterprises, the Rejection Error is the more common of the two. Ideas for new products and services should be rejected because they are silly, stupid, impractical, too expensive to implement, too far ahead of their time, or for any number of good and sufficient reasons. The Rejection Error comes into play when such ideas are rejected because they conflict with old ideas (or company policy), because some corporate priest finds them offensive to his or her cherished beliefs, or for any of the reasons Tom Fitzgerald outlined. The power of negative thinking is strongly and destructively at work when the Rejection Error occurs.

The Acceptance Error is less well recognized but still very much present. We also call it "the same old stuff" error. It occurs especially when ideas for programs, products, services, or plans are accepted because of the prestige and importance—the clout—of the individual presenting them without particular regard for the merit of the ideas. This error is even more likely to occur in a new and emerging entrepreneurial venture because of the solo concept of the Entrepreneur. Frequently, individuals with good, new ideas work alone. When their ideas are attacked, they will often adopt a "mountain man" strategy; i.e., retreat to some high ground and fight off all of the opponents. Such a defensive, reactive approach historically has proved to be far less effective than an offensive, proactive one; moving into the environment and developing allies who can assist in overcoming negative thinking and who can help secure rejection of bad ideas and acceptance of good ones.

Erroneous Acceptance and Rejection

There are four possible outcomes to the presentation of new ideas: (1) correct acceptance, (2) correct rejection, (3) erroneous acceptance, and (4) erroneous rejection. These four outcomes are outlined in Table 2.1.

Table 2.1
Idea or Proposal Outcomes

Quality of New Idea or Proposal	Organizational Action on New Idea or Proposal	
	Accepts	Rejects
Good	Correct Acceptance (1)	Erroneous Rejection (3)
Bad	Erroneous Acceptance (4)	Correct Rejection (2)

As can be seen in Table 2.1, two elements are involved. The first is the quality of a new idea or proposal. For simplicity's sake, let's assume the quality can be a good quality or a bad quality. The second aspect is what the organization *does* with the idea or proposal. Here, once again, let's simplify so that the organization can either accept or reject the idea or proposal. Clearly, along the diagonal in Table 2.1, the set of correct responses exists. If an idea is good, then the organization should accept it. We call that *correct acceptance*, and it is located in Cell (1) of Table 2.1. Similarly, if an idea is bad, it should be rejected by the organization. That cell is identified as Cell (2) on the chart.

Two other outcomes, however, are also possible. First, and probably the less dangerous of the two, is when a good idea is rejected. That occurs in Cell (3) on the chart, and is called *erroneous rejection*. Examples of erroneous rejection might be a drug that would be effective for a particular condition but is not accepted by the drug companies for whatever reason (faulty testing, inaccurate measurement, etc.). These are missed opportunities in organizational life. They are difficult to assess because we can never know what it would have been like had the opportunity been fully exploited. Only over a long period of time, as organizational vitality is sapped, competitiveness drained, and organizational fat builds up can we begin to sense that there may well have been a sequence of missed opportunities. More immediately damaging to organizational activities, however, and an area that organizations try to avoid at all costs is the outcome in Cell (4): the *erroneous acceptance* of an idea or a proposal that is truly rotten, which should have been rejected for a variety of reasons. But the idea is accepted and, what is worse, it is sometimes continued for years. For a drug company this might be the case where a harmful drug was introduced into general use. The horrors of Thalidomide, for example, represent one example. On a more global and historical scale, Barbara Tuchman's book, *March of Folly* (1984), details disastrous policies followed by governments in a wide range of historical periods.

REMOVING BAD IDEAS

As the dialogue at the beginning of this chapter suggested, introducing new ideas into organizations is only half of the problem. The other half is removing old, tired, stale ideas, but ideas that at one time captured the imagination of individuals. Sometimes these old ideas are ensconced in semi-sacred concepts, such as, "It's our tradition," or "We've always done things this way." The problem, of course, is that you cannot know in all cases whether the original idea is valuable and should be retained or is hopelessly out of date and should be junked. It is in this sense that the *Marketplace of Ideas* concept helps out.

Organizations need to stimulate competition among ideas, approaches, and perspectives for products and services. This kind of competition is every bit as important as the competition for market and market shares. The organization that competes well internally most likely will compete well externally. The organization that is internally lack-lustre, that avoids challenges, that opts for self-satisfaction with its mission and roles is not likely to do well in other marketplaces. The problem of driving out old ideas, then, is really the other side of the coin we've just been discussing. The introduction of new ideas will, within a competitive climate, be the best mechanism for setting old ideas to rest. Entrepreneurs are, therefore, energy releasers in organizations because they represent a creative force involving new combinations, new permutations, and new configurations. These fresh approaches invigorate and inspirit big and small organizations. The climate of excitement that is produced by the regular infusion of new ideas and new perspectives creates a heady atmosphere that in some instances becomes its own reward. Think back to the places (and they may not be the current places) where you have had the greatest sense of fun in accomplishment—a sports team, perhaps, or a play, or even in a job. Frequently, these are not situations in which you were the boss. Regardless, what you will recall, if you are typical, is the energy that was released by the activity and energy that you could relate to and that you found engaging and uplifting. Almost without exception such recollections are of activities that involved joint participation in some kind of collective effort. Perhaps you played an important role in a crucial sports victory. Perhaps involvement in a high school play springs to your mind. Whether your role was a small one or a large one, you should try to recapture some of the magic you felt in the entrepreneurial setting.

The energy of thought has a second benefit that comes from the product itself. Think back to the time when the needle was finally accepted. Not only was there a climate created that new things could and would happen, but there were all the ancillary benefits generated by the specific new idea. Who can tell what social reorganization may have followed the invention of the needle? Certainly, divisions of labor involving hole punchers, gut pullers, needle makers, needle hole drillers, and so on would shortly arise. This would probably be followed by the question of which animal skins could and should (under God) be joined together. Doubtless, religious leaders found a helpful role for themselves almost immediately. And we haven't even begun to discuss the emergence of the entire fur fashion industry. Such changes are important ones and the structural change that follows them is, itself, an antidote to old and tired ideas. Therefore, the entrepreneurship process is indeed a freeing process, freedom from imprisonment in old concepts and approaches.

CONCLUSION

The energy of thought is released through planned, proactive steps. Maybe no one will come up with something as revolutionary as the needle, but there are lots of ideas out there that can help the organization achieve its goals, help introduce new products, new services, improvements, and refurbishments. The idea alone, however, is not enough. In new ventures, special attention needs to be given to intellectual, interpersonal, and organizational aspects if the idea is to bear fruit and not be relegated to some dumpster of "crazy suggestions" that is perennially full.

The first step is to recognize the energy of thought. The next is to enhance, increase, and legitimize the supply of new ideas in order to create an organization that welcomes new approaches and perspectives. There is much more than this, of course, but without the supply, little that happens later makes much difference.

NOTES

1. For a discussion of early man, see Pfeiffer, 1984.

2. You can just imagine what people must have said to him: "What'cha gonna do with that bulk, Hiram? You gonna run wires to every house in the gosh darned country? Smarten up!"

3. And "dress down" has a negative connotation. That's what happens when you criticize someone else.

The Supply of Ideas: Success and Failure—The Mountain Man and the Wagon Train

Beyond the routine problems of survival in rugged countryside and brutal weather, mountain men were confronted with a great variety of special ones endemic to their work. Jim Bridger, for example, once went about for three years with a long, barbed Blackfoot arrowhead buried in the muscles of his back. Finally Bridger ran into the missionary-physician Marcus Whitman, who dug out the arrowhead, presumably without any anesthetic except, perhaps, a bottle of whiskey.

> —*The Trailblazers* (p. 73), a volume in *The Old West* series,
> New York: Time-Life Books, 1973.

With their wagons loaded and their animals assembled, all that remained for the pioneers to do at the jump-off point was to organize themselves. Here the American town-meeting tradition proved useful. As if by reflex, they would nominate candidates, hold elections and set up temporary governments.... Alonzo Delano heard of one [wagon train trail government] that contained a court of appeals, an executive branch and a legislative body, all set forth in a written constitution.

> —*The Pioneers* (p. 89), another volume in *The Old West* series,
> New York: Time-Life Books, 1974.

INTRODUCTION

Introducing new ideas, getting them accepted, and transforming a new idea into a viable product or service is a crucial task, perhaps *the* crucial task for the Entrepreneurial Manager. This is true whether you are starting a venture or working within an existing organization. In new ventures staff come with pictures in their heads, with various kinds of cultural baggage, or with sets

Figure 3.1
The One Dimensional/Theoretical Failure-Success Grid

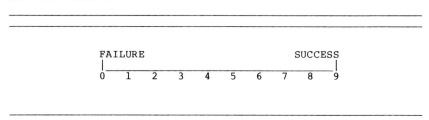

of ideas about the way things should be, about processing facts, or about who's ahead and who's behind. These can and often do inhibit the development of the new venture. Indeed, one of the principal reasons new ventures fail is the inability of Entrepreneurs to instill an appropriate set of ideas and purposes in the minds of those they recruit to work with them (Hardacer and White, 1987). Part of the problem comes from a misunderstanding of the components of success and failure. Part is derived from the misconception of the Entrepreneur as a "mountain man" instead of the head of a wagon train.

SUCCESS AND FAILURE

The problem is compounded in ongoing organizations where there is not only the general set of cultural orientations but also special forms of culture and structure that must be considered. Thinking up new ideas, products, and services by itself does not insure successful development. Although many Firms fail after start up, there are doubtless millions more new ideas with tremendous productivity potential that have been generated in big, existing firms that never get anywhere—ideas that are lying unused and ignored in some forgotten report or that have been scribbled on scraps of paper in somebody's desk. The examples of Transitron, Penn Central, Eastern Airlines, and Osborn Computer clearly illustrate that past success is no certain guarantee of future success. There is also no certain guarantee that an individual who has made a string of good decisions in the past will continue to do so. The problem can be graphically illustrated in the Success/Failure grid displayed in Figure 3.1.

Most people think of success as a line along which they can move. As they move in one direction, increments of success develop. As they move in the other direction, they encounter increments of failure. As Figure 3.1 suggests, success and failure in this conceptualization are at opposite ends of a pole. Though this idea is a very popular one among business people, it contains a potentially lethal hidden assumption. It intimates that, if you are exhibiting success behaviors you are automatically not exhibiting failure

Figure 3.2
The Multidimensional/Actual Failure-Success Grid

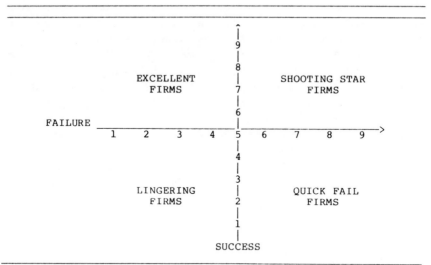

behaviors. Every increment of success is a decrement of failure—every success activity makes failure less likely. The idea is preposterous on its face. What actually happens is demonstrated in Figure 3.2.

As Figure 3.2 suggests, success and failure involve the *two* sets of behaviors that operate simultaneously. You can have lots of successful behaviors or a few; you can engage in high success behavior or low success behavior. What is important to understand, however, is that low or even neutral success behaviors are *not* failure behaviors. Success behaviors are those activities that are going to yield some measure of success, whether it be a tiny bit or a great deal; but success is always the outcome.

Failure behaviors are something quite different. They are activities that are going to cause serious problems. Furthermore, *not* engaging in those failure behaviors will not necessarily insure success.

If you play this scheme out just a bit, Figure 3.2 is the logical conclusion. There is one line of success behaviors, High to Low. There is another line of failure behaviors, High to Low. This leads to a four-fold table with different sectors of performance and different types of success and failure available. In the upper left-hand quadrant, with High Success behaviors and Low Failure behaviors, we find the enduringly successful Firms that continue to outperform others time after time. No doubt, Peters and Waterman (1982) would call these "the excellent companies."

In the upper right-hand corner, where High Failure activities and High Success behaviors operate simultaneously within a Firm, are the "shooting star" companies—those firms that enjoy brilliant success followed by spectacular failure. One may rightly wonder what happens in these kinds of cases, how a firm that was so successful could so suddenly go belly up. Part of the answer lies in the fact that at the same time such Firms were engaging in lots of success behaviors and doing lots of things right, they were also engaging in a lot of failure behaviors and doing lots of things wrong.

In the lower right-hand quarter of the grid are the quick-fail firms. Those are characterized by high amounts of failure behavior and low amounts of success behavior. Such Firms have almost nothing going for them, and we would not expect them to last very long.

In the lower right-hand quadrant are the lingering, slow-fail Firms—the "punk" Firms. That term comes from the slow burning stick that is often used to light firecrackers—there's a low glow, it may go on for a long time, but it's not terribly spectacular. Firms in this sector are characterized by few success behaviors and low failure behaviors. They're not doing much right, but they're not doing much wrong either. Depending on environmental circumstances, such Firms can go on for years, slowly dying until some catastrophic or cataclysmic event occurs that at last pushes them under.

Organizational renewal involves moving into the upper right-hand corner. Developing a sound organizational foundation and fostering creativity with a Firm requires the identification of the kinds of success behaviors that are needed to yield success behaviors and the identification and avoidance of failure behaviors that are so characteristic of new Firms.

Entrepreneurial Management seeks to remedy at least some of the failure behaviors and to introduce, at the same time, some success behaviors. The principal failure behavior that the Entrepreneurial Manager seeks to reduce is the pattern of negative rejection of new ideas. The principal pattern of behavior that the Entrepreneurial Manager seeks to introduce is aimed at developing and thinking about new ideas. It involves the recognition that ideas are not enough, that ideas need to be managed, massaged, developed, championed, walked through. Without these activities the ideas will fail and, as a consequence, the new or old venture will fail.

We believe that the problems of American business today—or the problems of American government or the problems of the nonprofit sector—do not really lie in a lack of creativity. There is an almost limitless number of good, new ideas all around us. There is an ample supply of creative people available, capable of coming up with new approaches and new perspectives as they are required. Our difficulty—our failing—is that we are not using the creativity that is already present in the system. The example of Edward Demming makes this clear.

Edward Demming is an American who developed innovative quality control ideas that American industry rejected during the early 1950s. With success burgeoning on every hand and in a classic application of the myth of "if it ain't broke, don't fix it" philosophy—a philosophy that may have destroyed more organizations, ruined more products, brought the eclipse of more services, and stifled efficient government in more ways than any other—American industry seemed to find Demming's ideas too radical, too new. The Japanese thought otherwise. At that time the imprint, "made in Japan" was synonymous with a shoddy, tinny, short lasting, poor quality product. Japanese industry embraced both Demming's ideas and Demming himself. (Even today he is regarded as an honored hero.) Japan's application of Demming's concepts is given major credit for the high quality we now generally associate with Japanese products.

It is not that American business and industry lack creativity. What is lacking are the systems for putting ideas into practice. More importantly, perhaps, what is lacking are the appropriate perspectives and mechanisms necessary for implementing such systems.

THE MOUNTAIN MAN

The all too prevalent perception of the Entrepreneur is that of the "Mountain Man"—the rugged individualist, "Please, Mom, I'd rather do it myself." This should not surprise anyone. Throughout our history we have extolled the virtues of such an individual. Self-reliance is among our most esteemed virtues, and our great folk heros embody that characteristic: Daniel Boone, Kit Carson, John Fremont, Jeremiah Johnson—the trail blazers. The Entrepreneurial Mountain Man (we think) develops new ideas alone. Our vision of the "great inventor" is a half-crazed genius sequestered by himself in his basement or his garage, thinking up new things, growing new ideas from the fertile soil of his solitude. To be sure, history has occasionally produced such giants, such bigger-than-life souls. But they are rare, and the belief in such individuals places a business enterprise at considerable risk. Because of it, some Firms try to wait for such a Mountain Man to come along, much like the traveling preacher, with a set of new ideas to save them. This perspective, centering as it does on both creativity and idea development in a single person while setting aside our own possible contributions, leads to many organizational problems. Worse, still, it gives rise to a number of problematic organizational types. Let's take a look at a few of these.

The Aimless Organization. This is an organization with no particular ideas. Whatever happens to be current, whatever happens to be a fad, is something that this organization will try to do. It doesn't stick to its knitting, it has no knitting.

The Ritualistic Organization. This organization does the same old stuff (S.O.S.), day in day out, year in year out. Unlike the aimless organization, which doesn't do the same thing for more than twenty minutes, the ritualistic organization always does the same thing.

The Hostile Organization. This conservative organization actively campaigns against new ideas, new procedures, new processes, new products, new services, and so on.

They epitomize the "if it ain't broke, don't fix it school," and they often don't know that it *is* broken.

The Action Organization. This is the firm that says, "Just don't stand there. Do something." What is done is far less important than that there be an appearance of activity at all times.

There are many more, of course, but all of them represent a failure of ideas; a failure to use, to involve, to develop new ideas within their organizations. In large part, blame the Mountain Man perspective. These problematic organizational types cannot shake the belief that sometime, somehow, somewhere some individual, possibly charismatic, will come along with the complete package. They give little or no attention to what their organization, itself, needs, what it might do, or what it should do.

THE WAGON TRAIN

Another image that we celebrate from American history in general and the American West in particular is "the Wagon Train." Where the Mountain Man presents a solo image, the Wagon Train conjures up visions of a collective action to achieve a difficult goal. The Wagon Train is every bit as much a treasured historical image as the Mountain Man; and its staying power is phenomenal, at least if measured by its ability to survive as a continuing series on television. The Wagon Train had an elegant unity about it that was an effective blend of cooperation and community self-reliance. Because it covered vast distances for the march, encountering little other humanity between small settlements and Indian encampments, it could not and it did not expect outside intervention, save an often fickle Providence, to solve its problems and meet its community responsibilities. The cooperation of everyone was essential to survival.[1]

Much entrepreneurial literature looks to the Mountain Man image. Not only is innovation presumed to be located in the individual; but, as we noted before, the individual must have certain characteristics—the right stuff and so on. Taylor (1985), in a piece called "Do You Have What It Takes (to Be an Entrepreneur?)," talks about six characteristics she feels are associated with Entrepreneurs. These are: (1) life experiences (family history and business background); (2) personality; (3) motivations that drive a person; (4) live cycle [positives] (age, health, and general family situation); (5) role assumption capability (willingness to take on entirely new responsibilities; and (6) business readiness (in terms of financial and managerial knowledge).

Although it is certainly true that these characteristics are helpful, we don't know whether they really *create* success or are simply *associated* with success. Neither do we know much about the competencies, conditions, and context that are involved. And Taylor does not suggest anything about working with others as crucial. Our own perspective is well expressed by Coach John

Wooden in a little piece he wrote called "On Staying Power," published in the *New York Times Magazine* as an essay paid for by The Panhandle Eastern Corporation. In a paragraph called "The Main Ingredient Of Stardom," Wooden says the following:

I always taught players that the main ingredient of stardom is the rest of the team. It is amazing how much can be accomplished if no one cares who gets the credit. That's why I was as concerned with the player's character as I was with his ability.

While it may be possible to reach the top of one's profession on sheer ability it is impossible to stay there without hard work. . . . I look for young men who would play the game hard but clean but who would always be trying to improve themselves to help the team. (The "Business World" section, Part Two, June 8, 1986, p. 60)

Indeed, as DeVries (1985) points out, the very energy that is characterized by an Entrepreneur—what Wooden calls "ability"—may well have a negative impact on an organization if it cannot be channeled and used. This "One Man Band" theory of entrepreneurship needs to be modified to involve others.

Maidique (1980) talks about this point in an article on "Entrepreneurs, Champions, and Technological Innovations." He points out four roles that are needed for the successful, overall development of an idea. First, there is the technical innovator, who is the individual who comes up with the idea in the first place. Then there is the business innovator, who is the person within the organization who helps make it happen. The third role is the product champion. This is the person who pushes the actual idea within the organization. Finally, there is the executive champion. He or she prepares the organizational decision apparatus to be receptive to—and to receive—the Entrepreneur's new idea.

Cohen, March, and Olsen (1972), in the "Garbage Can Model of Decision Making," see organizations being made up of four kinds of people—four vectors: people who know the problems, people who know solutions, people who control the resources, and decision makers looking for work. They all need to come together at the same time and in the same place for high quality decisions to emerge. Failure to achieve such articulation and or- chestration in the groups studied, they argued, resulted in the garbage can model of decision making in which these elements were combined more or less at random. What their point tells us about Entrepreneurial Management is the same thing Maidique talks about; there needs to be a group of skills, a wagon train, that can be assembled on a planning, a project, or a product basis. It can both initiate ideas and carry them through. This is really a task accomplished in collective context.

Those who would introduce new ideas, then, often face a series of con- tradictions. They may come up with an idea of their own (the Mountain Man), but they absolutely require the contribution of others to flesh out, support, and implement that new idea (the Wagon Train). So, coming up with the idea is insufficient on its own for entrepreneurial success. Individuals who do think up new ideas may be operating in uncharted territory. Still, they need activities of a day-to-day nature to sustain their activity. Similarly, as DeVries (1985) suggests, innovators who can see new things may, like Maxim, exhibit characteristics that are also destructive. For these reasons the Entrepreneurial Wagon Train approach is stronger and more important than the Entrepreneurial Mountain Man.

Elements of the Wagon Train

Wissema, Van der Pol, and Messer (1980) give us a pretty good idea of what such a Wagon Train ought to look like. In their piece on strategic management art types, they identify six types needed by firms. These are: (1) the Pioneer, (2) the Conqueror, (3) the Level-Headed Ruler, (4) the Administrator, (5) the Economizer, and (6) the Insistent Diplomat. Wissema, Van der Pol, and Messer talk about these as personality types and link them to stages of organizational growth. The Pioneer, they argued, links to explosive growth, the Conqueror to expansion, the Level-Headed Administrator to continuous growth and consolidation, the Economizer to a period of slippage along the organization's trajectory, and the Insistent Diplomat to that period when the industry is contracting. We suggest that it is more appropriate to regard these as skills rather than people or as functions rather than personalities. In the true Entrepreneurial Wagon Train, all of them are required at all phases of an organization's activity. In fact, these functions *are* the Wagon Train that the Entrepreneurial Manager must assemble.

The Pioneer embodies those competencies and characteristics that support risk, that are daring, and that go counter to the accepted course. Offsetting these to some extent may be a lack of consistency and staying power here as well. The Pioneer is characterized by the initiation of new products, services, and ventures.

The Conqueror consolidates new products, services, and ventures and puts them into practice. The Conqueror is something like the Executive Champion in that there's an openness to new ideas but a recognition, as well, of what is needed to make them viable. Whereas the Pioneer may initiate new directions, the Conqueror develops the strategy for development and implementation.

The Level-Headed Administrator is the tactician for the Conqueror's strategy. Level-Headed Administration focuses on day-to-day, relatively routine administrative tasks and goals. In spite of appearances, the completion of this function is absolutely essential to the smooth operation of any big or small organization.

The Economizer displays certain negative aspects. There is a bureaucratic rigidity in this function, a lack of willingness to bend, a minimalistic performance of organizational activities, and a narrow construction of opportunities and responsibilities. All of these might look like a collection of traits to be avoided. It might be if it was all by itself. It serves, however, as a kind of brake on the Wagon Train, just as the Pioneer and the Conqueror serve as both lead team on the front wagon and wagonmasters. Without the Pioneer and Conqueror, the Economizer—the brake—is almost entirely negative and hostile and many organizations are characterized by only brakes. If, on the other hand, the lead wagon has no brake, then slowing, stopping, and shaping become more difficult, if not impossible. Functions that appear negative in solo, therefore, can be quite positive within the full Wagon Train context.

The Insistent Diplomat, like the Conqueror, represents a consolidating, integrating function. Gently persuasive, finding ways to accomplish larger focuses within current rules, pressing to expand those rules: all are concepts contained in the word, *Diplomat*. The addition of *Insistent* confers a proactive, assertive quality on the function but not as aggressive as either the Pioneer or the Conqueror.

These functions, or persons, or personalities comprise a fairly good Entrepreneurial Wagon Train. All must be present if a venture is to succeed. Should any one of them assume overwhelming prominence, a new venture, a new product, a new service is likely to be in trouble. Typically, we identify the Pioneer or the Conqueror as the Entrepreneur. Unfortunately, this tends to associate entrepreneurship only with development, while ignoring the successful introduction of new ideas, products, or services.

Sometimes an innovative individual will have all of these skills and will be able to move from one to the other as needed. Most often, however, the individual will have only one or two of them. In such cases the entrepreneurial team—The Wagon Train—needs to be brought together to accomplish the Entrepreneur's total purpose. The Entrepreneurial Manager is the one who orchestrates, coordinates, sequences, and articulates all these functions, replacing them when they are missing, bolstering them when they are not working effectively, and keeping all functions in balance.

The maintenance of appropriate balance among the functions is the key to virtually everything in successful entrepreneurship. We tend to ascribe a special goodness to the Pioneer; but, when out of balance with the rest of the system, the Pioneer can be a real pain in the posterior if she or he simply supplies a stream of new ideas and never follows up on them. (Maxim was like that.) The Economizer can be similarly troubling if there is no forward moving force to keep the Economizer from strangling the organization. But the apparently negative Economizer can be useful in slowing down a pell-mell, forward rush.

These, then, are the components of the entrepreneurial team. These are

the components that the Entrepreneurial Manager needs to manage, whether
that management is the arrangement of a sequence of roles within oneself
or the arrangement and orchestration of a number of different individuals.

THE ENTREPRENEURIAL MANAGER AND THE
ENTREPRENEURIAL WAGON TRAIN

The Entrepreneurial Manager needs to be able to do several things well,
simultaneously. The first of these is to recognize the different skills, competencies, and characteristics that are needed for entrepreneurial success and
be able either to develop or recruit them so that there can be an entrepreneurial team in place. This recognition requires setting aside old, individ-
ualistic perspectives and seeing the likelihood and necessity that several
individuals will need to be involved. This awareness allows the Entrepreneurial Manager to build the kind of entrepreneurial group that will lead to
the success of the new product or service.

This is not the only skill Entrepreneurial Managers require for assembling
entrepreneurial groups. Another includes the ability to package new wine
in old bottles in order to secure support. In their own work of public administration, Simon, Smithberg, and Thompson (1956) point out that new proposals linked to values are most likely to insure success. In this particular
case, if the Entrepreneurial Manager is able to show others in the organization
or venture capitalists that there has already been a base of work in a particular
area, acceptance is likely to be increased.

A third skill the Entrepreneurial Manager needs is the ability to secure
sponsorship. Here the Insistent Diplomat can be a useful person/skill to
invoke. Sponsorship refers not only to securing support from individuals
outside the organization but, perhaps even more importantly, from within
it, as well. As Morita says in *Made In Japan* (1986):

The concept of consensus is natural to the Japanese, but it does not necessarily mean
that every decision comes out of a spontaneous group impulse. Gaining consensus
in a Japanese company often means spending time preparing the ground work for
it, and very often the consensus is formed from the top down, not from the bottom
up. (P. 198)

Sayles and Chandler (1971) point out some of the tasks that they believe
the Entrepreneurial Manager must undertake, including monitoring and influencing of decisions. Their "project manager" corresponds to our Entrepreneurial Manager. They comment that "the project manager must
constantly seek to penetrate the organizations upon which he is dependent
but which he does not directly supervise" (p. 494). They continue:

Thus, project management is not a curious blend of the old and the not-so-old; it
calls for a new set of skills and procedures. . . . It requires a capacity on the part of

the manager to put together an organizational mechanism within which timely and relevant decisions are likely to be reached (as distinct from individual decision making), a conceptual scheme for "working" interfaces and for predicting where structural changes should be introduced if the response is inadequate, untimely or insubstantial. (P. 495)

With respect to decision making, they outline some key responsibilities worth noting here:

1. Give problems their "proper" weight and context.
2. Tackle problems in the right sequence and at the right time.
3. Shift the decision criteria.
4. Boundary settings: boundary widening and/or narrowing. (P. 492)

How different this kind of concept is from the traditional Entrepreneur building a prototype in some garage and then offering it to a big concern.

Sayles and Chandler (1971) suggest a number of specific techniques that the Entrepreneurial Manager (project manager) needs. Among these are bargaining, coaching, cajoling, confrontation, and intervention. Still others are quarter giving, inspiriting, motivating, enabling, and trapping. *Bargaining* involves the give and take of reciprocal goods that the Entrepreneurial Manager can trade with other employees to build a project team and accomplish the development of new ideas and their implementation. *Coaching* involves working through others, rather than doing it yourself. *Cajoling* involves "selling" the idea, "pitching the concept," and is useful at the beginning states (getting your foot in the door) and in seeking to overcome strong resistance. *Intervention* involves taking a proactive, involving stance rather than waiting for problems to come to you. *Quarter Giving* means allowing individuals enough room to function. *Inspiriting* and *Motivating* suggest the need to provide the culture in which workers and others want to join you and perform. *Enabling*, like coaching, means helping the "other guy" do the task and, thus, increasing task accomplishment and self-esteem. *Trapping*, like confrontation, means dealing with unpleasantness. In this case it involves making an agreement with the employee in question to meet certain standards or performance measures. Appropriate action can be taken if the standards are not met. *Confrontation* involves coming to grips with performance problems—of people or products that are in trouble—before things become too serious.

If you are to be a manager, each of these is a reasonable technique to use on occasion, especially when working with a diverse group of Pioneers, Conquerors, Level-Headed Administrators, Economizers, and Insistent Diplomats. What should be clear from the list is that it involves working *through* other people as much as or more than doing the actual job yourself. It is this kind of orientation—productivity through others—that is the fundamental aspect of the Entrepreneurial Manager's role. The Entrepreneurial Manager may, indeed, contribute at a particular point as a result of a particular skill, just as an orchestra conductor may, on occasion, fill in for an instrument on which he or she is proficient. We can also think of the Entrepreneurial Manager as the subtle leader of a string quintet group in which the actual leader is also a performer who acts to guide, measure, and structure the work of others. Meetings are a particular vehicle for this achievement. We discuss them in some detail in a later chapter.

CONCLUSION

Supplying new ideas to the ongoing business and keeping that business and new ventures alive and well requires an understanding of at least two important principles. The first is the duality and simultaneous nature of success and failure. All kinds of things are going on within the entrepreneurial effort, some success focused, some failure focused. It is the combination that makes the ultimate difference.

The second principle is that there is a difference between the Mountain Man approach and the Wagon Train approach. This difference must be understood. The Wagon Train is a person-in-context perspective on the entrepreneurial function. Popular images of entrepreneurship are not only heavily based in personality typologies. In addition, they seem to focus on the individual Entrepreneur in some kind of solo performance—the Mountain Man—as the key element in the entrepreneurial function. Unfortunately, this perspective is not only bad as an analytic tool, but conjures up a potentially lethal model for fledgling or established Entrepreneurs to follow.

A more balanced view suggests that a whole range of skills is needed for the successful introduction of new products and services. There is, of course, need for generating new ideas through the application of the energy of thought. But there is also the need for developing organizational pathways through which ideas can pass for building commitment to new products and services. Morita (1986), Board Chairman of the Sony Company, tells of the difficulties he had personally in getting acceptance of the Walkman™ concept in his own company. Finally, through the use of the many techniques described here—bargaining, coaching, trapping, threatening—he managed to get the concept accepted and production underway. It took a great deal of effort on his part. In retrospect, all of this may seem strange to us, for the Walkman™ has revolutionized listening habits for the entire world. At the time he proposed it, however, it was just one more crazy new product, competing with other new possible directions and developments, that the company might or might not choose to undertake.

NOTE

1. Historically, we tend to think of the west as being settled by individual pioneers. In fact, the actual settlement occurred through groups of people in wagon trains.

This migration was structured differently from the first migration from Europe to America. The historian, Daniel Boorstin (1958, 1965, 1973), suggested that the very vehicle of migration may have caused some difference in orientation. The first migrants came in boats, passive passengers while the crew worked. The second migrants went together in wagon trains with everybody working. Because of the fact that everyone had to be involved in a wagon train mode of migration, Boorstin believes that this might have caused a more positive attitude toward the public weal in group activities in the west.

4

The Entrepreneurial Staircase

What goes around comes round again.
—From Carol Stack, *All Our Kin*

For the humorist, timing is everything.
—Comic (anonymous), New York, 1986

INTRODUCTION

In Chapter 2 we talked about the need for new ideas to be introduced regularly in the Firm. In Chapter 3 we talked about the need for collective effort in accomplishing organizational ends. The individual-in-context was the important focus for the process of introducing new ideas. This chapter focuses on the steps in the development of new ideas, products and services, or forms. Think of it as the Entrepreneurial Staircase.

Cycles exist both in idea development and in the Firm, itself. There will be variations, of course, from case to case, from Firm to Firm, in the set of phases through which ideas and Firms pass, but in general there is a certain regularity to the steps.

THE ENTREPRENEURIAL STAIRCASE

Entrepreneurship exists in steps. Carol Moore (1986) identified three of these: Innovation, Implementation, and Growth. There are, as well, at least two other phases that also need to be addressed: Stabilization and Renewal. Services, products, and programs all go through these stages, which collectively make up the product cycle, the service cycle, or the Firm cycle. Whole organizations, in fact, go through these steps from the beginning of a new

Figure 4.1
Steps in the Entrepreneurial Process

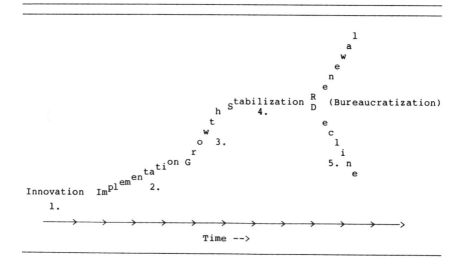

concept, to bringing that concept into practice, to growing, to plateauing out, and then into being refurbished and renewed. Figure 4.1 gives a graphic idea of this process.

There are at least three reasons why it is crucial to know the stages of this Entrepreneurial Process. First, each stage has key tasks, key roles, and key activities that must be carried out. Second, each stage has particular tasks and particular conditions to be concerned with, particular tasks to be accomplished, particular competencies to be learned. Third, there are *important* problems in the transition between one phase and another.

Each stage and each transition holds the possibility of failure. The Innovation is not able to be implemented, for example, and remains in the talking stage. Or, the Innovation, though implemented, has problems with Growth, either not growing enough and not being able to get into the Growth Stage, or growing too fast and not being able to manage Growth.

After Growth comes a period of Stabilization. Many ventures (products, services, or whole Firms) are not able to move from the Growth Stage into the Stabilization Stage. Different leadership may be required or other important changes may have to be made before Stabilization is possible. Without Stabilization, the quickly implemented new ideas may resemble a shooting star—flaring brilliantly for a few moments, then burning themselves out.

Finally, after Stabilization must come Renewal. Firms or products or services that move through the Entrepreneurial Cycle need to be constantly refurbished and renewed. One cannot continue to use the same old stuff (S.O.S.) all the time. Let's examine each of these stages in a bit more detail.

The Innovation Stage

The key task during the Innovation Stage is coming up with the new idea. Problems are those of creativity (how to come up with the new idea in the first place) and with managing (or engineering) the supply of new ideas or creative thoughts about new products or services. The problems focus on the difficulties surrounding the new idea. New ideas, remember, are often half-baked and incomplete. They are easy to attack and criticize. Thus, one must be especially persuasive and especially convincing in inviting others to consider the possibilities of a new approach before they reject it prematurely.

It is Innovation (or invention) that distinguishes the Entrepreneur from the small business person. Consider, for example, someone who secures a McDonald's franchise. Although that individual may face some financial risk, there will be little, if any, intellectual risk. The decisions have already been made: The products to be marketed, the marketing strategy, even the location of the business have all been predetermined. Thus, such an individual would not be an Entrepreneur within the definition being developed in this book.

Many ideas for products and services die at the Innovation Stage. Just because someone suggests them does not necessarily mean that anything is going to happen to them. Thus, the Entrepreneur must not only be able to think up or present new ideas, he or she must also be able to move the suggestion from the Innovation or Invention Stage into the Implementation Stage. It is this aspect that differentiates the Entrepreneur from the visionary—that individual who keeps supplying new ideas but does not take them to the next step.

The Implementation Stage

The Implementation Stage involves moving the product or service into production. Production does not necessarily mean gearing up the factories and turning out a product full tilt, or marketing a service to the maximum. It can mean both of these things, of course; but it can also mean nothing more than test marketing a product on a very small scale—trying a few examples of the new product or service within a limited and focused context. Prototypes are sometimes built at this phase and, often, tried and improved. One can, for example, begin by offering pizza for delivery at a single store in a single location, as Domino's did back in the middle 1960s. Similarly, in a big Firm one might circulate something new internally, testing the waters to see whether a particular product idea can pass muster among colleagues within the organization, as the developers of Post-Its™ did at 3M Corporation.

Key problems at this stage center on the actual putting together of something that others can see—a new game, for example, or a new toy; perhaps a training program on how to run meetings effectively or a pizza or travel service. As with all stages in the Entrepreneurial Cycle, during Implementation you must not only give close attention to the immediate task at hand, you must also be anticipating the next step along the way. Even as the Innovation is being suggested, you must immediately start thinking about Implementation. As Implementation is progressing, a lot of attention must be given to Growth. It is at this time that you begin to plan and shape the ways in which Growth might occur, the particular markets that would be most appropriate for the kind of Growth you envision, and so on.

All of the Implementation activities, then, must be designed with the next stage clearly in mind. This facilitates the process of transition to the next stage. For many Firms who ignore or are unmindful of the need to keep one eye on the present and the other on what's coming up, their ideas peak out at the Implementation Stage. They wind up offering a small set of products or services being offered to a very limited market. To be sure, some innovators may be satisfied with this because it suits their lifestyle or other interests; some may become fixated at this stage because mild success has brought with it a heightened fear of failure or has simply sapped any desire to take further risks. Such Firms have no particular plan nor any apparent desire to grow. They are demonstrating "arrested entrepreneurialism" in which the full potential of the product or service is not exploited but remains latent or underdeveloped.

The Growth Stage

During the Growth Stage, the third step of the Entrepreneurial Staircase, the product or service really begins to take off. Managing Growth becomes a key problem during this period. Such specific difficulties as adding staff, developing facilities, responding to orders, dealing with customer complaints and demands are all very new and develop in a context of high pressure. There is often a "crisis management" ambiance in such a situation. The inability of many entrepreneurs to deal with these kinds of pressures, coming as they do all at once and with such high intensity, often sounds the death knell for many Firms, products, and services.

But simply managing Growth is not enough. One eye must again be squarely on the future, when Growth will give way to Stabilization. Firms that survive, thrive, and prosper are those that shape Growth in such a way that it focuses on Stabilization.

It is important in thinking about the issues of Growth to be aware that Growth may not occur in the same shape or pattern. The illustrations in

Figure 4.2
Various Ways Organizational Development Can Occur

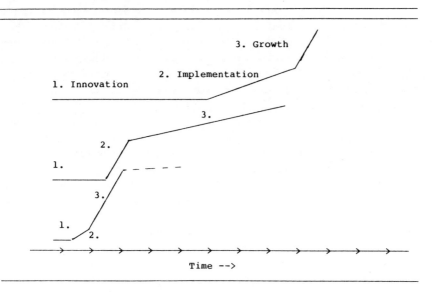

Figure 4.2 suggest several ways that the first three stages can arrange themselves. There could be, for example, a relatively long Innovation Stage,
followed by a long Implementation Stage, followed by a sharp Growth Stage.
Alternatively, the Innovation might be implemented quickly, followed then
by a long period of development before Growth occurs. A still different
approach occurs when an Innovation is introduced and takes the market by
storm. It's quickly picked up and Growth is explosive and immediate.

When constructing your own scenarios, you should keep these different
models in mind. More often than not, Entrepreneurs are fairly self-indulgent
about their own ideas. They believe in them, and they believe that they
will take the market by storm. Sometimes it really happens. And, if it
happens to you, you had better be prepared for it both intellectually and
psychologically. Failure, however, happens sometimes too. And one needs
to have at least prepared mentally for that eventuality. The lifeless carcasses
of Firms that enjoyed quick success are strewn widely across the landscape
of American business history, physically represented by boarded up buildings, empty stores and factories, and disconnected telephone numbers.

The Stabilization Stage

Stabilization involves bringing regularity and routine to the product or
service. The rate of Growth has now tapered off. The issues are continuity

and consistency rather than response to an explosive and dynamic market situation.

The key problems center on responding to regularity. Frequently, the individual who can handle Innovation, Implementation, and Growth does not find the Stabilization Stage a terribly comfortable one. It seems boring and routine. What should be a relatively tranquil and resource replenishing phase is often troubled and truculent. The Entrepreneurial Manager, so accustomed to the swift pace and pressure up to this phase, continues with a management style geared to the pressure cooker instead of a slow simmer. This gives rise to behaviors that are often inappropriate for the present circumstances. Flamholtz (1986) saw this as a transition stage signaling a change in emphasis from entrepreneurial management to *professional management*. This change may or may not involve a change in personnel. It certainly involves change in behavior, pace, and focus. Here too, as Stabilization occurs, Entrepreneurs need to think about the next stage: Renewal.

Stabilization can be a very long phase in the Entrepreneurial Cycle. It can be (and often is) boring, but it can also be (and often is) deadly; for, as the time increases, the environment continues to shift. A product or service that met needs at the beginning of the Stabilization Stage, may cease to meet them as the Stabilization Stage continues. In some cases, as with the computer industry, the cycle of environmental change is very fast. Competitors are developing and introducing new products at an incredible rate, and Renewal must occur on at least a yearly basis in order to remain competitive. In other cases, the product life cycle is longer. Whatever the case may be, Renewal is necessary. That Renewal links the Entrepreneurial Cycle back to Innovation.

The Renewal Stage

The last step in the Entrepreneurial Staircase that completes entrepreneurial activities is Renewal. Pareto, the famous Italian economist, talked about something like this in his parable of the lions and the foxes. He called it the *circulation of elites* (Parsons, 1949, p. 283). At some point foxes would be in power; and lions, rough and ready, would overthrow them and take over the government. According to Pareto, however, in the long run more than strength was needed. Guile and wiles were essential, and foxes were brought back in. After a period of time, foxes would be in the dominant position, and another group of lions would move in and overthrow them.

Pareto was using metaphor to differentiate between human characteristics: the strong vs. the clever; the employer of brute force vs. the employer of cunning and guile. What Pareto was pointing out, however, was that governments begin, develop, become fixed in their position, and eventually get thrown out. The process from the point of view of those who study the history of Firms is considerably more extended than the few steps Pareto suggested. He has, nevertheless, provided us with an essential insight. Governments go on, although the people in them may change. Firms, often, do not; and without Renewal—repositioning, refocusing, recharging—Firms may moss over, as has happened with some aspects of the automobile industry in the United States and some other industrial segments with which we are all generally familiar. Firms tend to grow, add staff, become plump, then overweight, and in the process cease to become competitive.[1]

Renewal is necessary in order to avoid organizational *depositioning*. Depositioning occurs when the environment shifts. Sometimes the shift occurs slowly, as the incident of the boiled frog illustrates. Sometimes it can occur with what seems like lightning swiftness, as in the shift from the use of tubes to the use of transistors in electronic products. In both cases a Firm that once found itself in the middle of its market, now finds itself on the periphery.

Renewal is also needed to activate the development of new purposes to counteract the tendency of all organizations to drift. Organizational drift occurs when an organization responds to handy rather than strategic aspects of the environment; it goes for this government contract or that market niche because it is handy and immediately profitable, or at least sufficient to maintain the status quo. Such a Firm frequently winds up having a product or service stew and has not, as Peters and Waterman (1982) suggested, stuck to its knitting.

In short, the Renewal Stage is a juncture. Renewal is as much of a hoped for consequence as is Innovation, Implementation, Growth, and Stabilization. Organizational debt at Renewal time occurs when the mossed over organization no longer competes. Herbert Kaufman illustrates this problem in a series of question-answer titles in his book, *Time, Chance, and Organizations* (1985):

Question: Why Do Organizations Die?

Answer: Because Their Engines Stop.

Question: Why Do Their Engines Stop?

Answer: Usually Because They Develop Resource Problems.

Question: Why Do They Develop Resource Problems?

Answer: Because Their Environment Is Volatile and Adjusting to It Is Not Easy. (PP. vii–viii)

As the last step in the Entrepreneurial Staircase, Renewal links back to Innovation and permits the organization to go ahead. Renewal has a positive sound to it; and, indeed, that is what one hopes for. But a positive result, one in which the Firm really does "re-new" itself is not always what happens. In Figure 4.1 two other options are also indicated: Bureaucratization and Decline.

The bureaucratization option, essentially, is a continuation of stabilization but with increasing rigidity, multiplication of layers, insistence on procedures regardless of what the procedures were for initially (if any one can remember what they were for initially—this process, by the way, is what sociologist Robert K. Merton (1957) calls *means ritualization*) and other manifestations with which most of us are familiar. Firms can go on for a long time this way; but often, as in the auto industry, they suffer eventually from depositioning and go into decline.

Decline is the other alternative. It can occur (and does occur) as a possible result of any stage. But, unless the cycle is renewed here, as Kaufman (1985) suggests, problems arise. Organizational illness develops—high turnover, negative and hostile cultures, declining financial performance—that for some reason cannot be dealt with readily. Decline has set in. Death is on the way.

STEP-LINKED TASKS AND ROLES

The Entrepreneurial Staircase allows us to see the major steps through which the entrepreneurial process goes. Each stage has a characteristic problem associated with it. That problem must be solved before the venture can go to the next step on the staircase. It is useful to examine those step-related problems in more detail, and a wide range of authors have contributed to this task. Looking at what various people have written in general, the various books and articles suggest that there are four levels at which these problems must be solved. First, at the level of the Firm solutions must be found and a goodly number of Firm-level tasks must be completed. Second, at the level of business activity there are also tasks to be completed and a number of competencies to be acquired. Third, at the level of ideas each stage focuses on areas of thought to be explored and completed. Fourth, and finally, each step on the Entrepreneurial Staircase almost always requires different roles to be played by each member of the staff. These tasks, linked to steps on the Entrepreneurial Staircase are displayed in Table 4.1.

Table 4.1 also shows the relationships among the ideas of various authors who have explored the problems associated with the various steps of the Entrepreneurial Staircase concept. It is now possible to look at the specific tasks that need to be accomplished at the Firm level.

FIRM TASKS

As we've already noted, each step on the Entrepreneurial Staircase creates special problems for Firms. So, too, does the transition from step to step. It is often more likely, in fact, that you will trip in the movement from one step to another than while remaining in a particular step.

Table 4.1
The Entrepreneurial Staircase—Step-Linked Firm, Business, and Idea Tasks as Viewed by Various Authors

Steps in the Staircase / Tropman (1)	Key Problem	Firm Tasks (Conditions)		Business Tasks (Competencies)			Idea Tasks (Competencies)	
		Churchill and Lewis (2)	Famholtz (3)	Gartner (4)	Famholtz (5)	Hosmer (6)	Vesper (7)	Tropman (8)
Innovation	Thinking up the idea	Existence	New venture	Locate business opportunity	Identify market niche	Get the idea Evaluate opportunities	Acquire technical knowledge	Problem proposal Decision
Implementation	Starting viable production	Survival success		Acquire resources Market the product/service	Develop product/service Secure recourses	Plan the activity Structure the opportunity Solve problems	Develop connections Obtain manpower and physical resources Obtain customer orders	Planning PERTing Program
Growth	Manage growth	Success/takeoff	Expansion	Build organization	Develop operating system - Develop Mgt systems	Manage growth		
Stabilization	Responding to regularity	Maturity	Professional-ization Consolidation		Develop corporate culture			Oversight Assessment
Renewal	Repursory reconfiguring	Rejuvenation		Respond to society				Evaluation

Innovation

At the Innovation stage the Firm has just come into existence. It is a new venture. Everything is fresh and exciting. In most instances if the Firm is new, the Firm is small. If the new idea or new approach is a subpart of a larger organization, there is still the freshness and excitement of taking first steps. To be sure, many organizations stumble here because the individual Entrepreneurial Innovator is not able to survive the criticisms and negative reviews that often accompany the introduction or suggestion of new ideas for products and for services. Technically, it is unlikely that these ventures are ever counted as venture failures because they may have existed only for a very short period of time. As with our Neanderthal Man and the needle, the idea never got to the Implementation Stage.

Implementation

Once the idea or Innovation has gained some credibility, Implementation is the next step. It is here that production of products begins, new procedures are tried, new approaches set into motion, and new services offered. Here, the market is tested and the Firm experiments with prices. Here, too, survival of the venture, rather than survival of the idea, is the characteristic concern.

Because Implementation requires the establishment of some organizational form and the investment of some capital, survival becomes the crucial question. It is often here that the classic entrepreneurial scenario evolves—working day and night, involving all family members, and so on—in a desparate process to make everything work at least adequately.

Growth

A key point in a Firm's transition comes during the Growth Stage. This is the point that Flamholtz (1986) sees as the "fulcrum of transition" into a period of Stabilization—that solid time when things are regular and routine, and excitement is held to a minimum.

This transition can cause special difficulties for founding members. Often individuals who found organizations possess tremendously high energy and drive. They have come to believe through the earlier developmental phases of their organization that they, and they alone, must have their hands in everything. This means that the distribution and reorganization of power that is so very important in the Stabilization Stage can be potentially problematic for such individuals. Furthermore, they tend to identify the Firm as "their" personal property—recalling the days, perhaps, when they were swimming upstream with a small product or service that no one cared about whatsoever. They now sit at a pinnacle of some success and resist mightily attempts to stabilize that might involve replacing them. Such replacement may be necessary, however, particularly if they tend to manage by force of personality, so diverse, choppy, jerky, and episodic that a regular business or organization cannot run with them at the helm. Special roles may need to be found or developed for founding members, therefore, during the transitional phase.

Such a problem befell Steve Jobs, one of the founders of the Apple Computer Company. Ultimately excluded from his own Firm, he founded another called Next. His interest is probably more in the developmental than the regularized. The transition from now to Next, however, was not as peaceful as it might have been.[2]

Stabilization

What is important in achieving the relative quiet of the Stabilization Stage is to make provision also for Innovation and development to occur so that the next stage, Renewal, can be stimulated. All too often the overlap and simultaneity of the entrepreneurial stages is not perceived by organizational builders. Consequently, they make no provision for some subsectors of the organization to continue to engage in Innovation; to continue supplying the kinds of conceptual resources that the organization will need at the next stage. The self-satisfied feeling that usually comes with Stabilization may be cut short as the Firm or organization runs out of momentum from the lack of internal energy or finds to its distress that environmental shifts make it impossible to continue doing what it has been doing, and it hasn't the foggiest idea what to do "next."

The organizational subparts that continue to supply fresh ideas and perspectives during the Stabilization Stage become more dominant during the Renewal Stage. It is the fresh ideas they generate that must now catch on within the organization to provide the organization with the necessary conceptual energy to engage in Renewal.

The difficulties of Renewal are legend. One of the reasons for these difficulties stems from the fact that the officers of the organization, during Stabilization, tend to entrench themselves deeply into the organizational power structure; they *become*, in fact, the organizational power structure. The kinds of permissions—the kinds of "champions"—at the executive level that are needed to supply resources so that a period of Innovation may begin again are not present. All people interested in new ideas get negative responses as a matter of course. I know of a case where an executive had a large oil painting made to hang over his desk. It was composed of a single word—"No"—prominently displayed against a neutral background. When employees approached him, they had to sit facing that sign. Hardly an auspicious beginning for a whacky or crazy proposal.

In some organizations the Stabilization Stage has excluded organizational subparts, which are doing important developmental work. The executive cadre, therefore, has nothing to say "no" to. But if there has been that provision, then moving into the Renewal Stage is likely to generate a different kind of conflict—one between the innovators (the next-steppers, the futurists) and the "here and now*ists*," the current power structure. As Galbraith (1982) observes, "here and nowists" aren't that sympathetic to change. Not only are those in the current power structure in a good organizational position to control or deny access to innovative activities, they may also perceive that such activities will change the nature and focus of the organization that they have come to cherish and embody. Rather than seeing themselves (and placing themselves) in a position to lead into the next stage, they perceive the next stage as displacing them from power, influence, and authority. They see it as replacing them with others. Unfortunately, that view becomes a self-fulfilling prophecy. An organizational conflict develops that can either lead to the demise of the organization or create the fact of those executives replacements, which were not a necessary prerequisite in the first place.

Renewal

Organizational maturity implies a certain regularity as the central problem of that step on the Entrepreneurial Staircase suggests. The key difficulty is that doing things regularly is not necessarily predictive of doing something different once, and the organization must confront issues of rejuvenation. Although survival and the issue of success are critical matters to be addressed in the Implementation and Growth Stages, rejuvenation is the key task in the Renewal Stage. Rejuvenation implies a range of fresh perspectives and fresh approaches that are inventive and innovative rather than cosmetic. Model changes in the automobile industry represent something new, but the amount of newness is, in reality, marginal; and, with the exception of certain fulcrum years, generally speaking they are cosmetic.

BUSINESS TASKS

As you ascend the Entrepreneurial Staircase, and harkening back to Table 4.1, there are a number of specific tasks that relate to each of the steps on the stairs. A range of authors, including Churchill and Lewis (1983), Flamholtz (1986), Gartner (1985), Hosmer (1985), Tropman (1984), and Vesper (1980), have made a range of suggestions about business tasks within the entrepreneurial process that fit the Entrepreneurial Staircase concept fairly well. We must emphasize that these suggested tasks are both illustrative and ordered according to priority. By that we mean they are suggestive rather than definitive of all the tasks that might need to be accomplished during a particular step. We mention them with respect to one area of organizational development, but this does not mean that they would not be needed elsewhere. In this sense they may have their highest priorities at one particular step or level, but they are also useful or needed at other steps.

Innovation

A number of authors, including those we cite in Figure 4.2, have suggested the kinds of business tasks that are most appropriate at the beginning stage of an entrepreneurial process or venture. First, of course, is getting the idea. Involved with that idea are other procedures, including crystallizing the venture that will be required to deal with the particular idea in question, locating and evaluating the business opportunities involved, identifying the market niche, and acquiring the technical means for Implementation.

These are crucial beginning tasks. Without completing them, it is unlikely that the venture will proceed successfully.

Implementation

Once you have identified a particular product or service and have a sense where and in what ways it might fit, Implementation begins. A variety of resources need to be acquired. Connections need to be developed. Physical resources and orders need to be obtained and a variety of practical problems, including financing, space, specific marketing technologies and techniques, need to be taken into account.

In the Implementation Stage of product or service development, a range of connections with other organizations on the output side (for sales and distribution) and on the input side (for resources, raw materials, staffing) needs to be articulated. It is at this point that the product or service is "off the ground."

Growth

After introduction, a product or service may die a quick and natural death. The earlier work may have contained errors and mistakes. The market may not present, or there may have been a variety of specific problems within the Implementation activities that forestall or truncate Growth. In this case, *failure management* is required. It is as important to successfully manage failure as it is to manage success. Both place stresses upon people and the Firm. Both represent difficulties for the individual and for the Firm. In the most severe failures, failure management takes the form of bankruptcy proceedings and other personally and legally difficult activities. But sometimes failure is only within a segment or an aspect of a business, or failure may be in a venture that is only a sideline or second occupation for some individuals. In any case, failure and its implications need to be confronted.

Managing Failure. From time to time the experience of failure (so long as it isn't lethal) can be good for a Firm. Sam Zell of Equity Financial Management stresses this point. Failure forces management to look at areas where problems occurred. As I indicated previously, failure behaviors and success behaviors tend to go on simultaneously. It is not particularly unusual for difficult and problematic failure bahaviors to be overshadowed by success behaviors. In such situations, examination of the failure behaviors is often avoided (it's an unpleasant task at best). Denial then replaces failure analysis. The assessment of failure that does occur is usually directed at the assignment of blame and belongs to the "You-Idiot!-What-Did-You-Do-That For?" school of management. It results in a great deal of negative affect, often giving rise to anger and personal and organizational sulking. Focusing on *who* is to blame rarely, if ever, has a positive outcome. It is almost always destructive.

But failure is always symptomatic of some kind of disease in the organization: a system that has failed, a critical subsystem that is not performing its function properly, timing that is out of phase with the rhythm of the organization, an unrecognized need for some missing organizational element (Drucker, 1985). Sometimes the disease is incurable, and the Firm will die no matter what is done in the name of a cure. Far more often, however, once the causes that give rise to the symptom are understood, effective remediation and correction (a cure) are possible. Consequently, curing the disease requires diagnostic procedures, implementation of a treatment program, and the constant monitoring of progress toward recovery.

Every organization, therefore, requires some mechanism for the *objective* analysis and management of failures that do occur and of areas where potential failure may occur (Failure Mode and Effect Analysis). With such a mechanism in place, analysis of failure can lead to positive results through reassessment, readjustment, and fresh attempts at success. The failure analysis and management could take any of a number of forms, depending on what the organization feels most comfortable with—a board of review, for example, or an inspector general, or simply an outside consulting Firm. Whatever its form, its primary focus should be on *what* caused the failure, never upon *who*. There will always be a *what*. Sometimes it's difficult to find, giving rise to a temptation to fall back on the assignment of blame. Resisting that temptation will yield a minimum of resentment on the part of the staff (even when part of the cure requires replacing one or more staff members), and it will give rise to positive results that can be seen and measured.

An effective failure analysis and management system allows the Firm to side-step the near obsession that American society has with notion of *perseverance*: "keep on keeping on," "don't give up the ship," "press on regardless," "when the going gets tough, the tough get going," and so on. To persevere is to be virtuous, to give up is to be a coward or a quitter. An effective failure analysis and management system permits the Firm to make a more nearly rational assessment of when it is appropriate and necessary to try again and when it is appropriate and necessary to stop that particular line of endeavor and move on to something else.[3] All decisions in questions such as these are judgment calls. It is important that the decision maker has enough information and sufficient perspective to make an informed judgment rather than one based in emotion and the pressures of the immediate instant. Providing that information and assisting in the development of that perspective are the purposes of the failure analysis and management system or mechanism.

Managing Success. It is one thing to become successful. It is quite another to stay that way. Just as failure needs careful management, so too does success—all the more so if success comes very quickly. Success must be accompanied by a certain amount of organization building. Differentiation and integration become extremely important. Resources must be secured and supplied on a regular, continuing basis. The development of operational and management systems becomes a necessity. Much of the success management problem occurs within a high pressured context in which the environment is making lots of demands, of varying levels of specificity, that often conflict with one another. Keeping good relationships with the social context also becomes a crucial issue.

One problem with success, especially quick, sharply focused success, is that its management alone becomes totally time-consuming. As I have suggested before, entrepreneurial management involves always preparing for the next phase while dealing with the current phase. It is in the explosive Growth period of a product or service that doing both those activities becomes very very difficult. All one's attention is focused on the here and now. The next seems far off.

Stabilization

As a Firm enters the Stabilization Stage, a number of specific activities need to be considered in order to make the Firm reasonably successful. Although the authors, displayed in Table 4.1, do not comment much about it, Flamholtz (1986) speaks of developing corporate culture. Although this may have occurred earlier, there is a refining aspect that may go on; and specific attention may now be given to the issue of corporate culture.

As important as the development of corporate culture may be (and it is extremely important), there are other matters that must also be attended to during Stabilization. These include the development of regularization and organizational policy, sorting out of that policy, developing training programs for staff, and taking a fresh look at incentive programs.

Stabilization is also the time to begin looking ahead to Renewal, though it is not a particularly popular activity at this time. Individuals just out of an effective Growth Stage often do not wish to begin looking ahead. Nevertheless, it must be done, though it may not necessarily be a full-time activity and may be consistent with certain other Stabilization-type activities. In the rush of meeting customers' orders and demands for the product or service, there may simply not have been enough time for indepth analyses of customers and clients, or to adequately examine market feedback. Stabilization is the time for those activities to begin in earnest.

If anything, Stabilization means a greater efficiency. The same level of the product or service is being maintained at a lower per unit cost. There is often a tendency on the part of an organization to waste these gains. That tendency must be resisted, for the Firm now has resources that can be used not only for managing the status quo, but for directing considerations for the next phase of organizational existence.

Problems develop during the Stabilization Stage that need to be attended to. Consider as one simple example, Domino's Pizza. In 1986 its projected earnings were $1.5 billion. In that year the assistant to President Tom Monahan retired. She was the first person ever to retire from Domino's. She had been with the company for ten years. One might speculate about the kind of organization that has achieved such a blizzard of organizational Growth without anyone having worked long enough to retire. In addition to personnel problems, the kind of corporate culture that an organization like that might have would doubtless be very different from one in which there had been a longtime commitment of longtime employees. Domino's is now entering the Stabilization Stage; and their crucial problem, of course, is responding to regularity. Doing the same kinds of tasks over and over and over again will be one part of the stabilization challenge. A second will be dealing with the competition. Some of that competition will be national in nature from existing chains and from others that may develop and decide to compete vigorously. Other kinds of home delivered foods may compete, as well. At the moment, for example, there is not a particular American market (nationally) for home delivered Japanese sushi, but there's no particular reason why in an increasingly health conscious America a preference for a wide range of sushi products might not develop.[4]

Other competition may occur locally. You will need to decide how much your product should vary, how many new products you should add (recall that there was a time when McDonald's did not serve breakfast), and how these products are to be added.

The challenges of Stabilization, then, are essentially the challenges of regularity with appropriate adjustments to prevent falling behind. No one thinks of Stabilization as incredibly exciting or particularly innovative. Flamholtz (1986) calls this the *professional stage*, and we all understand that a professional at anything is someone who can turn in a high performance with some regularity in a wide range of operating conditions. This is true for the professional golfer on a variety of courses, a football player on a vareity of teams and playing fields, or a concert violinist in a variety of settings and with a variety of repertoire. It is equally true for the attorney facing a variety of client legal problems, a physician confronting a variety of physical conditions, or an accountant reconciling a variety of financial situations. It is also true for the succesful business dealing with various market demands.

Within the Stabilization Stage are the seeds for Renewal or for decline. The Entrepreneurial Manager needs to be aware of these possibilities and emphasize the tendencies toward Renewal.

Renewal

Strangely enough, the wide range of authors who talk about the overall entrepreneurial process or Firm and business tasks that are required at various steps on the Enterpreneurial Staircase do not talk a great deal about the Renewal process. Some helpful insights are provided, however by Drucker in his book, *Innovation and Entrepreneurship* (1985), and by Brandt in *Entrepreneuring in Established Companies* (1985). It may be the youth orientation of America that causes us to stress the "organizational child" rather than the "organizational adult." Alternatively, it may be that our fear of older organizations is similar to our fear of older people—something that David Hackett Fischer (1978) calls *gerontophobia*. Whatever the reason, American society seems to overvalue the young and overattend to them. This is true whether the young are people or organizations. Our society also tends to inappropriately dismiss the older social unit, whether that unit is a person or an organization. Certainly, with respect to American business enterprise, the performance picture of older companies is mixed. Some people refer to "arteriosclerosis" of a company and to a "hardening of the categories" with respect to management, labor, culture, and so on. However, organizations, like people, can experience what some speak of as being "born again" (though such organizational repurposing may not have the same kind of religious overtone).

The first point about organization Renewal, then, is that it is possible, desireable, and appropriate. We should not automatically assume that the older organization is *out* of the picture, anymore than we should assume that the younger organization is *in* the picture. It well may be that our inattention to the procedures and processes of organizational Renewal are, themselves, partly to blame. Organizational Renewal means rejuvenation and reconfiguration, but what, one might ask, would such attention be? What are the kinds of business tasks that organizational Renewal requires? Certainly, if Kaufman (1985) is right, environmental scanning is very important. Most organizations don't really know much about what is going on in their environment. The popularity of John Naisbitt's book on national trends is clear evidence of this. For most students of American society, Naisbitt's conclusions were neither terribly surprising nor terribly complete. Indeed, Naisbitt's trends come from a monitoring of 6,000 local newspapers each month (Naisbitt, 1983, p. 8). None of his data required the Freedom of Information

Act to pry it out. Yet, the sales of that book indicated that people were intrigued and impressed by what he wrote. That can only mean that our level of ignorance about our environment was greater than might have been hoped. A number of other trends might be added to the ten Naisbitt suggested. One, for example, has to do with the aging of the population. He does mention the aging issue, because Florida is one of his "bellweather" states, but the fact that our nation now has about as many older adults as Canadians (about 11%) and will have considerably more (some trends are up as high as 20% by the year 2000) does not make his list of major trends. One problem that the environmental scan can deal with, then, is the avoidance of the boiled frog phenomenon.

Knowing the trends, however, is not enough. You have to do something about them. It is in this context that the Four C's Conference becomes, once again, a useful mode of operation. It forces trend attention; it demands trend action. At the very worst, the mature Firms can engage in reaction to the trends they spot. Even better, though, would be an operating structure that permitted proaction. Anticipating trends, being ahead of the game, and in some cases even setting the trends is a desirable goal.

IDEA TASKS

A third group of tasks that are linked to the steps in the Entrepreneurial Staircase are sets of ideas and intellectual orientations. These undoubtedly overlap to some extent with Firm tasks and business tasks, but from our point of view they are sufficiently separate to deserve special attention. As Firms and ventures proceed up the Entrepreneurial Staircase, different intellectual orientations and foci are required. It is important to keep in mind the different types of intellectual tasks one needs to attend to as the entrepreneurial process proceeds.

Innovation

The Innovation Phase has a lot of idea-related steps because Innovation is primarily an idea. First, of course, is defining the problem.

The problem for business can be either finding a service or product that the market needs or finding a market for the service or product that one has. Given the problem, various proposals are usually developed to meet the problem. The generation of these options is crucial. One great problem in idea generation is that there is premature closure on a solution; individuals quickly state the problem and move immediately to an action step without considering the range of options and the range of implications that might be involved. Paradoxically, moving too quickly to a solution often leads to disaffection and subsequent disavowal. This in turn delays a decision longer than would be the case if one took the time to deal with some of the available alternatives. It is from these various proposals that a decision is made—and a decision must come before Implementation begins.

It is not at all unusual for organizations and individuals to start projects before there is any sort of agreement that the project will go forward. Often, this involves the "politics of the deed" in which one gets an enterprise underway and hopes that its momentum and the disinclination of managers to stop something already started will be sufficient to keep it going.

The other problem, of course, is postmature decision making in which alternatives and options are studied and discussed in far greater depth than necessary and over a far longer period of time than necessary. So much time is taken up with such evaluations that new ideas wither on the vine. One of the most important tasks of Entrepreneurial Management in the idea processing stage, therefore, is to see to it that options are developed on the one hand and that a timely decision is made on the other. As we are often reminded on wall posters "not to decide is to decide."

Implementation

Once the problem has been explored and the decision made, a new set of tasks comes up in the Implementation phase. Here, planning and design ideas and programmatic structures are proposed. To the extent that the original decision was strategic, the Implementation activities are tactical. In the new idea stage the question of what to do is primary. That having been decided, the Implementation Stage concentrates on how to do what has been agreed upon. There are a number of intellectual activities that focus on the actual process of Implementation. *Flow Charting*, for example, which deals with the specification of the series of steps that are required in Implementation, is a useful technique that can be employed. In a great many applications even more useful is *PERT* (Program Evaluation and Review Technique. See Allen, 1978).

PERT is a method for outlining the steps to be accomplished in the achievement of a particular goal. With PERT one works backward from the desired date/time that a product is needed and outlines the steps that need to be accomplished by specific dates or times in order for that final goal to be met. The preparation of a Thanksgiving dinner—the turkey, all of the trimmings, and the guests—provides a clear illustration of PERT. Let's say everything needs to be assembled by five o'clock. That is the time at which the guests and the meal are to come together. To accomplish this feat, different activities will need to be initiated at different points in time. We'll be serving a giant, twenty-five pound turkey with stuffing, which our well-thumbed copy of the *Joy of Cooking* tells us should take about fifteen minutes a pound. That translates into approximately six and a half hours of cooking time, allowing for a bit of standing time so it carves more easily. For the bird to be on the table at five, we'll have to stick it in the oven at 11:30 A.M. Similarly, thirty other foods go in to be cooked at different, carefully calculated times (potatoes, squash, beans, yams, three different kinds of pies, and so on). By the time five o'clock rolls around all is in readiness, and our guests "oooh" and "aaah" at our efficiency. They will be particularly impressed if we have taken into consideration all of the dozens of other Implementation activities that are required for the Thanksgiving dinner, and start each of them at the appropriate times. These would include setting the table, buying wine and other liquid refreshments, all of which must be carefully orchestrated to meet our five o'clock sit down time.[5]

PERTing is just one example of what Delbecq and Van de Ven (1971) would include in the whole area of program design or the structuring in advance of a particular set of activities and interactions designed to produce a good or service. They also emphasize program activation and program orientation and diffusion as intellectually focused activities of the Implementation Stage.

These are the essential elements in the Implementation process. Whether one uses a PERT technique or some other planning technique, the key point here is to keep in mind that Implementation requires planning, design, organization, orchestration, activation, operation, and diffusion so that all of the activities can be introduced at the appropriate time, all coming out at once. Although these are, in one sense at least, business tasks that people do, they are also intellectual tasks that people think about. If the intellectual set of tasks is ignored, there are likely to be a host of problems on the operational side. Whatever the preparatory activities might be—large or small, complex, or simple—the crucial feature of Implementation is that they are usually all aimed at a product or service being put on the market, completely ready for purchaser use at a particular point in time.

Growth

In the Growth Stage the idea is already in operation and may even be in an expanding phase. Three fundamental ideas need to be considered here: paradox reduction, perspective retention and principle generation.

Paradox reduction focuses on the competing and often inconsistent demands, problems, and difficulties that attend to an explosive Growth situation. Cash is coming in, but more cash is needed to finance Growth. Growth is needed to generate more cash. A wide range of paradoxes of the "no job, no work permit; no work permit, no job" variety develop, and they need resolution. These problems are particularly difficult during the Growth Stage because so much is going on simultaneously.

This organizational disharmony requires a second important set of ideas: perspective retention. In a Growth period, probably more than any other time, one is often running from pillar to post, dealing with all manner of business "fires." It is extremely difficult to grasp an overall sense of what might be happening. In fact, a failure to retain perspective and have some sense of the past, current, and future trajectories causes some Firms to fail at this particular stage. These are almost always Firms offering a very good product or service desired by a significant subset of customers (their growth testifies to this). Ideas about the overall business and about the Growth process, itself, make it possible to deal both with the present and the future.

This perspective allows a third set of ideas to emerge: *principle generation.* Principle generation is a kind of precursor to policy. It focuses on drawing general operating conclusions from the first three stages, using them as the first step toward Stabilization. Based on experience, certain things are *known* to work. Using them provides a good basis for moving ahead. And the Four C's Conference keeps you from getting in a rut.

Stabilization

Stabilization requires a different set of ideas. Because regularity is the hallmark of the Stabilization stage, what is needed are ideas about the ways in which what is being done can be checked on and the results of those checks used to guide the process even further. Monitoring, oversight, assessment, and appraisal ideas seem to be crucial. (For more detail, see the section on Evaluation Structures, Chapter 8.)

Monitoring is simply checking the numbers and flows. It involves simple counts and tabulations—"how many are we making, using, serving, etc."

Oversight involves checking for compliance. A bit of measurement and comparison enters.

Assessment involves judgment over a batch of time, products, people. "This process has (or has not) worked well. It is close to (or far from) our level of performance." Mid-course corrections can be instituted here.

Appraisal is fateful. It involves go/no-go decisions—-continue (or undertake) vs. stop (or don't activate). It blends all the information from the previous process into a judgment decision.

From the perspective of the cycle of ideas, the Stabilization phase is quite important because it is within this aspect of the entrepreneurial cycle that preparation is made for the next phase. Although in the cycle of activities tasks may be going forward that bring routine, regularity, and smoothness to the supply of the product or service, in the realm of ideas only a small amount of energy is placed on these things. For the most part, in fact, most energy is directed toward refurbishment and redirection. This is partly possible, because information about needed improvements, changes, and refurbishments becomes available in the evaluation process. Just because a company makes a decision to continue with a particular product line or service, or the individual Entrepreneur decides to keep on going with his particular line of work, does not preclude there being pieces of information about how to improve that product or service that are still consistent with a "go" evaluation. It is these pieces of information that are used to improve the product or service and start the product on its next set of travels through its life cycle.

Renewal

Within the cycle of ideas, of course, activities in the Stabilization phase meld into those in the Renewal phase. The difference simply lies in focus. In the Stabilization phase ideas about product refurbishment stem from the evaluations done in the Growth phase. In the Renewal Stage, new societal trends are the primary focus. If firms have a way to store ideas for future use, now is a good time to take a fresh look at them. It is primarily here in the Renewal Stage that the material in such storage is brought out and examined. Attention moves away from the specific idea and broadens to a collection of other possible ideas, approaches, and things to do. A lot of individuals and Firms don't do anything different because they don't have any idea about what *to* do. It is not so much that they are hostile to Innovations—although there certainly may be some of that. Their minds simply draw blanks. They are not imaginative or creative in that way. Everyone knows families who have vacationed in the same spot year after year, not necessarily because it is the only option they have, but because they never thought of doing anything else. They have let the energy of thought disappear from their decision-making process.

Ruts quickly become perilous chasms for business enterprises. It is very important, therefore, for Firms and the individuals connected with them to maintain the energy of thought—to maintain a list, a file, a box, a big envelope, any place where new ideas, crazy suggestions, weird perspectives can be stored. The Four C's Conference may help in liberating them, but they achieve their real importance in the Renewal Stage. That is the time to pull out and give serious consideration to all those ideas, approaches, and concerns that no one had time to deal with before. Many will seem as preposterous as when they were first suggested. Put them away until later. To your astonishment, some will probably strike a responsive chord. Either conditions will have changed since they were first proposed, or the passage of time will allow you to view them from a different perspective. Then, when these fresh and untried ideas (or old ideas whose time has finally come) are combined with information flowing out of the evaluation activities on current products or services, the necessary conditions will have been re-created for the new existence of business life.

What is important, therefore, in the whole Renewal area is that there be a formal and an informal research and development effort that is called on at this time to feed new ideas, perspectives, and concepts into the organization. When we use the phrase *research and development*, we realize that it has a big Firm, big buck connotation. Put that connotation aside. What we actually mean is that new ideas must be suggested continually as part of the ongoing organizational enterprise. Although this may not be research in the minds of some, nevertheless it is an exploratory, suggestive enterprise. On an ongoing basis new ideas should be flowing in. Some—and this is the development part—will be tried. As you will see in the chapter on Organizational Structure, we suggest incubator or reservation sections where new ideas can be tried out a bit. These trials need not be fancy or costly, nor are large laboratories required with many scientists. What is needed is a mechanism for tapping the creativity of people working in the organization instead of stifling that creativity and letting it go to waste.

ROLE LINKS TO THE ENTREPRENEURIAL STAIRCASE

A last aspect to the Entrepreneurial Staircase involves a focus on the kinds of roles or characteristics that individuals in the enterprise may need. For our purposes here, the word *roles* is preferred. It sounds more flexible and more open than the more permanent term *Characteristics*. Understand, however, that these role types can be either different individuals or the same individual changing roles or orientations and repositioning themselves to meet new needs. Two discussions are particularly helpful with respect to role change over the Entrepreneurial Staircase, those of Wissema, Van der Pol, and Messer (1980) and Maidique (1980).

Innovation

In the Innovation Stage, a pioneer-type orientation is useful. This orientation is very "flexible, very creative, very divergent" (Wissema, Van der Pol, and Messer, 1980, p. 42).[6] Maidique talks about the "Market Gatekeeper," the "Technological Gatekeeper," and the "Creative Scientist" as being needed in the Innovation Stage. Notice that these terms seem to focus on persons rather than roles. To the extent that the person orientation is taken, intellectual limitations develop because one thinks of the person as totally characterized by this particular modality. Rather, orientations are needed that have a pioneer spirit to them, a technological, creative orientation, to get products off the ground.

Implementation

To implement ideas a somewhat different but possibly overlapping set of characteristics is needed. The pioneer may continue to be important, but what Wissema, Van der Pol, and Messer call "The Conqueror" is also important. Such an individual is "appropriately non-conformist, creatively structured toward anything new" but also "capable of seeing beyond limits, generalist, and rational" (Wissema, Van der Pol, and Messer, 1980, p. 43). Maidique refers to these same kinds of characteristics contained in the Technological Champion (i.e., the individual who has an idea for a particular product or service from a technical service orientation point of view) and the Executive Champion (i.e., the individual who frees up resources and creates a climate of organizational permission for activities to go forward). A Project Manager is also a useful orientation to have in the Implementation stage (Sayles and Chandler, 1971). All of these talk about the need to push ahead creatively but in doing so to take into account the practical steps that are necessary to get a Thanksgiving dinner on the table, even if roast peacock is being substituted for turkey.

Growth

In the Growth Stage the Conqueror continues to be important, and Market Gatekeeping talents are added to Executive Champion talents in order to manage the growth matrix. It is here that the Level-Headed Ruler may also be Helpful. Wissema, Van der Pol, and Messer (1980) outline characteristics as, "strongly structured according to the time table" with a "solid, systematic, penetrating, specialist" orientation (p. 43). Such an individual should not be the only one in charge in an explosive growth situation or the Growth may be arbitrarily truncated in favor of orderliness and tidiness. Still, in such an explosive situation, the dynamic orientation of the Conqueror matched with the more routine orientation of the Level-Headed Ruler is what is needed.

Stabilization

In the Stabilization Stage the Level-Headed Ruler will continue to be important. Wissema, Van der Pol, and Messer identify two others: the *Administrator* and the *Economizer*, both of whom can be crucial at the Stabilization step. The Administrator is "routine, reproducible and docile" with "solid and conformist vision" (p. 44). The Economizer is "legalistic, everything according to precedent" (p. 44).

If the Stabilization Stage is a continuing one at the same level, then a combination of the Level-Headed Ruler and the Administrator will work well. If consolidation is required, however, then the characteristics of an Economizer might be important.

Renewal

Renewal requires the Pioneer to surface once again. Because we are now discussing renewing an ongoing organization, however, what Wissema, Van der Pol, and Messer call the *Insistent Diplomat* needs to be added to the pot. The Insistent Diplomat has "maximal flexibility within a fixed objective, accepts restrictions," but "is more strategic-directed towards the long-term than tactical-directed toward the short term" and is "broad, relativistic, and many sided" (p. 44). Such characteristics are needed in order to open up clogged organizational systems, to reconfigure frozen organizational structures, and to get people to see different perspectives in a different way. As most of us are well aware, it does precious little good to demand that people see things in different ways. Rather there must be the continuous kind of pressure (some may call it nudging) that might be characterized by the Insistent Diplomat role. However, the characteristics of the Insistent Diplomat are not likely to be associated with an innovation. Instead, they make a consideration of innovations that are already present possible.

As one moves up the steps of the Entrepreneurial Staircase, different characteristics become prominent. These can come either from individual change—setting aside old characteristics and taking on new ones—or by bringing in new employees who have the desired characteristics. It is our observation that individuals do have a role repertoire (and we'll be talking more about this in the chapter on Style), but it is a somewhat focused repertoire; individuals may be a Pioneer and a Conqueror, but they may not move into the Level-Headed Ruler, Administrator categories. Similarly, those individuals have difficulties with the orientations of an Economizer. Those orientations may in turn clash with those of the Insistent Diplomat. In short, individuals are most likely to have available for use roles close to those they are typically using. Similarly, skills that are linked to skills we already have are relatively easy to develop. Skills that are quite different from those that we already have may take a greater period of time to develop and may not even be within our reach. A combination, therefore, of both a role repertoire and a personnel repertoire may be necessary in order to have a successful journey up the Entrepreneurial Staircase.

CONCLUSION

This chapter has presented an overall sketch of the Entrepreneurial Staircase. Fundamentally, that process is made up of several parts: the entrepreneurial steps and entrepreneurial tasks. The stages—Innovation, Implementation, Growth, Stabilization, and Renewal—represent the major echelons through which products or Firms go as they move from an idea in somebody's head—or gleam in somebody's eye—through development, expansion, and maturation; after which they stand in need of improvement or refurbishment.

The tasks vary by steps. At different steps different tasks are required. Firms have different problems at different steps. Business tasks differ with different steps. Intellectual tasks and roles are step-related.

Generally speaking, in Entrepreneurial Management, two key tasks emerge as extremely important aspects of the overall Entrepreneurial Manager's assignment: *intracycle management* and *intercycle management.* Intracycle management focuses on those tasks within each cycle. The activities and ideas appropriate to each cycle must be stimulated and generated. Intercycle management is the orchestration of the transitions between one cycle and the next.

All transitions or passages are difficult and some are treacherous, and represent the points where many Firms fail. Such failure does not necessarily come about because their products or services are replaced by something better or have become less appealing. Often failure comes because the Firms do not recognize the phases and stages through which they must pass. Therefore, they are unable to move from one stage to the next. On an individual level we call this *arrested development,* and the person who is enjoying a prolonged adolescence is a prime example: activities permissable in the late teens and early twenties, though no longer expected or even permissible in the late twenties and beyond, continue to persist. To survive effectively in our society, it is imperative that individuals articulate reasonably well with their environment, forgoing some of their older ways, adopting some newer behaviors, and attending to some of the fresh expectations of their new position in the life stage or the life cycle.

It is equally important with Firms and products. For some Firms, moving forward is an extremely difficult and sometimes impossible feat to accomplish. Such movement may involve a new constellation of talents that has not developed. Sometimes the old talent isn't ready to be reconfigured. Sometimes the necessary new talent isn't available.

A cautionary note, however, is in order: actual clock time on these sequences varies considerably, depending on industry. Some of them can be many years in length. Others, in extremely fast moving industries, may be very short—for them a year, or even several months may be a long time. The key point is to be aware of the nature of the cycles and the different demands that surface and become prominent within each of them. An idea manager or a policy manager in the larger Firm at least will enable the business to be aware of cyclical location and to adjust the entrepreneurial process to fit, articulate and even anticipate that location. As people have frequently said, "If you don't know where you're going, any route will take you there." In a case of business development the velocity may differ, but the direction seems to be much the same. Awareness of the entrepreneurial cycle will enhance the ability of the Entrepreneur to be successful, will enable new ideas to be introduced, will prevent (or at least down play) the possibility of stagnation during the Stabilization and Renewal phases, and can introduce Renewal activities at an appropriate juncture.

NOTES

1. Firms grow for a number of reasons. Some stimuli, however, may have nothing to do with relationship to the marketplace. The Tropman "Two Martini" Theory of Firm Growth, for example, argues that, after this historical two-martini lunch, most executives and middle managers are not in a terribly good position to complete the afternoon's work. In fact, after returning to the office, they are very likely to say something like, "Good Lord! Look at all this work. I need an assistant." In due course they get a new assistant who, in time, begets another assistant, and so on. The Two-Martini Theory of Firm Growth suggests that, as time goes on, everyone in the organization is working halftime. Thus, twice as many people are needed at full salary to do the work that needs to be done by half. As applied to government, the theory appears especially persuasive. In both cases, however, evidence remains to be established by "rigorous scientific research."

2. This problem is common in all organizations. For religious organizations it is known as the difficulty of transition from sect to church; i.e., from the young, developing, perhaps vigorous and vibrant small conjur of committed religious to an organized, bureaucratized "Church Central." Emphasis in this transition is on the building of large church structures and is sometimes called, "The Edifice Complex."

3. Perseverance in the face of adversity is not uniquely an American Trait. The Japanese have it also. See for example the work of Ivan Morris, *On the Nobility of Failure: Tragic Heroes in the History of Japan* (1975).

4. By way of explanation, sushi is a staple of the Japanese diet made with rice. Essentially, it is a packed rice ball with something in the center, which could be a vegatable or fish or almost anything else, and which may have a wrapping of flaked seaweed called *nori*. There are an almost limitless number of variations. We mention the possibility of home delivered sushi only because, as a product, it would be ideally suited to the home delivery market: it is not bulky, it does not require a warming apparatus, and it is extremely tasty. It should be distinguished from sashimi, which is specifically raw fish, although some sushi may contain raw fish. The authors would appreciate generous expressions of gratitude from any readers who act on this idea and derive fabulous fortunes thereby.

5. Another important Implementation technique—some argue it is a Stabilization technique—is the "Just-in-Time" approach. Just-in-Time, or JIT as it is usually called, is exactly what its name implies; things to be used in a process arrive just in time exactly as they are needed, not before or after they are needed. The development of JIT has been attributed independently both to Edward Demming, initially sent by Gen. Douglas MacArthur to assist the Japanese redevelop their industry after World War II (probably a false attribution) and to Taiichi Ohno, former vice-president of the Toyota Motor Company in Japan (probably the correct attribution). Though generally thought of in connection with manufacturing, the approach is widely applied in Japan (and is rapidly growing in application in the U.S.) to a broad range of processes where elements can be added to the process on an as-needed basis. Looking

for all the world like the real time implementation of the Program Evaluation and Review Technique (PERT), according to Gwe (1985),

Just-in-time is a strategy for achieving significant, continuing improvement in performance by elimination of all waste of time and resources in the total business process. It requires and stimulates simultaneous improvement in quality and productivity of all activities. It develops the latent capabilities of all people in the company. It improves speed and flexibility of response to change by collapsing total throughput time, involving the total network of customers and suppliers.

In a 1986 personal communication, Fadra Towers reported on the work of John Towers, Senior Industrial Engineer and Systems Research Supervisor with Martin Marietta Aerospace:

JIT is a philosophy, a state of mind, as well as tangible techniques. The philosophy of JIT does not use "band-aids" to cover up excess inventory, safety stocks or padded lead times. Instead, JIT solves problems as they happen and encourages workers to help solve those problems. Vendors are also involved in the JIT philosophy. Their cooperation in the JIT process is vital for JIT to work correctly. The vendor helps to bring about the goal of JIT which is to have "all external materials required to produce a product arrive at only the proper time in the schedule when needed and only in the quantity desired."

Towers continued to explain:

Many different elements of a business must work well together in order to make JIT work. These elements include the business staff, the quality control process, the supply process (including outside vendors), the purchasing and production control processes, plant design, and the Japanese concept of "kanban" which means essentially dealing with all problems, however large or small, the instant they arise—and employing whatever people and resources are needed to deal with those problems—in order to assure the quality needed in the production process and the finished product. Failure, inefficiency, or recalcitrance in connection with any of these elements dooms the JIT approach.

Though elegantly simple in concept and enormously powerful in its application to Japanese industry and to an ever increasing number of American organizations, a significant segment of American business has questioned it. This segment claims that it makes forecasting more difficult (customers are not reliable in providing estimates of their needs), that it places too heavy a reliance on the quality of the thing supplied by a vendor (even a minor part improperly supplied can shut down an entire plant, which accompanies a general climate of distrust of outside suppliers), that labor union contracts with their rigid and inflexible definitions of job categories prevent each employee having a total view of the company (which is essential if JIT is to work), and that the American work force needs to be completely reeducated before JIT can work (i.e., a change in the way productivity is viewed from a stress on the productivity of pieces per hour per employee to an emphasis on the productivity of the plant as a whole and a change in the way employees are evaluated from being based on how many parts he or she has produced to how closely total production—without excess inventory or waste—matches the required production.

According to Towers, there are some striking success stories among American companies that have adopted JIT. General Electric, for example, was one of the first in the United States to use JIT. By 1983, GE was using JIT in 40 plants. At the company's dishwasher plant it permitted a 40% reduction in parts, 50% reduction for in-warranty service calls, 50% reduction in scrap-rework, 40% less space, 15% increase in capacity, and an improved market penetration (to 40%). At its switchgear plant it reduced major setup time from 56 minutes to 1.5 minutes, reduced work-in-process from 10 weeks to 1.5 weeks, and did it with a 22% decrease in overall factory inventory. And at Digital Equipment Corporation's Diversified Disk Product plant, after only two months of JIT, the plant showed an 85% reduction in work in process, a 63% improvement in productivity, the elmination of rework inventory, almost 400% reduction in overtime, and a 52% reduction in plant costs.

Generally speaking, then, JIT is the most efficient production technique in today's manufacturing technology. The success of JIT requires all elements and concepts of JIT working together at the same time. Success depends on the commitment of everyone in a business where JIT is used. Where JIT has been implemented and its precepts closely adhered to it has invariably resulted in cost reduction, increased productivity, and happier customers.

For excellent discussions of JIT consult any of the following: Yashuiro Monden, *Toyota Production System*, Industrial Engineering and Management Press, Norcross, GA, 1983; Henry E. Riggs, *Managing High-Technology Companies*, Lifetime Learning Publications, Belmont, CA, 1983; R. Dave Garwood, "Explaining JIT, MRP II, Kanban," *P&IM Review*, October, 1964, vol. 12, pp. 66, 68–69, 88; Carl Kirkland, "Just-In-Time Manufacturing: What You Need to Know and Why," *Plastics Technology*, August 1984, pp. 63–68; Leon B. Crosby, "The Just-in-Time Manufacturing Process: Control of Quality and Quantity," Production and Inventory Management, *The Journal of the American Production and Inventory Control Society*, Fourth Quarter 1985, Vol. 26, No. 4, pp. 94–100; and Robert A. Parmalee, "JIT Implementation by the Numbers," American Production and Inventory Control Society, Twenty-Eighth Annual International Conference *Proceedings*, October 21–25, Toronto, Ontario, 1985, pp. 457–461.

6. In their article, Wissema, Van der Pol, and Messer (1980) place a different series of steps on the Entrepreneurial Staircase. They begin with Explosive Growth, to which they link the Pioneer, then to Expansion, then to Continuous Growth, Consolidation, what they call "Slip Strategy," and finally Contraction. We are reorganizing their managerial types into somewhat different steps on the staircase offered here. They have three steps within the Growth Stage, for example. They may well be right, but for our purposes a five-step overview rather than substeps within each step seems to be more appropriate.

II

THE TEN-S SYSTEM

In Part I of this volume we introduced the idea of Entrepreneurship in a slightly different way than many people think about it. Because our view is somewhat out of the ordinary, the differences between our perspective and the more traditional one are worth a brief review.

First, we take the position that Entrepreneurship is not simply a matter of personality characteristics but—and more importantly—of competencies, conditions, and context, as well. This focus highlights entrepreneurial skills as things that are achieved rather than things ascribed. It seeks to identify the kinds of things that individuals need to do in order to enhance entrepreneurial potential and activity. We emphasized, particularly in Part I, that Entrepreneurship is as much a function of the organization and environment as it is of the person undertaking the entrepreneurial enterprise. We must think of the Entrepreneur, therefore, not as someone who flies solo but, rather, as a manager—particularly a manager concerned with the introduction of new ideas, new products, and new services into systems, whether those systems require the development of a new organization or whether they are, in fact, an extant organization.

Second, we see Entrepreneurship as a process of new idea introduction, development, and stabilization. Simply establishing your own business does not qualify you as an Entrepreneur. Rather, you have to take risks both financially and intellectually in order to fit our definition. Furthermore, there is a definite need for others to fill out the entrepreneurial package.

Finally, ideas of cycle, stage, and process were introduced in Part I. These provide an overall framework in which entrepreneurially interested individuals can locate themselves.

Part II provides a checklist of things to do in the entrepreneurial enterprise.

As you might expect, these are not so different from what is required of enterprises in general. The things an Entrepreneurial Manager needs to attend to are, by and large, the same kinds of things that all managers need to attend to. The key difference is that for the Entrepreneurial Manager they are more complicated and more difficult, more tenuous and less certain. The introduction of new products, new services, or new ideas is always potentially problematic. It is that very excitement that draws some individuals to these enterprises and repels others.

The Entrepreneurial Manager needs to attend to ten areas of focal concern. Each is important in and of itself. All need to be orchestrated together. The system we discuss is an elaboration on the one reported by Peters and Waterman (1982) and by Pascale and Athos (1982), among others. The design is a relatively simple, *Seven-S system*. Each S represents an important area for management attention. Three of the S's are called *hard* S's: Strategy, Structure, and Systems. These are widely thought of as being favored by American-style management orientations. Three of the S's are *soft* S's: Style, Staff, and Skills. These are widely thought to be favored by Japanese-style managers. One S—Subordinate values—is seen as an integrating feature of the other S's. A drawing of the Seven-S System from Peters and Waterman's *In Search of Excellence* (1982) is reproduced as Figure II.1.

The system we present here refines and expands the view, adding three S's to the original Seven-S System: Self, Superordinate Structure, and Superordinate Values. In addition, our focus is on the management of ideas, innovations, new products, and new services. This Ten-S System is best visualized as a pie with a two-circle center cut into six equal sizes and with a very thick crust. It is displayed in Figure II.2.

Self is at the center. Although we will not spend a great deal of time talking about the self, it certainly cannot be ignored. Surrounding the Self are Skills and Style. Both of these elements are personal in the sense that they are in the possession of the person and can be used by the Entrepreneurial Manager to advance her or his interests.

Beyond Skills, Style, and Self lie four organizational elements: Strategy, Structure, Staff, and Systems. These are the elements on which Skills, Style, and Self work and focus. A fifth organizational element, Subculture, is also a focus of Entrepreneurial Management effort. It is described here as a ring that integrates persona and organization and links them to the external—superordinate—environment.

The third major ring is Superordinate Culture and Structure. These elements represent the environment, the external conditions of markets, regulations, public opinion, values, and attitudes that can be responded to and occasionally shaped.

As one moves from the center to the edge of the pie, there is less and less control, and it becomes clear that Self is only a part of the pie. Although there may be some set of given or natural abilities, they are a minor element

II.I. Seven-S System from Peters and Waterman

McKINSEY 7-S FRAMEWORK ©

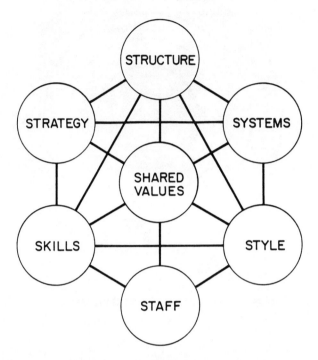

[1] Source: T. J. Peters and Robert H. Waterman, Jr., *In Search of Excellence*, (Harper and Row: New York, 1982). p 10
Reproduced with permission

in the entrepreneurial package. Acquired orientations, like willingness to work hard, persistence, and so on are much more important. Skills and Styles can certainly be acquired, although acquiring Styles is not as popular an idea as acquiring Skills.

Within the middle circle is the Firm, itself. There are great opportunities for influence and direction here. Indeed, when one thinks of management, it is to this area that attention is usually drawn.

The external environment is less in one's usual sphere of influence. Occasionally, of course, it is possible to have some measureable impact upon it. Even then, however, that impact is usually on a small segment of a very large arena. Generally the environment is managed by adaptation rather than by direction.

The chapters in this section outline some of the concerns that need to be addressed by the Entrepreneur in the introduction of entrepreneurial systems.

II.2. The Tropman Ten-S System

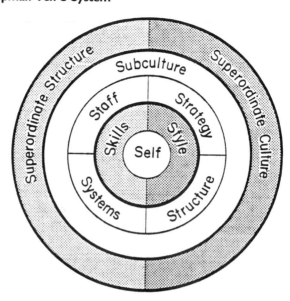

Adapted from the 7-S System of McKinsey and Company
T. J. Peters and Robert Waterman Jr., *In Search of Excellence* (New York: Harper and Row, 1982).

By John E. Tropman. M. Levin contributed to this design.

Chapter 5 deals with the "crusts" of the pie, outlining some major changes in social structure and social culture that are demanding of attention.

Chapter 6 examines organizational subculture, that integrating feature of organizations that ties all the parts together. Chapters 7, 8, 9 and 10 pick up on Strategy, Structure, System, and Skills, respectively, and Chapters 11 and 12 focus on Staff and Styles. Self has already been discussed. Each chapter in this group has "Creating" in its title—"Creating Organizational Subculture," "Creating Organizational Strategy," and so on—in order to emphasize the active and interventive nature of the chapter focus.

5

Society: Social Structure and Social Culture

#1: "Action is what makes the world go round. Thought never helped anyone." North-Going ZAX

#2: "Fool! Thought guides action. Without thought no one would know what to do." South-Going ZAX

#1: "Listen, noodle noggin, what people think is determined by what people do, how people act. Our values conform to our situation. When in Rome..."

#2: "You're missing the point; values cause preselection of a range of actions!"

#1: "Even Aristotle understood ideas came second! So did Marx."

#2: "Plato knew better! Max Weber knew better!"

—John E. Tropman
The ZAXes are courtesy of Dr. Seuss

INTRODUCTION

Steven Leacock once observed, "All things considered and there being few incidents to the contrary that I can immediately recall, it is very likely that the future lies ahead of us." Charles Kettering cautioned us, "We should all be concerned about the future because we will have to spend the rest of our lives there." Certainly, for the field of business, it would be extremely helpful if we could discern some of the shape and texture of the future in order to prepare ourselves better for what lies ahead. This is particularly important for the Entrepreneur because it is emerging trends that represent the market niches open for new products and services.

Too often, in the crush of daily business, we do not look ahead to reflect on what may be in the future. We give little thought to how we can best adjust ourselves both to prepare for what is coming and to take advantage of it. On those rare occasions when we do find ourselves anticipating our journeys on the road ahead, all too frequently we see trends and developments that we don't like or that we find difficult to accept. And so we reject them. We emulate Michael Flanders' ostrich, burying our heads in the sand and adopting a posture of supreme contentment, secure in the mistaken belief that what we cannot see cannot possibly harm us. We all know companies that can be characterized in this way. It is for philosopher Friedrich Nietzsche to bring us back to earth, reminding us that "it is our future that lays down the law of our today." By orienting ourselves to change now we can prevent precisely those kinds of developments that we believe will be troubling, and we can take advantage of those trends and developments that are coming whether we like it or not. As Longfellow suggested, "Go forth and meet the shadowy future without fear."

There is no question that our society—indeed the world—is changing rapidly. Those changes can be divided generally into two major kinds: changes in social structure and changes in social culture. Changes in social structure are concerned with changes in the patterns of things we do, the laws we have, the way we act. Changes in social culture center on the things we believe, the values we hold, and the attitudes we profess. Although it is true to some extent that actions shape beliefs and beliefs direct action, it is important to understand that the relationship between what we believe and what we do is open and conflicting. American society, for example, celebrates equality worldwide; and we are probably better at supporting equality than most other countries. In spite of that professed and supported position, racial and gender discrimination are still prominent features of our social landscape. It would seem that our values have not completely permeated our actions.

In spite of these historic discriminations (remember that blacks were counted as three fifths of a person in the constitution for census purposes), our beliefs in the *importance* of equality and equal opportunity have not dimmed much over the years, actions to the contrary notwithstanding. It is probably because we behave as though our beliefs are largely independent of our actions—that we don't enact totally every belief nor do we adjust every belief to every action—that we observe so much openness and flexibility in our society. Many, indeed, are the Entrepreneurs who have gone ahead with a product or service despite lots of negative beliefs about whether that product or service would actually succeed. As Lawton (1983) writes:

The kernel of my message, however, is that the lack of predictability from one sector.
. . . to another even if we reduce measurement error to its bare minimum, is the

normal state of affairs to be expected for the human condition. Specifically we suggest that the relative autonomy among sectors is what makes human existence possible. If a change in one sector were to be immediately reflected in every other sector chaotic instability would be the result. (P. 355)

CHANGES IN SOCIAL STRUCTURE

What are the current changes affecting us within our social structure, and how do they effect Entrepreneurship? Let's consider once again the stimulating work of John Naisbitt in *Megatrends* (1983). We've already touched upon some of the things he mentions. We now add some others that aren't mentioned in his book. It is important to organize these trends in some kind of conceptual scheme. One useful one uses the acronym "POET" (Population, Organization, Environment and Technology). It provides a strong focus for thinking about social change.

Population

The population of the world and of American society is changing dramatically. There are estimates that the world population will approach seven billion people by the year 2000 (Hauser, 1976). Of these, about two billion will be in the more highly developed countries. The remaining five billion will be in the less well-developed countries.

Entrepreneurs need to think through the implications of the world market, especially if Naisbitt is right and we are moving from national to world economies. (We have more to say about this trend in a moment.) But there are some important demographic correlates in both the well-developed and the underdeveloped nations that are particularly worth noting. The population structure of well-developed countries, for example, will be older, with more people over 65 and fewer under 18. In addition, they will be more well to do. The underdeveloped countries will have a much younger population, and one which is relatively poor. Thus, the world marketplace in the year 2000 seems to be dividing itself into two major camps: relatively small but older and richer groups of nations and people on the one hand, and a relatively large younger and poorer group of nations and people on the other. Addressing the imperatives of these markets will require a great deal of ingenuity.

American society mirrors the changes of all well-developed nations. The population, for example, is aging. These older citizens represent a great potential market for Entrepreneurs, one that has so far been mainly exploited by the health care and housing industries.

Total population results from births, deaths, and in and out migrations. Each of these forces is working heavily to change the face of the American population. Births are decreasing, so the number of younger people is decreasing. (In contrast to the "Baby Boom" generation that followed World War II, this is sometimes called the "Baby Bust" generation.) Furthermore, medical advances and improved diet and nutrition programs are helping Americans to live longer. So, not only are there fewer younger Americans, there is a growing number of older Americans. Immigration, legal and illegal, is also a growth factor.

The final population of any country at any point in time is like a bank account. There are deposits (births, immigrations) and withdrawals (deaths, emigrations). However, these do not totally determine the net size of the account. Just as your money accounts tend to earn interest, so too do population accounts. In terms of population dynamics, demographers call that interest the "length of a generation." It is expressed as the average age of a woman in the society when she has her first child. If women have children at young ages, the population grows faster, almost without regard to any other factors—just as a bank account grows faster with a higher interest rate.[1] The length of a generation in American society is going up. Wise Entrepreneurs will be particularly sensitive to the needs of the older family. If women in their late twenties and early thirties are having children, then child care at work becomes a very important factor, something that might be less true if the average age of a woman having her first child were eighteen or nineteen.

There are other trends involving the American family that are worth examining. According to the *Wall Street Journal*, September 26, 1986, the population of working women is up to 54.7% from 36.7% in 1965 (p. 16). The fertility rate is going down. The marriage rate is going up, and the median age at marriage is going up for both men and women. The divorce rate has doubled since 1965, and the number of out-of-wedlock births is estimated to be three times that of 1965. With respect to the demographics of the American society, there is so much variation that we might say variation is now the norm. "People think they are seeing departures from the norm," says Peter Morrison, Director of Rand Corporation's Population Research Center, "but departures are now 75% of the norm" (*Wall Street Journal*, September 25, 1986, p. 1). Entrepreneurial Managers need to be aware of population trends, shifts, and movements in order to position themselves and their ventures to take advantage of new and different resources and contribute to finding answers to new and different needs.

Social Organization

Social organization reflects the way the society organizes itself to accomplish its various tasks. Several of the changes that John Naisbitt (1983) mentions can be located here. He notes that the changes in our social patterns and habits that fit into this category range from institutional to self-help, from short- to long-term orientation, from representation to participatory styles, from either/or orientations to multiple option ones, and from hierarchical perspectives to networking perspectives. To these we should also add changes from sex stereotyping to androgyny. Let's take a brief look at each of these.

Changes from Institutional Help to Self-Help. What once appeared to be increasing reliance on professionals and specialists seems now to be moving back to a focus on doing it one's self. This counter-move seems relatively pervasive, now encompassing self-help groups in finance, medical care, home birthing, and so on. Entrepreneurially oriented people might well find that products and services related to assisting this movement would be successful. Do-It-Yourself products are doubtless in for another big boom.

Changes from Short-Term to Long-Term. America has often been associated with the short-term, crisis-oriented mentality. This perspective has been widely cited as one of the important causes of our loss in product leadership status worldwide. We appear to be moving from a here-and-now mentality into a longer term perspective. This is apparent in the rise of strategic planning in business organizations. It is evident in the popularity of Individual Retirement Accounts and Keough Plans (even without tax deductability). We see it, too, in career consulting services that help individuals plan for a lifetime organizational activity, not just the next job.

Unfortunately, the "We Want It Yesterday" mentality, and the "I Don't Want It Good, I Want It Tuesday" orientation are still very much with us. Planning, it would seem, is not something we take very well to in our society. Still, as we are forced more to it, planning-oriented services should prosper.

Changes from Representative to Participatory Styles. We have long thought of ourselves as a representative democracy, a view that has permeated our relationship to many of our institutions. In the past we have tended not to deal directly with items of concern. Rather, we have a long tradition of designating representatives to ask on our behalf. Naisbitt purported that this trend is changing. More and more we appear to want to act directly on and in our own behalf. We want to take control of those areas of our lives that are of most concern to us and that most effect us. It is no anomaly that books such as Wayne Dyer's *Pulling Your Own Strings* (1978) are such runaway best sellers. Partly, of course, this orientation stems from a fear that our representatives often have done us dirt. Partly, too, a resurgence of self-interest and even narcissism may account for this trend, telling us over and over again that we are our own best friends.

Throughout business and industry, however, the ability of workers to participate directly in the making of their product and to be valued for that participation becomes an increasingly important focus. Entrepreneurial ventures will need to take this trend into account both in terms of designing and structuring employee participation plans and in setting up structures that allow for employees to contribute not only their physical labor but their ideas and perspectives, as well. Entrepreneurs can also offer services that help other businesses do this.

Changes from Either/Or to Multiple Options. Naisbitt (1983) suggested that American society is moving out of a posture in which one's choices are either *this* or *that*, a situation where the number of alternatives is limited. The result is what decision theorists call a *zero sum game*. The flip of a coin is a typical example of such a game: if we win, you lose; if you lose, we win. We appear to be moving toward a situation where we have more options available. Rigid and precise work schedules, for example, are being replaced in some quarters by *flex-time* in which the individual sets his or her own work schedule within previously agreed upon perimeters. There is also the development of *job sharing*, where the same job may be held by two different people for the convenience of both. Rigidly defined benefit plans are moving to veritable cafeterias of options. The creation of multiple options implies that individuals not only have a choice of the food displayed there, but in the design of the cafeteria. Entrepreneurs need to be aware of these new expectations, for opportunities in meeting multiple needs will abound.

Changes from Hierarchies to Networks. Although hierarchies have long characterized our organizations in America, they are no longer necessarily typical of organizational processes. More and more we see rigid, multilevel chains of command being replaced by participatory schemes, such as management by objectives and Quality Circles. The organizational circle, discussed in Chapter 8, is a good example of this different approach.

Increasingly we seek to rely on others who have had experience with problems similar to our own. This is networking, and it appears to be gradually replacing the reliance on those who are impersonal, distant experts, who may or may not have our interests at heart, and who may or may not care particularly about whether their advice is helpful or harmful. Networking involves getting together with others and engaging in collective problem solving, relying on each other for mutual support and encouragement. It also involves using the group as a resource—using group context, for example, in order to obtain preferential treatment in job seeking. Although the use of networks has been taken almost for granted among male business executives, in recent years we have seen a deliberate and growing effort among women to develop similar networks. As Rosabeth Moss Kanter points out in her book, *The Change Masters* (1983), shorter and flatter organizations are likely to be more innovative, responsive, and resourceful than the tall and skinny ones. The chains of command that hold the structure up also bind the individuals in it, freezing them into particular positions, views, and dispositions.

Changes from Sex Stereotyping to Androgyny. Traditional wisdom has it that men are men and women are women. The roles associated with that notion are no longer as pervasive in organizations as they once were. Increasingly in today's society the view that some jobs are for women and some for men, that business roles have immutable sex-linked characteristics, is out of date. A kind of gender commonality is occurring, with both males and females taking on or expressing some of the characteristics of the other gender. Women have gone into the paid workforce in large numbers. The number of house-husbands is certainly not as great as the number of working wives, but it is not as insignificant as it was at one time. Some men are choosing to stay at home while their wives, for whatever reason unique to that family, bring in the income.

But even if complete role reversal of traditional roles does not occur, there is often a melding and a blending. The result is that men are doing much more of what we have historically thought of as woman's work. In addition, we see more and more women undertaking the activities regarded as peculiarly male only a few years ago. Popular music stars, such as Boy George, deliberately adopt an androgynous costume. Popular movies, such as *Tootsie* and *Victor Victoria*, celebrate gender disguise where men become women and women become men. Lest one think these trends are reserved for the arts, successful individuals in business today—especially managers—seem to be able to combine styles of men and women. Sargent's book, *The Androgynous Manager* (1981), focuses on this trend. Entrepreneurs who recognize this will have more flexibility in staffing their new ventures.

Environment

Changes in the environment, for purposes here, are changes in the locations of business and the way business is organized in the landscape. Naisbitt (1983) mentions movement from north to south as a major trend; and clearly at the time he wrote, that seemed reasonable. With changes in oil prices, however, some of the booming southern cities have now gone into eclipse. At the same time, some regions—New England is a notable example—have come back in relatively spectacular ways. Even the Midwestern "Rust Belt" may become burnished up in time. Some authorities predict that in the years to come, fresh water will become an extraordinarily valuable commodity. Those states bordering the Great Lakes then may be sitting on a resource far more valuable than oil.

Our point is simply that the physical environment of business changes. Sometimes resources that were once plentiful dry up. Sometimes resources, once unattended, become valuable. Particular market geographies once taken for granted become changed, changing marketing requirements radically. This leads logically to Naisbitt's suggestion that we are changing from a national economy to a world economy.

Changes from a National to a World Economy. It is clear that America must reposition itself vis-à-vis world economy. American business must find those things that we do well and specialize in them more than we have in the past. Such specialization and differentiation is not new. It has been a constant process within the country as a whole *intra*nationally. Dealing *inter*nationally, however, requires us to face a number of problematic and difficult restrictions and hurdles that we have not had to confront before. Still, there are numerous opportunities not only with respect to on-shore or off-shore business occasions and their combinations and permutations, but also in business ventures assisting other businesses in developing and enhancing the necessary coping skills.

From Ecological Ignorance to Environmental Sensitivity. Although our national emphasis on production and the material side of life is still extremely strong, more and more of it is accompanied by a sensitivity to the environment in which we live. There is a growing awareness of the quality of life that includes not only the material things, but the natural setting in which we live our lives, as well. Slowly but surely we're taking measurable steps to improve that environment, and the pace of such improvement is gradually accelerating. In time, perhaps, individuals will come from all parts of the world to view our varied magnificent scenery and to enjoy our upgrade in environmental quality. Opportunities abound in developing the products and services to service this environmental consciousness. Entrepreneurs in other businesses need to take environmental concern into account.

Technology

Basically, technology is a more efficient way of doing work. It is a pattern of transformation of materials through the use of energy. With respect to contemporary American society, changes in modes of production and in focal industrial activities are appropriately thought of as changes in technology. Naisbitt mentions three that are especially relevant: changes from industrial society to information society, changes from force technology to high technology, and changes from centralization to decentralization.

Changes from an Industrial Society to an Information Society. Many years ago most Americans were farmers. Only a few were engaged in the production process. With the passage of the Civil War and the development of steam power, industrial technology—"force technology"—became the major mode of production. Most Americans moved into jobs in the production process, and only a minority remained farmers. As we have moved from the production of food to the production of materials, we may expect that we will next move from the production of materials to the production of information. This is what Naisbitt means when he refers to the movement from the industrial society to information society. Already we have begun to see a decline in manufacturing as a fraction of our total human energy and effort and an accompanying increase in automated manufacturing plants.

With the shift away from an industrial society, the new locus of activity will be to collection, storage, analysis, and dissemination of information. These will build on new computer and telecommunication technology. Making such a prediction in 1950 would surely have seemed more far-out than far-reaching. At that time the computer was a room filling, cumbersome, clumsy, expensive piece of apparatus. But all of that was before the transistor, intregrated circuitry, and the microchip. The home computer that Radio Shack marketed in 1979 for about $1500 was eight times more powerful than the computer that controlled the defense of the entire United States in 1955, a computer that cost $11 million.

Entrepreneurs will surely find ways to exploit this trend toward an information society. Already, computer shopping and electronic mail are becoming relatively commonplace. The interstate highways of the future may contain a tiny band running down the center of each lane that links to and activates with on-board automotive computers. You will get in your car, hit the main drag, program in your destination, and settle back with a good book. Your car will slip into the ongoing stream of "car trains," controlled by computer operated sensors. Chips containing maps of the United States will already be built into the vehicle. The automobile is only one of an almost infinite number of possibilities that will ultimately rely on the new information technology.

All libraries one day will be stored on or in mass storage devices, addressable by computer, and accessible from an unlimited number of computerized locations. Apart from the storage of information and its quick retrieval, entrepreneurial premiums will be placed upon mechanisms for selecting, digesting, and synthesizing this vast amount of information. After all, even with search time counted in microseconds, the amount of information on most topics will be vast. Relevance, appropriateness, timeliness, focus, and analysis will be at a premium.

Changes from Force Technology to High Tech-High Touch. Contained within the change from an industrial to an information society is a shift from force technology to high technology. This shift is of considerable importance to individuals who work for any particular organization. Industrial society was the era of force technology. Physical work was their premium. In the information age high technology is the focal element, and high technology requires a sophisticated and intelligent work force. Workers cannot simply be replaced willy-nilly, as so often happened in the industrial era. Leaving aside the humanitarian considerations, physical strength is easier to replace than the sum costs of intellectual development or specialized high technology training. Given our increasingly complex computer-based technology, the amount of time it takes to train workers becomes an extremely crucial element. Entrepreneurial activity involving worker training, retraining, and so on is likely to be a burgeoning field. Having made those investments employers will be much more chary about making employees "walk the plank." Special efforts will have to be made at coming to accommodations between management and labor, because labor is too valuable now to be set aside in a casual manner. This opens additional opportunities for interpersonally oriented entrepreneurial types in the whole area of employee relations.

The employee has finally been recognized as the complex machine she or he always has been. The throw away society ("if it doesn't work, throw it out and get one that does"), characteristic of the industrial age, may be on the decline. In part, at least, this is because the ability to replace depends on having a stock of expensive pieces of equipment waiting in the wings. With people we don't have "extras" waiting around until one of us breaks.

Changes from Centralization to Decentralization. Correlated with these two other trends is a movement toward decentralization. Naisbitt (1983) sees a decided movement away from large centers and toward smaller, more efficient units. In recent years, for example, we have seen a movement away from large mental hospitals toward small, community-based foster care units. Population has been moving out of our larger cities and into smaller, more useable spaces where individuals can relate to one another more easily. We have seen some erosion of the consolidated political power in Washington with some influence (albeit small) flowing back to the states. Peters and Waterman (1982) allude to this particular trend in two of the features they find characteristic of excellent companies. One, a feature that they call a *loose-tight property*, implies some centralized control (the tight part) with a lot of abilities to deal individually with local situations flowing to subunits (the loose part). In addition, their orientation toward *simple form, lean staff* bespeaks a similar focus. To the extent, at least, that hierarchies represent centralization and networking represents subnodules within the organizational structure, this is another version of the shift from hierarchies to networking.

Doubtless entrepreneurs will find opportunities here. These might include specially training the smaller units and working with them on an individual unit by unit basis to improve their efficiency and productivity.

THE ENTREPRENEURIAL ADVANTAGE

Are these trends the key ones? To be frank, we are not sure. Some may prove to be enduring; others, passing. Trend forecasting is a risky business, especially in the area of social patterns and social behavior. To some extent, however, whether they are right or not right is beside the point. They suggest the types of changes that Entrepreneurs might look for. As one begins to sit down and think about what kinds of market niches might be available in current trends or other trends or local variations of national trends, fresh ones will come into view. The central point here is that new patterns of social behavior, social relationships, create demand for new products and new services. By examining social trends proactively and by considering how you might relate to them, you will automatically be a step ahead of your competitors.

CHANGES IN SOCIAL CULTURE

If changes in social structure, such as Naisbitt (1983) describes, are in the works—or likely eventually to be in the works—then it is also true that changes in the system's beliefs, attitudes, and values are likely to be occurring as well. Some, as we indicated at the beginning of this chapter, are inter-related. Others may be proceeding quite interdependently but are stimu-lating some changes.

The Patterns of Culture

One of the more important features of the value system—and the one that hasn't been talked about very much—is its structure. Before examining the changes, let's take a brief look at some of the features of the structure of culture.

Values, commitments, beliefs, attitudes are all more than just lists. They are patterns, shapes, and structures. For every list of values—like a dictionary—there is a grammar, a set of rules, for putting them together. From our perspective—and that of a number of others (e.g., Robert Lynd,1939, and Seymour Lipset, 1963)—values come in sets; i.e., pairs of competing commitments. For example, in *The First New Nation* (1963), Sey-mour Lipset sees our whole nation unfolding as a tension between values of achievement on the one hand and values of equality on the other.

An important feature of this value structure is that it is not concerned simply with two ends of a continuum—achievement is not simply the other end of equality; permission is not simply the other end of control. It is much like the success/failure grid we mentioned earlier. Rather, we must think of high (and low) achievement societies in the same way we think about high (and low) achievement individuals. Those societies and persons who are not motivated to achieve, however, are not necessarily egalitarian, either.

The best way to think about these value structures is in the form of a plus with intersecting axes. This leads to a four-fold design as displayed in the Figure 5.1.

One axis is achievement orientation, as present in a particular culture. A second axis is egalitarian orientation. Both dimensions run from high to low. What this means is that there are four cells that characterize most cultures. *High-high*, a culture that is high on egalitarianism and high on achievement. There are certainly companies where this is the case. There are also *low-low* cultures where neither achievement nor egalitarianism seem to be par-ticularly prominent. In addition, we can identify companies that are high on achievement and low on egalitarianism. These display corporate cultures that are tremendously competitive and cut throat.

There are also those companies where achievement orientation is low and egalitarianism is high. Typical of such Firms and businesses are those of a life-style nature. Individuals enter them less to make money or achieve a high rank in society than for the intrinsic pleasure that participating in the culture provides. Many musical careers may fall into this category (although there is a considerable amount of competition in music, as well).

Figure 5.1
The Conflict between Achievement and Equality as American Values

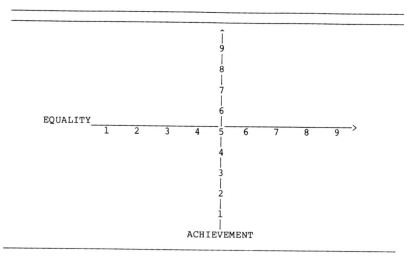

Finally, there are those Firms low on achievement and on equality. Because they are not moving and have relatively hostile cultures, they are among the worst places to work.

The fact that there are paired values within organizational cultures does not exhaust the things that we can say about them. In fact, this perspective expands our ability to understand the dynamics of organizational culture in ways heretofore only hinted at. Four other points are worthy of special mention.

First, the achievement-equality dichotomy is only one of many. (From an entrepreneurial point of view, another particularly important value conflict is between the permission to innovate and the control of innovation. In Chapter 6, we discuss a number of others.) Achievement and equality is a useful and appropriate one for business, but competition between values of permission on the one hand and control on the other, particularly of the innovated processes and products, is another universal competitive element that characterizes a wide range of organizations.

Second, in any given pair one or another value may be more dominant. Within the American culture, for example, we might conclude that achievement is the more dominant value with egalitarianism being a strong competitor but less prominent than achievement. It is the presence of both *plus* their differential importance that allows for organizational cultures to be located differentially within the value matrix.

Third, in spite of the fact that dominance or prominence of one value of the pair exists, organizational cultures change over time. Partly this change is in response to internal dynamics. Partly it is in response to external pressures and frictions. Over time emphasis on one value creates a tension or a stress within the organization or culture because competing commitments require that both value orientations be honored in some way and in some time. Thus, over time attention to achievement will produce pressures to emphasize more egalitarian and democratic values. As this pressure builds up and manifestations of these values become evident, they begin to threaten the achievement values. Emphasis on them then begins to reassert itself. The dual value framework, therefore, creates a constant friction of values internal to the organizational culture that allows for—and in fact requires—some degree of value change and alterations. Hence, in the value matrix described in Figure 5.1, the organization, once located in a particular position, does not remain in that position and will change over time. Any location or dot within a matrix representing a particular organization's position and a particular point of view must be seen as a stroboscopic capturing of a dynamic organizational situation in which the culture at an earlier point of time had a different position and will have a different position still at a later point in time.

Societal values shift in similar ways. Any location of a society at a particular point in time on these views will be decidedly different if we look at that society at a later or an earlier point in its history.

The great economist, Albert O. Hirshman (1981), also indicates a source of value change deriving from dual or competing value commitments. In his book *Shifting Involvements* (1981), Hirshman points out that disappointment, in particular value commitments, which are almost certain to occur is, itself, a generative force in beginning to explore other perspectives. He talks about "shifting involvements" from public to private orientation as a particularly salient and contemporary example. This disappointment can occur both within the society at large and within any particular organizational subculture.

We have mentioned two engines of change for values: tension between competing commitments and disappointment in the achievement or the accomplishment of a particular value. But when one thinks of values as located within different organizational parts—in a society as a whole, in communities, and in organizations—then a third engine of change presents itself. Friction between organizational values and community values, between organizational values and societal values are two specific examples of that engine of change. An organization that emphasizes achievement orientation, for example, fits well in a society that also emphasizes achievement. For this reason, as Daniel Boorstin (1974) and DeHartog (1971) suggested, the Quakers found themselves at odds with Philadelphia culture. Generally speaking, as a matter of fact, communal or collective approaches to living and problem solving, being disjunctive as they are with major American orientations, have rarely been able to plant themselves successfully here.

But examples of cultural clash like the Quakers or, more dramatically, like the Mormons, are in the extreme. Typically, organizations struggle with such value conflict problems as organizational gain versus citizenship responsibilities to the communities in which they do their business; commitments to stockholders versus commitments to employees; and so on.

Fourth, we're seeking to apply the concept of competition that is well-understood in the business community to the area of culture. There is much talk about the marketplace of products. We even hear about the marketplace of ideas. What we need to begin thinking about now is the marketplace of commitments and, indeed, the competition for and of commitments. Cultural conflict does not simply exist between us and some undetermined "them." Rather, it exists within our Firms, within our communities, and even within ourselves.

We have spent a great deal of time discussing the structure of culture and the tensions between competing values. Our reasons will become clear shortly when we discuss business subcultures. As we outline some of the changes that seem to be occurring in our belief and attitude system, it may appear sometimes that we are merely changing what we already believe in. Indeed, popular magazines often refer to the "retraditionalizing" of our culture. But retraditionalization must be understood in this very specific context; a switch in emphasis from one value to another closely related but somewhat competing value. Cultural change is much less the substitution of completely new values for completely old ones than it is the submergence of some value for a while only to have it resurface at a later time to claim attention and commitment. At the same time more recent values take on the appearance of being dated. They submerge for a while and will at some future time emerge and lay their claims upon the society. The nostalgia boom, "golden oldies" radio, the rerelease of old movies are just a few examples of ways Entrepreneurs have profited from this clash of cultures. With this sense of the pattern of culture in mind, let's look at some specific shifts.

From Public to Private Orientation

One of the great cultural changes that has occurred in the last fifty years is a change from private orientation to public orientation and now, back again, to private. Before the Great Depression and the presidency of Franklin D. Roosevelt the federal government was a relatively small operation. The combined efforts of the social programs initiated in the 1930s and subsequent years, and the large military effort begun in World War II and continuing today, has put the government in a leadership role with respect to revenues, employment, and influence. But that period now seems to be one that is going into eclipse. Substantial doubt about the efficacy of public bureaucracies has been voiced by a number of writers (Lipset and Schneider, 1983; Tropman, 1987; Yankelovich, 1981). Popular belief has it that there is something like "paradoxical counterproductivity," especially in the public arena. Educational institutions fail to educate; medical institutions fail to heal; institutions of criminal justice fail to be corrective. Not only are such institutions failing, but those who become involved with them often become worse: I.Q.'s fall in school; illness becomes more severe in hospitals; criminality is exacerbated in prison.

Entrepreneurs are among the major beneficiaries of this move toward privatization. There is talk of private prisons, leased by the government. Private schools are a growing area. Private social services supported by tax dollars is another example. And there are doubtless many more ways Entrepreneurs could exploit this trend toward privatization.

From Bigness to Smallness

Some of the suspicions of government very likely stem from a suspicion of bigness. As Lipset and Schneider point out in their book *The Confidence Gap* (1983), the American public is not only suspicious of big government, but of big business and big labor as well. Certainly, the giants of the American corporate world have given us every reason for suspicion and distrust. As one student put it recently, "We thought they knew what they were doing. How could we have been so blind?" A celebration of smaller but better would unquestionably benefit the entrepreneurial impulse.

From Collectivism to Individualism

In the 1950s, when William F. Whyte wrote *The Organization Man* (1957), the popular view of the large organization was that everyone was completely the same. All had become completely "the man in the gray flannel suit." Interchangeable people, like interchangeable parts, could be substituted one for the other without anyone knowing the difference. To house these new employees, tract housing, like Levittown, went up so quickly and with houses so similar that there were numerous reports of men coming home at night and entering the wrong house by mistake, unable to distinguish theirs from their neighbors. In response a reaction emphasizing the individual and his or her unique aspects developed. Daniel Yankelovich (1981) talks about it as follows:

In the 60's cross-section surveys showed that the shifts in culture barely touched the lives of the majority of Americans (a fact those enmeshed in the "60's Revolution" found difficult to comprehend). By the 70's however, most Americans were involved in projects to prove that life can be more than a grim chore. Americans from every walk of life were suddenly eager to give more meaning to their lives, to find fuller self-expression and to add a touch of adventure and grace to their lives and those of others. Where strict norms had prevailed in the 50's and 60's, now all was pluralism and freedom of choice: to marry or live together; to have children early or to postpone them, pehaps forever; to come out of the closet or stay in; to keep the old job or return to school; to make commitments or hang loose; to change careers, houses, spouses, states of residence, states of mind.

In the 1970's all national surveys showed an increase in preoccupation with self. By the late 70's, my firm's studies showed that more than seven out of ten Americans (72%) spent a great deal of time thinking about themselves and their inner lives—this in a nation once notorious for its impatience with inwardness. The rage for self-fulfillment, our surveys indicated, had now spread to virtually the entire U.S. population. (P. 5)

Yankelovich's summary is as good as any to capture this shift to personalized preoccupation. Enterpreneurs have seized the advantage here in providing personal development courses. The whole health movement is related in part to this. Trimming up one's body, after all, is related to self-improvement and preoccupation. The shift to upscale products and high quality goods fits in here as well. Americans, preoccupied with themselves, are no longer satisfied with shoddy workmanship. Entrepreneurs can seek advantage here.

From Instrumental to Sacred

Yankelovich also points out that values in American society are changing to put greater worth on the intrinsic as opposed to the purpose aspect. He comments:

We adopt an instrumental philosophy whenever we ask about something: What is it good for? From this perspective a tree is good for lumber, or to give shade, or to enhance the appearance of the landscape. A forest that no one harvests or sees is not good for anything. It is not valued in itself. From an instrumental perspective a person is valued because he or she is a good worker, or provider, or sex object, or is useful in meeting one's needs in some other fashion. Everyone knows someone about whom you can say, "Oh, he's only interested in you if you can do something for him, otherwise you don't exist." This is an instrumental outlook. . . . Our studies suggest that seekers for self-fulfillment are reassessing what is sacred and what is instrumental in American life. Should people in the workplace be exploited exclusively for instrumental purposes, or do they have intrinsic value as well? Should we value certain aspects of nature and society—a wilderness, a vanishing species, a primitive culture, old automobiles, old buildings—for themselves, apart from their instrumental value? (P. 7)

Our answer is, yes! Part of the new American cultural value system involves a reemphasis not only on the individual person but the value and worth of that individual person independent of what she or he can deliver in the form of goods or services. There is an intrinsicalness worth attending to. Entrepreneurs can find numerous opportunities in assisting the society to manage these developing values. But Entrepreneurs should also be aware that employees will think of themselves not only as units to service the entrepreneurial venture but as people with intrinsic value, not to be shuttled and shunted from here to there for the simple and often unjustifiable pleasure of the Firm.

The Getting/Giving Compact

Yankelovich also discusses the Getting/Giving Compact as it has historically developed in American society and as it is now changing. The Getting/Giving Compact, according to Yankelovich (1981):

The old getting/giving compact might be paraphrased this way: "I give hard work, loyalty, and steadfastness. I swallow my frustrations and suppress my impulse to do what I would enjoy and do what is expected of me instead. I do not put myself first. I put the needs of others ahead of my own. I give a lot, but what I get in return is worth it. I receive an ever growing standard of living and a family with a devoted spouse and decent kids. Our children will take care of us in our old age if we really need it, which, thank goodness, we will not. I have a nice home, a good job, the respect of my friends and neighbors; a sense of accomplishment of having made something of my life. Last but not least, as an American I am proud to be a citizen of the finest country in the world." (P. 9)

Yankelovich stresses the importance of this implicit contract in sustaining the American growth pattern. But there is considerable disquiet. The string of American victories began to be broken when the War on Poverty failed and the Vietnamese War came to a halting conclusion. Things just seemed to get worse from then on. American productivity leveled off. Very large corporations—like General Motors and United States Steel—ran into serious trouble. A large number of Americans were discovered to be homeless. Others were discovered to be illiterate. For the first time it appeared that parents might not be able to expect, other things being equal, their children to do better than they had done. The price of single family homes seemed to soar out of the reach of many Americans. Faced with these possible and actual problems, the future began to dissolve. Hope began to erode. Yankelovich comments:

Sensing this contradiction between their goals and their strategies and being aware of the change for the worse in economic conditions, what most Americans fear today is coming up empty handed. Many of us suspect that at the very moment in our history when we are psychologically ready to satisfy our hunger for the best of the material and spiritual worlds, we may in fact be confronted with the worst of each.

Americans fear we may have to endure in exacerbated form all of the familiar ills of advanced technological society—from high blood pressure and urban decay to the absence of community—and also to put up with an unstable economy and a lower standard of living. (P. 11)

It is in this context that Entrepreneurship will surely flourish. If the Giving/ Getting Compact that seems to have sustained a lot of self-repression over a number of years is now being set aside, then the time is right for individuals to try to do those things they have always wanted to do. Many among us have wanted the freedom, the independence, the self-direction of a personal venture fueled by ideas that we believe are profitably marketable—but which others have often doubted and rejected. Furthermore, dependence on self now seems much more realistic than dependence on the larger culture to produce for us. Both white collar and blue collar employees have found that organizations have short memories. When an organization is taken over, individuals who have devoted much of their lives to its development and enhancement are summarily dismissed. Sane people conclude that organizational loyalty under conditions we observe is foolish. Relying on ourselves and our own ideas has at least one advantage: We are probably not going to take ourselves over and lay ourselves off.

The Concert of Cultures

We have spoken here of large-scale trends in belief and attitude and value systems that affect the entire country. But one must approach this kind of prognostication with more than a grain of salt. After all, in a socially pluralistic society, one would expect a pluralism of values too. It is important that Entrepreneurs especially recognize that opportunities lie not only within the realm of values that characterize the entire culture but value packages that characterize minority groups within the culture as well. Teen values and YUPPIE values represent two groups of values that have been strongly recognized already by the business community. Values of the black population and the opportunities they might present for marketing and sales have also been in the spotlight in recent years. Values of older Americans and regional, sectional, and other subsectional values can represent important niches in the market that Entrepreneurs can use. Faith Popcorn (1986), a consultant who specializes in keeping businesses apprised of new values, speaks in general of nostalgia, loyalty, patriotism, and family as values that will emerge within some sectors of the population. And, if history is any guide, other values will emerge in other sectors and be strong.

As with the Social Structure, the Entrepreneur must be constantly alert to changes in the Social Culture. These changes represent both dangers and opportunities. Failure to take them into account can be quickly fatal.

CONCLUSION

Entrepreneurial Managers need to be aware of the outer ring of culture and structure. It is the crust of the entrepreneurial pie. Things people do, actions people take, interact with beliefs that people have and orientations that people profess.

Changes in population, organization, and environment and technology are part of the contextual kit that creates new conditions for organizations. They require new competencies from individuals even if the organization and the individuals in question are doing as much as they always did.

Changes in beliefs are another part of the contextual change. The system of values tends to be locked into sets of competing commitments. Commitments tend to alternate between elements in the set, even though one element may be more valued than the other. Thus, societies and organizations may swing between achievement and equality, for example, or permission and control even though achievement and permission may be the more dominant values.

Change conditions and change values stimulate the occasion for new ideas—either inventions (things that have not been developed before) or new applications of older ideas now being shaped to new occasions and opportunities. The Four C's Conference, in its focus on the Context, should pick up and reflect within the organization some of the cultural and structural shifts that are going on. It is important not only to be aware of what's happening but to adjust your own operations in order to take advantage of those shifts. It is to this end that the other eight S's come into play.

Entrepreneurial Managers need always to ask the following questions:

1. What is happening in the structure? What changes, developments, and shifts are occurring?

2. What is happening in the culture? What changes, recombinations, readjustments are occurring?

3. What do we need to do in terms of: (1) organizational subculture, (2) strategy, systems, and structure, style, skills, and staff to make ourselves more relevant to, or articulated with, or profitable through these large-scale changes?

It is not always the case, of course, that adjustments in the remaining eight S's are stimulated because of environmental shifts. Sometimes organizational culture is, itself, out of date. Organizational structure needs improvement. Organizational staff needs refurbishing, and so on, but contextual assessment is the place to start.

NOTE

1. An example of this is as follows: If a woman has her first child at fifteen, and if this cycle is repeated, she is a grandmother at thirty and a great grandmother at forty five and a great, great grandmother at sixty (and a great, great, great grandmother at seventy five). If a woman has her first child at thirty, and if this cycle is repeated, she is a grandmother at sixty and a great grandmother at ninety.

6

Creating Entrepreneurial Subculture

Deutsch: The culture of any organization—group, business, or nation—however large or small can be characterized by its machines.

Morningstar: You mean, of course, any *modern* organization.

Deutsch: No, I mean *any* organization. Time is irrelevant.

Morningstar: What about ancient Greece?

Deutsch: Easy. Teaching machines.

Morningstar: You're kidding.

Deutsch: Not at all. The ancient Greeks had wonderful teaching machines. They just weren't very careful with them. In fact, they had the greatest single teaching machine ever invented. They called it "Socrates," but they broke it.

> —Luncheon exchange with sociologist and social philosopher
> Carl Deutsch, University of Michigan, Mental Health Research
> Institute, 1962.

INTRODUCTION

Corporate subculture—what Peters and Waterman (1982) call *superordinate values*—serves as the integrating center for Structure, Strategy, Systems, and Staff on the one hand and Skill and Style on the other. Entrepreneurial Management is crucially concerned with crafting an appropriate subculture not only because of those integrating properties, but also because the belief system of an organization inspirits and vivifies organizational participation. Entrepreneurial Managers are quite aware that people work for money, *but* they also work for a number of other less tangible but no less real gains. As

Tracey Kidder points out in his book *The Soul of a New Machine* (1981), the essential reward for the computer development that he discusses was to be able to "play again," just like the pinball machines and arcade games that pay players not in money but in free games. Part of the management of organizational culture, therefore, is to find out the kinds of cultural rewards any particular staff values and cherishes and to begin to make those available within the system. These should be in addition to—as a supplement to—cash.[1]

MANAGING ORGANIZATIONAL CULTURE

Part of the proper management of organizational culture is to create a balance among the competing values we discussed earlier. There must not be an overemphasis on achievement, for example, to the detriment of egalitarianism and cooperation; nor is cooperation emphasized to such an extent that individual motivation to achieve is blunted (or worse, negated).

In his book *Organizational Culture* (1985), Schein defines it as:

a pattern of basic assumptions invented, discovered, or developed by a given group, as it is learning to cope with its problems of external adaptation [what we have called *context*] and internal integration—that has worked well enough to be considered valid, and therefore to be taught to new members as a correct way to perceive, think, and feel in relation to these problems. (P. 9)

He describes a three-step pattern outlining the two elements in organizational culture. The first step is basic assumptions. These are "taken-for-granted" and "pre-conscious" points of view. These are the ones that are often revealed in an assumptions audit.

The second step centers on organizational values. These are built on the basic assumptions and enjoy a more general level of awareness.

At the third step are artifacts and creations. These are products of basic assumptions that Schein speaks of as being "visible but not decipherable," at least without reference to some understanding of those values and assumptions. We would include organizational policies in this last group. Policies are a product of assumptions and values and represent a solidification of organizational ideas and foresight. Because they also serve to direct the specific day-to-day activities of the organization, policies represent a concrete point of the cultural fulcrum—the transition matrix between ideas and directions. The conditions and contingencies often specified in policy can be understood as attempts to explain to policy implementors the different value conditions under which different actions are permissible, desirable, or required. It is true, however, as Schein suggests, that values and assumptions are often implicit in policy rather than stated directly. Therefore, the Entrepreneurial Manager who approaches culture via policy needs to be analytically discerning.

Policy, of course, is one way in which culture is made manifest within the organizational context. It is one way, therefore, that culture manages the organization in the sense of setting the parameters, norms, and values within which organizational activity occurs. Culture needs to be and can be managed. However, with the creation of a climate of values—an organizational character—that, as Schein suggests, comes to typify the organization.

The first step that you, as an Entrepreneurial Manager, need to undertake is to find out what values are desired here. You can proceed in two steps: *metavalues* and *organizational* values.

Metavalues are general values that would serve any organization. Commitment to quality, presence of a work ethic among staff, integrity, and so on are among the overall values you would probably want to espouse. You also need to address what mix of organizational values would be appropriate and helpful for kinds of products and services that will characterize your enterprise (as well as for the organization itself). Consider, for an example, a value that might be called "organizational loyalty." It is important for staff to be loyal to the organization in a positive, proactive sense. Loyalty does not simply mean the absence of your employees selling secrets to your competitors.

It also means trying to find ways to improve your organization's performance and competence and bringing those ways to the attention of the appropriate organization officials. Your employees should do this as a matter of course—as a matter of their jobs—because they want to be associated with a winning team. We call these *social values* because their focus is on the organization. The Entrepreneurial Manager also needs to be sensitive to personal values. These are the ones we were referring to earlier when we spoke of values as rewards.

After outlining the desired values, the Entrepreneurial Manager seeks to assess where the staff is with respect to a values orientation: what they think personally and what they think others in the organization think. What is important in making this organizational values assessment is to try to tap competing values. By paying close attention to the competing conceptions we will be discussing in a moment, you can chart out the value matrix of your organization, rather than simply giving a list of values and observing that there is some kind of competition and contention among them. The values identified in any values list, of course, will be key in the development of any assessment form.

Once you have identified the set of values and the kind of organizational posture you need with respect to them, you can go about the task of introducing new value orientations into the organization. These will be orientations that will support new innovations, new ideas, new approaches, and organizational change, at least in the entrepreneurial context. They will free up what might be called the "prison of values" or the "boxes of values" that contain and limit the individual perspectives of the members of the organization and that subvert organizational purposes and efforts.

Culture, therefore, can be managed. Small towns do it. Propaganda is an example of how societies do it. Public relations is another example of how organizations often do it. Much of cultural management, however, is episodic and unfocused. A cult may be one example of culture that is so powerful when managed and focused that individuals are captured totally. Brain washing, which is probably an appropriate word for what occurs there, then requires deprogramming in order to bring the individual back to a culturally realistic view of the world around them. But what is managed for evil purposes can be managed for good, as well. Organizational cultures can enhance and inspirit us. They can remove us from the boxes and traps in which we exist, making our lives richer and giving meaning to our daily tasks. It is this that we have in mind as the goal of cultural management. The payoff, of course, will be an excellent and successful organization. That organization will be characterized by an adequate supply of new ideas and a set of norms that is receptive to trying those new ideas, playing with them, and seeing which ones make sense and which ones don't.

THE MATRIX OF CORPORATE VALUES: THE CLASH OF CULTURE

We have spoken of the conflict of values between different commitments that individuals within the organization and the organization itself may have. A good outline of these is presented by Lawrence Miller in his book, *The American Spirit* (1984). Miller does not present the organizational choices that he outlines as competing value commitments. Rather, he presents them more as choices between good directions and bad ones. Still, with a little modification, they fit very nicely our purposes here. They illustrate the kinds of choices that organizations continually need to make within their cultures. They also exemplify the need for balance. In no case, from this point of view at any rate, would you pick solely one of Miller's alternatives. You would, rather, seek to emphasize one over the other while taking account of the one being underemphasized. He calls them *primary values*. With some very slight modifications, Miller's list consists essentially of the following:

1. Multipurpose vs. Unipurpose,
2. Comfort and Satisfaction vs. Excellence Ethic,
3. Unity of Interest vs. Class Interest,
4. Personal Purpose vs. Organizational Purpose,
5. Command Decision Making vs. Consensus Decision Making,

6. Empirical vs. Qualitative Decision Making,

7. Disposable Labor vs. Intimate Concerns,

8. Expediency vs. Integrity,

9. Performance Based Rewards vs. Power/Tenure Based Rewards,

10. Career vs. Job.

Let's take a brief look at each of these.

Multipurpose vs. Unipurpose

Miller's discussion of these two values was originally titled "Purpose Driven versus Lacking Purpose." The clear choice here is between organizational purpose and no organizational purpose. For most organizations it is not simply a case of one or the other. Rather the difference is between having a single, overriding organizational purpose and multiple purposes. What is actually required is a blend between a single overriding purpose and the many other purposes that organizations have to accomplish. The single, "no diversions permitted" orientation is certainly to be valued. Such single-mindedness of purpose, however, can often lead us to ignore other strategic goals.

The Entrepreneurial Manager, therefore, must create a balance between the single overriding purpose on the one hand and other organizational purposes on the other. Frequently, of course, setting priorities, selecting goals, and goal refurbishment are what are needed here. Even if you do have a single purpose, it may change due to environmental shifts, internal composition adjustments, and so on. To the extent that purposes are expressions of values, however, then discussions of purposes, selection, articulation, and the setting of priorities are in fact discussions of values and their orchestration within the organizational framework.

Comfort and Satisfaction vs. Excellence Ethic

On one hand, most of us are committed to excellence and superlative performance whenever possible. On the other, we recognize that that kind of perfectionism can destroy a corporation or an individual if pushed to extremes. It is not possible to be excellent day in and day out in every product line or innovation. Similarly, it is important to have some things that one does well enough—not necessarily as well as others or the very best, but a place to relax a bit and to enjoy the fruits of previous labors. As Miller (1984) suggests, the question here has more to do with the dominance of one or another of these ethics rather than the choice. Most of us would recognize the need for both.

But the areas one selects for excellent performance are important, and the measurement systems one sets up are crucial to consider. Certain areas may be set aside as "good enough" areas of organizational performance. It is certainly not shameful to recognize that both values need expression. The question is how to accommodate them? Sometimes simultaneity is the way; that is, some products are selected for excellence, others to be satisfactory. Most manufacturers of consumer products, for example, manufacture products according to a hierarchy of excellence. For the most part VCR manufacturers offer a basic line that is inexpensive, offers minimal features, and is built to minimum acceptable standards. They also offer progressively more expensive and feature laden models, culminating with a "top of the line" model that is very expensive (relative to its cheapest model), that is manufactured according to the highest possible standards of engineering and quality control, and that does everything but provide a critique of the videotaped material one plays on it. Virtually all car manufacturers do the same thing.

Another way is sequence. For awhile our product will be the best. Then others will take over while we retool, at the same time maintaining a good level of product or service. We will then compete for excellence once again in the market.

There may be other ways. The key point, however, once again is the *balance* between excellence and comfort-satisfaction rather than total dominance of either. If comfort and satisfaction become dominant, the organization is in a dangerous position. Comfort and satisfaction levels have a tendency to sink, at least with respect to product quality. "Good enough" becomes acceptable; then "poor" takes over. Specific measures of the levels of product-service performance, therefore, should be set for both the comfort-satisfaction value area and the excellence value.

Unity of Interest vs. Class Interest

One view of organizations, celebrated a bit in the Japanese management tradition, is that organizations are like families or tribes. They secure the same kind of commitment, the same kind of participatory involvement that would occur in a family or tribal situation. Others view organizations as loosely coupled systems, full of diverse interests, class conflicts, and competitions. Conflicts between blacks and whites, for example, or conflicts between men and women, or conflicts between those who are getting ahead and those who are not are typical.

One would expect, we suppose, that the organizations that serve a country would reflect a country. If, as in the case of Japan, there is a greater degree of homogeneity and commonality among the citizenry, then one would expect commonality and unity to a degree at least to be characteristic features of that country's organizations. Likewise, organizations that serve a divided society might well be expected to be divided themselves. Thus, again to some degree at least, American corporations are microcosmic exemplars of the society as a whole.[2] In this particular situation culturally dominant values become organizationally dominant values. The job of the Entrepreneurial Manager is to seek to act as a counterweight or counter force (much as an outrigger on a Polynesian canoe is used to create balance), which will allow for accomplishment and achievement. The job of the Entrepreneurial Manager within the American context, therefore, is to find bases and realms of unity, commonality, similarity so that to some extent the differences can be submerged or at least set aside while attention is paid to the organizational purpose and the activities that will serve that purpose. However, in a firm where a unity of interest is the dominant theme, emphasis on the creating of some diversity, heterogeneity, and internal organizational friction is required in order to get the supply of new ideas required for continual achievement.

Personal Purposes vs. Organizational Purposes

The value conflict that Miller (1984) attempts to define with his "Purpose Driven vs. Lacking Purpose" value pair also defines a conflict between organizational goals and personal ones. We can think of this conflict as one between commitments to the organizational purposes, missions, goals, and orientations on the one hand and personal purposes on the other. These words are all plural because organizations do not have single purposes any more than individuals. To be sure, the Entrepreneurial Manager must help the organization to clarify its own purposes and give them proper priorities, but he or she must also help individual staff members to do the same.

The Entrepreneurial Manager's balancing functions require the creation of a proper articulation between organizational purposes and personal purposes. One way to achieve this balance is to create a fusion between some organizational purposes and some personal purposes. Some Japanese managers do this by taking the family on a company sponsored vacation. This probably would not fly in an American context, but there may be other ways to achieve a configuration that would be positive and useful.

Command Decision Making vs. Concensus Decision Making

It is popular today to think that decision making loosely described by the phrase *consensus decision making* is the way to go. It is thought that consensus decision making involves participation at all levels of the organization, brings in a variety of perspectives, and secures agreement from those who are required to carry out a particular business strategy before making an actual decision. Participation, at least, if not consensus entirely, certainly seems to be the wave of the future. Naisbett (1983) talks about this trend, as does Kanter in her book, *The Change Masters* (1983).

Consensus does not work in all kinds of situations. Sometimes in emergency and very difficult crisis situations a command mode is appropriate. When time pressure or other kinds of stresses are besetting the organization command may be appropriate. Furthermore, there are individuals who are at different levels of stake-holding commitment to the organization. The founder-owner, for example, may take a dim view of consensus on the simple ground that she or he was the individual who put up the money and energy to make the organization start and, therefore, should be able to say what happens. Whether one calls this command or not, it may closely approximate it.

Once again the issue is not either command or consensus but, rather, the conditions under which consensus or command are appropriate and the styles through which command or consensus are carried out. An important point about decision making (which we discuss in a later chapter) is that it has less to do with a style of command vs. consensus than with the setting and structure (organizational meetings) in which the decisions are made. All too frequently, organizational staff do not have the skills to manage the decision-making system—committees and meetings—and, thus, both command *and* consensus fail because, at some point, both require some kind of group activity.

Empirical vs. Qualitative Decision Making

In his original discussion, Miller (1984) labelled *non-rational* what we call *qualitative*. Unfortunately, his word skews the case badly. Clearly, organizations need an empirical base for decision making. They need to know the kinds of numbers that they have to generate, and all employees within the organization need to be aware of what these numbers mean and for which ones they are responsible. We should never forget, however, that numbers can be assessed in the same way we assess computer programs: garbage in, garbage out. The most sophistocated analytic techniques will not provide the right answers if the wrong questions have been asked. There is room, therefore, for qualitative discussion and sharing within the framework of question building and number orchestrating.

Moreover, there are certain kinds of questions that numbers can't answer at all. How many people, for example, would respond affirmatively to a market survey about a new product that they have not yet seen, used, or contemplated? What if a market survey had been done on Post Its™ before they were available? Even if people could conceive of a semisticky paper, they wouldn't have much idea as to the kinds of uses to which it might be put. Were we to rely on empirical methods—in this case a market survey—

with respect to this particular product, it's very likely that the results would be sadly different from those we have today.

To a certain extent, the qualitative side of a decision-making system brings in judgment, product knowledge, and emersion in the particular product or service industry. These are nontrivial, and a complete decision system should blend both. The difficulty is, of course, that qualitative judgments tend to become entrenched. The facts can't change them. This is a point made by Henry Rosovsky (1987), former Dean of the College at Harvard , in an article he wrote about being a dean. He cautions leaders never to underestimate the permanence of perception against facts. To the extent that qualitative approaches to decision making reflect entrenched features, permanent views that are simply declared over and over again, such as the one Rosovsky is referring to, then it is a poor method. But that is not because it is qualitative. There are also poor methods of empirical decision making.

The Entrepreneurial Manager needs to create a culture in which both numbers and judgment are respected. Each must be used to challenge the other. Each must supplement rather than supplant the competing method.

Disposable Labor vs. Intimate Concerns

Organizations can have different values regarding employees. One of them is that the employee is a quasi-family member or member of *the* tribe—a person for whom one has some kind of deep concern and to whom one has a personal commitment. Alternatively, the employee can be viewed as little more than a human analog to an interchangeable part. When one breaks down, get another one that works.

In the industrial society value system, the disposable labor focus was clearly the key element. It is against this perception that labor unions have labored long and mightily. It is against the cavalier and insensitive approach to individuals as human beings that they have fought significant battles. In the coming social structure of information society and high tech–high touch, individual workers become more important, if for no other reasons than for the knowledge and skills they have already learned and the difficulties that are involved in replacing those skills and that knowledge and getting quickly to the same level of functioning that the Firm was at before in the business.

Concern for individuals is appropriate and necessary. Entrepreneurial Managers must be aware of and sensitive to the crucial role individuals play in the development of a product or service. At the same time, concern for individuals (as all parents know) does not translate into a lack of standards, quotas, and job requisites. Therefore, managers need to strive for a blend of both orientations toward employees.

Expediency vs. Integrity

When Rosabeth Kanter (1984) speaks about a culture of pride, she means in part focusing on the fun and good feelings one has in being associated with a "winner" in a product or service. Beyond that, the culture of pride also includes working for an organization that both has and manifests integrity. It is associated with an organization that gets things done. Integrity involves open communication, open feedback, and visible demonstrations that the organization is honest and aboveboard in its dealings with its employees, its customers, and its community.

It sounds strange to speak of an alternative to integrity, and the word *alternative* here may be the wrong one. In the main, the pursuit of profit is an "end justifies the means" activity. It appears that organizations need to be watched so that they do not become overzealous in their pursuit of profit. The problem is not to allow one value to be an excuse for the other—not to allow the pursuit of profits to be an excuse for a lack of integrity or to stand on one's integrity to the point where appropriate action is delayed.

Performance Based Rewards vs. Power/Tenure Based Rewards

In a "can-do" society characterized especially by entrepreneurial activity the thought is always that rewards should go to people who "can do" the job. The operative cry, then, is "What have you done for me lately." Clearly, it is important to reward people who accomplish significant organizational achievements. It is also important not to forget that most employees most of the time will not fall into that category. Although it is true that leadership can exhort individuals to exceptional achievement, there still needs to be a group of standard bearers who do the various jobs of the organization regularly and reasonably well and who are characterized by organizational commitment and loyalty. Tenure, therefore, represents an amortized commitment, to some extent at least, and thus, can be recognized.

Although Miller (1984) lumps power and tenure together, we are inclined to distinguish between them. Power, as a basis for reward, certainly has a long history. And it may well be appropriate to reward individuals of greater power differentially, more on the grounds, principally, that such individuals have greater responsibilities.

The problem, particularly with power and tenure, is that these bases for organizational compensation and other rewards become entrenched and *separated from performance*. Therefore, Entrepreneurial Managers interested in creating a proper and viable organizational culture should seek to have differential bases for rewards, including at least these three elements. We believe the tilt should be toward performance. Nothwithstanding that belief, we also recognize the validity of power and tenure as important values. In your Entrepreneurial Management activities, you might want to give serious consideration to dividing up raise allotments into fractions for each. Alternatively, different kinds of rewards might be given for different types of contributions. Tenure, for example might be rewarded in part by money and in part by organizational celebrations (prestige and so on). To some extent access to further resources might be a reward for power. American executives in particular are now receiving astronomical compensations. Unfortunately, due to competition among executives for such rewards, the cost is high; and the feelings of self-worth and reward become minimal. As in most armament races, additional increments of compensation to topflight CEO's only serve to cancel out the premiums paid to other CEO's. A more variegated compensation system, basing itself as it might in different values rather than on a single value, could be a great step forward.

Career vs. Job

Miller (1984) does not talk specifically about a conflict of values between career orientation vs. job orientation, but it is an important one for us to keep in mind in the area of Entrepreneurial Management. Entrepreneurs are career-oriented. Frequently, they will invest lots of their own time, money, and energy in the development of products or services in the hope of developing gain later in their career. One of the problems that Entrepreneurs often face is that others are not so far committed or so far sighted. This is particularly true of employees. Entrepreneurs may find that employees are less willing than they to put in fourteen-hour days, to work weekends, and so on. Rather, the employee may take more of a job orientation; i.e., "I'm here to do a specific set of tasks for a specific salary. Give me the tasks, and let me go to work; and at five o'clock I'm out of here." Entrepreneurs need to be aware of the differences in attitudes that employees take and to adjust the jobs and rewards—at least to a certain extent—depending on these two orientations.

CULTURAL MIXING AND PHASING

Looking at the list of cultural conflicts overall, several general points need to be made. To begin with, those value dimensions on the left-hand side (Multipurpose, Comfort and Satisfaction, Unity of Purpose, Personal Purpose, Command Decision Making, Empirical Decision Making, Disposable Labor, Expediency, Performance Rewards, and Career) tend to be the ones that have characterized business organizations in this century. A cultural analysis of American business today would yield the legitimate conclusion that it is less the values of business that have caused the problems than the unbalanced emphasis on more dominant values that have been problematic. Overemphasis on Expediency, overemphasis on Empirical Decision Making,

Personal Gain, Disposable Labor and so on, may well have caused problems. And the question would arise: What about Performance? Surely Performance can't be faulted. We don't fault it, but there is an essential point that must be noted; namely, as a solo basis for evaluating an employee, Performance does not represent the total picture. Loyalty, for example, is very important. The fact that an employee has contributed over a number of years is also worth taking into account. This perspective does not mean that there are not parameters of performance, only that we recognize in business what we recognize in life: There are various bases that combine in a variety of ways to make a particular type of decision.

This observation leads to our second major point. Cultural management is really the management of cultural balance. Organizations, like people, sometimes go crazy. They become imbalanced when only one part of these cultural dualisms is recognized. Quinn (1979) points this out eloquently. It is the blending and melding of these various value packages that is the real test of entrepreneurial management. Sometimes Consensus needs to be generated, but sometimes it is Command. Sometimes Performance needs to be emphasized, but sometimes it is Power and Tenure. Sometimes Satisfaction needs to be emphasized and at other times the emphasis must be on Excellence. The point of all this is a simple one: You cannot always do one thing or the other. Conditions change. Personnel change. Variety is required.

Though it may appear difficult, in fact it is possible to manage culture. If the focus is on blending and melding, there are several possible courses available as options. Sometimes both values can be honored, as in the different levels of products mentioned in the excellence vs. comfort/satisfaction dilemma. Another strategy is *Averaging*. This simple expedient involves taking some of the influence of one value and some from the other value and splitting the difference. If some Command and some Consensus is needed, then an acceptable average is worked out.

Often, however, as in the case of Command and Consensus, Averaging is not the best option available to you. *Sectoring* or *Sequencing*, you determine, are better ways to proceed. Sectoring involves picking those particular areas where Command is to be used and other areas where Consensus is to be used. The very inconsistency is actually a refreshing bit of freedom from the unanimity of all one or all the other. Sequencing involves alternating value bases over time as opposed to the use of other conditions.

You may decide that none of these meet your particular need at a particular point in time. You still have Counterbalancing available to you. With Counterbalancing, the Entrepreneurial Manager seeks to provide the alternative perspective; if everyone is interested in Consensus, he or she may seek to involve a Command orientation; or, if everyone is Command-oriented, then the Entrepreneurial Manager might try for a Consensus orientation.

It is crucial for the Entrepreneurial Manager to be aware of the need for flexibility within the value matrix. A great number of values are required in any culture to keep it current, fluid, and relevant. As we noted earlier, Herbert Kaufman (1985) points out that organizations decline because they have problems with resources. They have problems with resources, he argues, because they are unable to adapt themselves to the changing environmental conditions. Although he doesn't use this particular term, it is possible to think of such organizational inertia as a *values ossification*. This means that if one particular set of attitudes, ideas, and beliefs that have characterized an organization over time continue to dominate, the organization ultimately finds itself out in left field and then out of the park.

THE FIRM LOGO AND MOTTO

Given all of these conflicting orientations, it is still necessary to pull all of these things together into a coherent and symbolized culture. One of the best ways to do this is through an exercise called an Organizational Logo and Motto. Every organization, no matter how large or small, should have both a logo and a motto. Attention to these, rather than being something delegated to a lowly subordinate, should at least occupy the central attention of the top individuals and, at best, of everyone connected with the enterprise. The logo in body symbolizes and represents the organization. And the few words that make up the motto symbolize the fundamental essence of the Firm. Many profitable discussions about organizational culture have come from attempts to either refurbish or generate a new logo and motto. When one is forced to say in a few words the essential focus of the organizational effort ("Quality is job one"—"The mark of excellence"—"Better things for better living"), it stimulates and gives concrete reality to thought. It forces organizations to answer the questions: "What business are we in?" (Naisbitt, 1983) and "How can we communicate that?" Often, people think the communication is only to others. This is not so. Communication via logo and motto is first and foremost to the organization itself and serves as an economical reminders of what the organization stands for and promises.

In defining a logo or a motto, care must be taken to embody both sides of the competing value frameworks. Overemphasis on a single value (excellence, for example) is likely to create a climate in which that promise cannot be sustained. This causes members of the organization to fall further short than they would have if a more balanced approach had been taken.

CONCLUSION

Organizational culture is a powerful—perhaps *the* most powerful—integrating force within the organization. This is especially true in a society like America where there are wide diversities, many different orientations, backgrounds, and interests. An important task for the business is to provide a ground where these can be set aside temporarily. One of the best ways to do this is to provide a belief system to which a wide range of diverse individuals can subscribe at least for the time during which they are associated with the organization in general and, more particularly, during the time they are at work. The difficulty, of course, is that there is not a single set of beliefs or values that will serve this purpose. Rather, the values of any corporate culture are a blend of conflicting dispositions that, if left to themselves, may "happen" to work out all right or may "happen" to clash so much that they cannot be overcome. These clashes can be very costly. Consider, for example, acquisitions and mergers, where two different cultures are suddenly brought together under the same corporate umbrella. Not infrequently, as many failed partnerships attest, a split is necessary; the differences are simply too great.

We are not suggesting that culture management can overcome all of these potential problems. Attention to culture as a specific and integrating force within the entrepreneurial venture, however, is a good place to start. One can ask about the kinds of culture one needs and about the kinds of values one wishes to embody. One can then systematically go about seeking to incorporate them.

Organizational ceremonies are an important part of culture management. Ceremonies convey to employees what is important, what is valued, and, as Schein suggested, part of the ways that we respond to the external problem and environment.

NOTES

1. The whole problem of the determination of what is rewarding is a tricky one and can represent a potential trap for Entrepreneurs. Pigeons, for example, can be taught to perform extraordinary acts. They learn these acts through a process of carefully structured rewards. But it is not the trainer who determines the rewards; it is the pigeon. And what is rewarding to some may be a source of indifference or even punishment to others. The same is true with employees. Employees will work for extended periods of time at maximum levels of productivity provided they receive timely and appropriate rewards. The bad news is, most employers haven't a clue as to what their employees find rewarding. They guess, based on what they, themselves, might like: free turkeys at Thanksgiving and Christmas, for example, when what the employees really want is slightly more extensive dental coverage on their medical insurance. The good news is that employers can quickly find out what their employees do find rewarding; all they have to do is *ask*.

2. This point awaits detailed research. The relationships between a superordinate culture and the organizations that are a part of it are, as yet, unclear. One hypothesis is the one mentioned: The organizations represent in microcosm the culture as a whole. There are undoubtedly some organizations like this. Organizations may counterbalance the culture, however, and become what Yinger (1982) called a *counterculture*. Again, doubtless there are some organizations like this. Most organizations may, in fact, be a mix both similar to and different from mainstream culture.

7

Creating Entrepreneurial Strategies

QUESTION: "How do you rate business and industry in product quality and price in competing with foreign companies?"

ANSWERS: "Fair/Poor"   61%
          "Good/Excellent"   34%

— Survey of the U.S. Adult Population by *Cambridge Reports*

A survey in 1981 reported that nearly 50% of U.S. consumers believed that the quality of U.S. products had dropped in the last 5 years.

— Garvin, 1987

INTRODUCTION

Strategy is a revision of expectations. Strategy focuses on the overarching set of ideas that guide and direct activities in a variety of subareas within the organization or, in the case of the new Entrepreneur, within the person's life or general framework of action. Strategy involves selection and choice. As people have frequently said, it is the difference between doing things right and doing the right thing. It is the difference between working smart and working hard. It is certainly useful to do things right, and it is useful to work hard. If one is not doing the right thing and working smart at the same time, however, then all of that energy and all of that effort will not have the kind of payoff that one expects.

Entrepreneurial strategy involves framing a set of choices and making decisions among those choices that will enable a new idea, product, or service to move from the idea stage into the actual production stage.

STRATEGIC DICTA

In the creation of entrepreneurial strategies there is a powerful set of strategic dicta—systematic ideas, if you will—that should be taken into account. Whatever the nature of your business or assignment, these ideas will help.

#1: Strategy Differs Depending on Stage of Growth

The first Strategic Dictum is: Take account of the sprint/pause cycle. In the material already discussed on the Entrepreneurial Staircase, an outline of organizational growth stages was provided. First there is the idea. Then, implementation follows. Next comes growth or expansion for those fortunate enough to survive the first two phases. The fourth stage is consolidation, and the fifth is renewal. What we did not discuss when we first presented this information is the alternation within and between stages of activity and rest. Much of strategy relates to these elements.

Mintzberg and Waters (1982) argue that growth occurs in *sprints* and *pauses*. Pauses are necessary in order to sustain entrepreneurial success. Tne long hours, the fatigue, the tensions cannot be continued without a break. The pause allows for some consolidation, for pulling together of gains and the discarding of losses and the general development of resources that can then be used to finance the next sprint. In this sense, growth is a choppy progression.

Sociologist Talcott Parsons (1951) had a formulation that arrives at a similar point. He had a four-step growth process, which he called the "AGIL Table"—Adaptation, Goal gratification, Integration, and Latency. Adaptation and goal gratification occur in the sprint phase. Integration and latency occur during a period of pause. (Parsons thought of latency as a period of rest and recreating of resources.) The important strategic message here is that Entrepreneurs need to have a strategy that accounts for both sprint and pause periods. That strategy requires definition of areas of adaptation and goal gratification followed by integrating and building in those achievements, healing the wounds caused by those achievements, and resting and recuperating.

#2: The Parts of Your Firm Are Different

The second Strategic Dictum is: take account of the different parts of the firm. Parsons (1960) provided a second insight into organizational strategy when he pointed out that organizations have three levels or parts. These levels are only loosely connected each to the other. The three sectors he saw were as follows: (1) a technical sector, which involves production and the actual "work" of the organization; (2) the managerial level, which involves the decision making and directing segments of the organization; and (3) the institutional level, which involves making connections with the wider environment.

It is quite likely that these three sectors will not necessarily grow at the same speed or at the same rate. Sprint-pause phases may be rather different for each. One might think, therefore, that the overall organization is characterized by the sprint-pause mode, but the subparts may actually have their own trajectories and these may be inverse to the overall one. Thus, the technical phase could be in sprint while managerial is in pause; and so on. A second aspect of entrepreneurial strategy, then, is to design a strategy to articulate different sprint-pause phases of the different subparts of the organization.

#3: The Firm Components Do Not Lead Naturally from One to the Other

A third Strategic Dictum needs to be explored here, as well. Parsons points out that aspects of the organization do not necessarily lead from one to the other. Those skilled in technical materials are not necessarily skilled in managerial materials. Similarily, good managers do not necessarily make good institutional connectors. Increasingly, organizations tend to separate these functions by locating them at different positions within an organizational hierarchy. This furthers the distance and difference that already exists. Part of the reason the "Peter Principle" ("individuals tend to rise to the level of their own incompetence," Lawrence Peter, 1970, 1972) may exist in organizations lies precisely here; the skills required at the next major level of the organization are rather different and may even be at variance with those at other organizational levels. A third aspect of entrepreneurial strategy— the third Strategic Dictum—is to prepare for intra-organizational stability and transition. This simultaneous strategy allows those individuals who are skilled within a particular level to remain and advance there, while identifying simultaneously those who are able to move and take on other responsibilities and prepare them for that.

#4: Have Different Strategic Approaches Available

Miles and his colleagues (1978) identified three orientations that are quite similar to the Parsonian trilogy. They talk about organizations having an entrepreneurial problem (which, because it focuses essentially on links with the environment, is similar to the institutional one), an administrative problem (which links to the management aspect that Parsons discussed), and an engineering problem (which focuses on the technical level). Thus, the fourth Strategic Dictum of entrepreneurial strategy is to design substrategies appropriate to each of the three problem levels within the organizational structure.

Miles and his colleagues developed four organizational response styles. These are (1) the Defender, (2) the Prospector, (3) the Analyzer, and (4) the Reactor. They offered these as ways organizations respond to environments in each of the three areas.

The first of these, the Defender, needs to secure a market on an institutional basis. On a managerial basis, the Defender needs to maintain organizational control and to insure efficiency. On a technical basis, the Defender produces and distributes goods efficiently. Organizational strategies for the Defender will focus on solving these problems.

The Prospector, on the institutional level, seeks ways to locate and exploit new opportunities. On a managerial basis, the Prospector wishes to facilitate and coordinate diverse operations. On a technical basis, the Prospector seeks to avoid long-term constraints of a single industrial program or process.

The Analyzer seeks to find and develop new entrepreneurial opportunities at the institutional level. At the same time, the Analyzer wishes to maintain a traditional base of customers and products. At the managerial level, the Analyzer seeks to design organizational systems that can accommodate both regular and innovative elements. At the technical level, the problem is how to stimulate both efficiency and stability.[1]

The Reactor, according to Miles et al., has no real strategy at the institutional level. At the managerial level management seeks to retain the "same old stuff" and retains old strategies and systems in spite of large-scale changes in the environment. At the technical level, production continues as it did in the past. Because there is no strategy to which technical changes can be fit, the inertia of history becomes dominant.

If one steps back a moment and looks at these four types—defense, prospecting, analysis, and reaction—one can see they comprise fairly general response modes to changes in the environment. At one level, one can ignore the external environment and react only when prodded and forced. A more adaptive strategy is defense; seek to locate oneself in a reasonably safe environment, fortify one's products and services, and wait out attacks. The analyzer strategy is more venturesome and allows one to retain anchors in traditional products and services while at the same time beginning to prospect for new and additional ways to penetrate the market.

The most venturesome (or risky!) of these strategies is the Prospector strategy. It focuses resources entirely on the development of new and innovative products.

#5: Mix and Phase Strategic Approaches

The best way to interpret these strategies is not to regard them as alternatives for whole companies. Rather, consider making two important variations on their application.

First, it is important to see that variations occur within the developmental arc of the organization. Hence, a different mix of these strategies may be used at different times in the organization's history. At a very beginning phase, for example, a Prospector strategy is appropriate. After all, there are no old products or services within which one can maintain a firm anchor. In the renewal phase of the organization, however (for a review of these stages, see Chapter 3), an Analyzer strategy might be important. There are variations over time. Part of the job of the Entrepreneurial Manager and the skills that person possesses involves reconfiguring the strategic matrix such that the appropriate dominant strategy can be operationalized at the appropriate time.

We mentioned the term *dominant strategy* because, to some extent, these strategies, like values, exist simultaneously. It is not a question of having only one and not the others. Rather, it is a question of which is prominent and dominant at a particular point in time. Indeed, their simultaneous presence acts as a plus for the organization. For example, even the Reactor strategy—hardly one that seems terribly elegant when studied in and of itself—might well have many benefits when present simultaneously with a Prospector strategy. The converse can be true as well: the Reactor and the Prospector, working together, may act as simultaneous controls each on the other. The problem, of course, is when one becomes totally dominant. At that time the company ceases to prospect at all if the Reaction strategy is the victor. In this case the company becomes—or can become—merely a shell of its former self. On the other hand, without the Reactor the Prospector may plunge headlong into a range of activities that prove to be unwise.

Similarly, the Defender and the Analyzer strategies may work in tandem. The Defender, moving more toward security and entrenched positions, the Analyzer recognizing virtues in that but moving out, can balance each other off reasonably well.

The second major perspective involves the parts of the organization that Parsons (1960) mentioned. It is not necessarily true that every part of the organization has the same strategy at any given moment in time. We all tend to talk as if that is so. One speaks, for example, of the X Company as having an aggressive strategy, or the Y Company as having a conservative strategy, and so on. Somehow, we talk as if all of this makes complete sense. And yet, on further examination and more detailed scrutiny, it turns out that X Company and the Y Company are *collectivities of strategies*. It may well be the case, for example, that the technical level has one particular strategic trajectory, the managerial another, and the institutional yet a third.

Part of these differences may depend on the nature of the environment. In the high tech area, for example, the technical level may be prospecting constantly while the managerial level may be seeking a defensive position with respect to products already established. The institutional level—represented by the Board of Directors—may be seeking an Analyzer strategy. Because different parts of the organization interact with and deal with different parts of the environment, it is rather likely (wise or not) that they will undertake formally or informally different strategic directions. Managerial orientation, for example, is heavily intraorganizational. Their primary focus is dealing upward with the institutional level on the one hand and dealing downward with the technical level on the other. They tend to be more insulated from external pressures either of customers (as the technical level would) or investors and general environmental politicians (as the institutional level would). Many at the managerial level, therefore, are more likely to adopt either the Defender strategy or the Reactor strategy in part because they are not confronted with the issues and problems as directly as the other two levels.

Part of the job of the Entrepreneurial Manager, therefore, is to understand what the strategic imperatives are at each level and to seek to orchestrate and fit all the parts and elements together. This task is not an enviable one nor is it easy. It is for this reason that the creation of organizational subculture becomes important as an integrating tool. If all of the organizational elements and parts at least have the same set of values and orientations, then it is possible to use those as a jumping off place for strategic articulation.

The first step, of course, is recognizing the likelihood that there will be different strategic points of view at the different organizational sectors. Considering the concept of the strategic matrix, it is quite possible to fit different strategies within a matrix and yet maintain an overall orientation or perspective toward one's line of work.

There may be times, however, when an Entrepreneurial Manager wants to stimulate differences in strategic perspectives. If, for example, the entire organization is dominated by a Reactor or Defender strategy, then one might seek an organizational niche where a Prospector or an Analyzer strategy could be introduced. Successful development of this strategy within a limited organizational domain, hopefully, will begin to create sufficient interest and envy to cause the generation of organizational change. Indeed, the virtue of simultaneous strategies with prominence and dominance rather than solo occupation of the strategic slot once again becomes evident. It is only with the friction generated by questions and hesitations that even a good strategy can become better. Without internal strategic competition as an ongoing part of organizational life, the likelihood of successful strategy for dealing with the external environment is diminished.

Strategy in organizations involves articulating compositional and contextual elements in a process of mutual adjustment such that their evolving needs and demands mesh. It is imperative not to see the context as a neutral thing to which one must respond but, in principle at least, as an element that one may shape to some degree. Phrases like "market creation" speak to part of this issue. Furthermore, strategy involves structuring and smoothing sprints and pauses so that the benefits can be gained from this unevenness rather than the problems. Cycles of heavy activity and rest can be beneficial if properly tuned. Then, as we suggested earlier, it involves linking different strategies with the different phases. One might concentrate on implementing more of a Prospector strategy during a sprint phase, for example, and more of an Analyzer strategy during a pause phase. Finally, it involves planning, configuring, and orchestrating the activities of distinct organizational components to create mutual support. In this sense, strategy implies and requires the creation of structure.

STRATEGIC TECHNIQUES FOR THE ENTREPRENEURIAL MANAGER

The overall discussion about how you, as an Entrepreneurial Manager, might proceed with organizational strategy comes up a bit short perhaps when you are seeking to figure out how to get your own ideas implemented into the system. For that reason, we provide the following suggestions. You may find one or more of them helpful.

There are two particular foci you might wish to consider. The first of these involves the personal presentation of self and things you, as an individual, might do. The second involves a discussion of successful organization strategies that Quinn (1979) compiled. We begin by discussing the personal strategies.

Individual Strategies for the Entrepreneurial Manager

As an individual, you can take certain actions that will enhance the impact of your ideas within the community and within the organization. These will be effective whether you are starting a new business and need venture capital and other support to get it going or you are already in an excellent business and are seeking to renew or refurbish it.

First, recognize that all new ideas advance the interests of some and retard the interests of others. You should begin with the notion, therefore, that most others in the community will be somewhere between neutral and hostile. This perspective may be overly cynical, and we're not suggesting that you become paranoid about potential opposition. Instead, as we indicated before, you should recognize that opposition is the most likely thing to occur and begin to seek ways to overcome that opposition. The first step is to assess it.

Assess Change Forces and Resistance Forces. As previously mentioned, in their 1958 book *The Dynamics of Planned Change*, Ronald Lippitt, Jeanne Watson, and Bruce Westly talk about assessing the change forces (those that would generally be counted on to support you) and the resistance forces (those that would generally be counted on to oppose you). Change forces and resistance forces may exist inside and outside of organizational locations that you are seeking to influence. It is important to do an initial assessment—a political assessment, if you will—of who is for you and who is against you. Politicians do this all the time, of course. It's called counting the votes. Often, however, innovators, captured as they may frequently be with the very interest and elegance of a new idea, do not spend time thinking about who may oppose the idea and why, and who might support it and why. Once you have change forces and resistance forces listed out, the next step becomes easier.

Use Techniques of Clearing, Checking, and Involving. Entrepreneurial Managers are often alone in proposing new ideas. Sometimes that is simply because they thought up the idea alone. Other times it's because they have not taken advantage of the support that is available. The aforementioned list suggests a number of allies. You can check through your proposal and idea with them and try to get their endorsement. Beyond that, you should also try to get their support and active lobbying help on behalf of the idea.

Part of this involves expanding your "person power." In addition, increasing the sheer number of supporters is extremely important, for numbers make the idea less easy to reject. It's always easy to turn one person down. It's a lot more difficult to turn down several people.

In the clearing process you not only check with other individuals, but you also seek to incorporate some of their ideas into the development of your proposals, themselves. This broadens the ownership of the idea in a real sense, and it enhances commitment.

Typically, this action is taken with friends, supporters (Lippett, Watson, and Westly's change forces). However, you should not rule out the possibility of converting the opposition by co-opting them into the plan. We have all had the experience of seeing people turned around as a proponent goes to those individuals, takes their criticism seriously, and seeks to address it. Not only are such individuals responsive because a particular criticism has been dealt with, but the prestige and deference generated by that exchange further builds support from individuals who might have been—and probably were—opposed.

Use In-Principle and Specification Discussion Styles. Two techniques are useful here: the *in-principle* technique and the *specification* technique. They tend to work together.

As a strategy the in-principle technique asks reviewers of any particular idea or plan to set aside detailed considerations and look, instead, at the overall principle—"Is this product, this direction, this service something that we wish to pursue?" You can often get an affirmative response in general without getting tied up in specifics. The problem is that new ideas often are shy on specifics. It's not that you never get to them, but it's very difficult to know whether or not to proceed without having some sense of overall approval.

The specification technique involves ways to address criticism if you get into a discussion of specifics (or, at the time you begin that level of discussion). Opposition to new ideas is often general and vague. Sometimes you have to work with that difficult situation. Sometimes, though, in the clearing and checking process, you can address opponents in a one-on-one, nonthreatening situation, saying something like, "What is it that you feel specifically is the problem? What kinds of specific changes can be made to address your concerns?" You may get ideas about ways to improve that will both make your proposal better and increase support for it.

It is imperative that you don't wait until opposition manifests itself. Successful Entrepreneurial Managers anticipate opposition and take steps like those we've just mentioned to enhance support and blunt the force of negative expression.

Develop Creative Program Design. There are certain features of the design of new proposals that may serve to enhance support and discourage opposition. Nobel Laureat, Herbert Simon (with Smithburg and Thompson, 1956) in the book, *Public Administration*, deals with this problem in a set of complementary ideas: (1) make compliance easy; (2) make noncompliance difficult. Simon and his colleagues were talking about ways to implement a plan, but the advice also applies to the very beginning design of a plan. If you can set up a plan that makes agreement easy and disagreement difficult, then you are going to enhance the ability of the proposal to succeed. One example they use is the tax deduction. Compliance is easy because you don't do it. Noncompliance is hard for the same reason.

Link Your Ideas to Current Values. Simon and his colleagues (1956) also argued that new ideas should be linked to prevailing values. This, as we've said before, involves securing of precedents, the general approach of putting new wine in old bottles. Linking to values, however, is a complex task. As we suggested in the section on subculture, values tend to come in linked pairs. Thus, when you seek to justify a proposal under a particular set of values, you should also be aware that there is going to be a competing set of values that will also need attention. Short-term gain and long-term gain, for example, is one case of potentially competing values. Linking a program to one of them could very well cause problems with supporters of the other. This perspective does not mean that you must always compromise your point of view. If a particular program has short-term gains, however, and is silent or even negative with respect to long-term gains, then you must be prepared for that kind of opposition and deal with it in advance.

Organizational Strategies for Entrepreneurial Managers

The brief suggestions mentioned previously concerning personal strategy characteristics can link with design or organizational strategy characteristics that will enhance the success of new ideas and proposals. A very useful list comes from James B. Quinn (1979).

Strong Incentives. It's very important in your Entrepreneurial Management business activities to provide incentives for establishing innovation. Without those incentives, performances tend to flatten out. This perspective does not mean that incentives have to be totally individual. They can also be oriented to group achievement. Individuals can be rewarded, but so can groups, task forces, committees, and other organizational collectivities. Furthermore, these rewards do not always have to be money. They can be, to be sure, but there are others that may be equally powerful: prestige, meetings with the boss, praise, permission to engage in other new projects, and so on.

The point is simple. Try to provide the kind of reinforcement within the structure that will support new ideas, products, and services.

Clearly Defined Need. It is important that you establish the need for a new product or service and the niche that it will occupy. Frequently the answers to these questions are so intuitively clear to the proposer, that she or he doesn't think to make the argument clear to others. Bearing in mind that others are likely to be neutral to hostile toward the idea, the requirement of establishing the need and the niche becomes doubly important.

Multiple Competing Approaches. Don't put all of your eggs in one basket with respect to new products or services development or their introduction. Instead, cast as broad a net as possible. All too frequently organizations believe that because they have an R & D center, ideas should come from there. Certainly, a lot of ideas do come from R & D centers, but the organization has to be fairly large even to have such a center. For the most part, in smaller organizations everyone should be invited to submit and explore ideas. If an organization permits a certain amount of time (5%, 10%, or 15%,) to be spent on idea development and product experimentation, everyone will have a chance to have a go at developing some innovative product or service.

There are several methods worth consideration. First, you might have a special telephone number and answering machine for new ideas that you promise to listen to as boss and to which you will respond. Although an answering machine might seem a bit impersonal, many individuals with whom we have worked have said something like, "I never can catch the boss long enough to tell him the idea." They could write to you, of course, but obviously they don't. This way they can tell you something using a voice communication mode that they know you will hear. This stimulates the creativity that they have rather than waiting for the R & D department to come up with something.

You can also send out a memo to staff—or, if the organization is small, simply tell them—saying something like, "We're having a problem with XYZ. Anyone who can solve it gets a bonus." And, when ideas are developed, synopses of them can be sent out for comment. This approach is likely to discover and, sometimes, remedy flaws.[2]

Multiple and competing approaches might seem like a waste of time and energy. In some specific instances it is, and for some extremely large projects, such multiplicity may be impractical. But the point here is to avoid getting into an organizational rut in which the same individuals who always do things, continue to do things, and continue to have the same perspectives, orientations, and points of view.

But more is needed than just to stimulate the input side. You, yourself, as an Entrepreneurial Manager, have to commit to accepting and processing some of these new ideas. If individuals make lots of suggestions and never see anything happening, they'll come to the conclusion that you didn't want the suggestions in the first place or wanted them only for the purposes of covering your own posterior. Thus, you must be willing to accept and try the best among the new ideas.

User Guidance. Throughout the process of new product or service development, close interaction with potential users is an important feature. In the book publishing business, as a case in point, the use of readers, test marketing, trial copies being used for particular classes (in the case of text books) all provide valuable information that allows for product shaping and sculpting, service adjustment, and refocusing.

There are always voices around you that will argue that the consumer doesn't know what is right. None of us like evaluations that are potentially negative and criticize efforts into which we have put lots of time. On the other hand, early feedback allows for adjustment, and that becomes crucial.

High Expertise. It is imperative to involve top talent in the introduction of new products or services. In the developmental and idea stage, such top talent may be "borrowed" from books, articles, and other authorities. In other words, rather than advancing an idea totally on your own, try to find others who have similar ideas or who have offered similar or related suggestions. Keep in mind that, if it is only Sam's idea, it has less credibility than if it is Sam and Peter Drucker's idea. We are not suggesting the inappropriate link-up with authorities and prestigious individuals, but, rather, doing so when it makes sense and when the links are clear.

As the product or service moves into the developmental and implementation stages, the very best individuals in your organization should be secured to develop and run the program. The reason for this need is that there is much less known about the new product or service than the standard one. As a result, individuals whose expertise is pretty much doing the same old thing are *not* the kind of individuals you need in product innovation and introduction.

Longer Time Horizon. Innovations require a longer time than many people realize to move finally through the whole process from idea to popularly accepted product or service. It's for this reason that advice to entrepreneurs to "persevere" is among the most common in the entrepreneurial literature. The material in this book if conscientiously applied will shorten the time. Nevertheless, as an Entrepreneurial Manager, you need to recognize that results from new ideas, new products, new services are likely to pay off in the longer term rather than in the immediate, shorter term. Although you should always be looking for immediate applications, total focus on that sector of the innovation pie results in relatively modest improvements rather than in larger, big scale innovations.

Committed Champions. In order for innovations to continue and for new products and services to be viable, individuals must be committed to the importance and need of the product or service and be willing to devote the time and interpersonal energy to push them through the system. Backers and supporters are always needed for any idea. You can't rely solely on committed champions, however. They are necessary but not sufficient conditions for organizational excellence in the new idea, new product, and new service department. Indeed, Entrepreneurial Management is designed in some degree to replace part of what is usually attributed to champions. Sometimes just the enthusiasm of your champions will cause you to prevail. More often organized and methodical management of the idea generating and transformation system is what is needed. And, that organized and methodical management cannot be located away in some remote R & D department but as part of the ongoing ambience of the organization, itself.

Top-Level Risk Taking. If you are a top-level manager in addition to being an Entrepreneurial Manager, then you will need to model risk-taking, innovative behavior. If the CEO is always walking around the room backed up against the wall, soon the staff will follow suit. It is important for top management to realize that it is perfectly acceptable for top management to be wrong sometimes. (Keep in mind that an executive is one who makes many decisions, some of which are right.) It is for this reason that top management should engage in a variety of innovative projects *on different scales*. Thus, a failure, particularly in a small-scale project, serves the modelling function without a great deal of loss. Large-scale loss is more difficult to tolerate. The likelihood of those losses will be sharply reduced if innovation is an ongoing part of the organization's culture.

Moral Delivery Mode. Finally, Quinn (1979) suggests that innovations were enhanced and have been successful where they fell into what he called a "moral delivery mode"; i.e., where the product was worthwhile, useful, made a contribution to the community and enhanced the common culture rather than detracted from it.

CONCLUSION

Strategy—the structure of expectations—is an important starting point for individuals who want to introduce new products, services, and ideas. This is true whether they are seeking funding for an original idea or they desire to introduce that idea into an ongoing concern.

A variety of Strategies are possible. In this chapter we have tried to suggest some common conceptualizations of Strategy—to look at some of the things that have been associated with successful Strategic postures relative to innovations. We have also offered some hints as to ways in which individual Entrepreneurial Managers can make their own ideas more likely to be accepted and acted on.

Strategy, however, is only one of six points of consideration. The others—Structure, Systems, Staff, Style, and Skill—are also needed to put the total package together. Typically, at least in most contemporary organizational thinking, Strategy is followed either by skill or structure. Structure is the second hard "S," and it is to a discussion of Structure that we now turn.

NOTES

1. The Analyzer, as Miles *et al.* (1978) describe that organization strategy, is a fairly good example of value dualism that we talked about in the last chapter. Both innovation and stability are sought to be developed and attended to on a recognized simultaneous basis.

2. The Walt Disney organization has a long history of involving its employees at every level in the problem-solving process, whether the problems are trivial or of major importance. The story is told that the tradition began back in the 30's under the following circumstances. Walt had received the story board for a new cartoon from his artists. (A story board is a succession of drawings depicting each of the major scenes from beginning to end.) He liked the concept of the cartoon and the way it was being executed generally. But something bothered him. He couldn't figure out what it was and neither could his professional artists. He left the drawings hanging on his wall when he went home that evening. Later, a cleaning woman came in to straighten up his office. She apparently studied the drawings, and then left Walt a note. The note said that the action depicted in one of the drawings was backwards and couldn't possibly work the way it was drawn. She left it paperclipped to the particular drawing in question. When Walt came in, he read the note and realized that the cleaning woman had seen what everyone else had missed. From that time onward, he and his company actively sought solutions to problems from employees.

Unfortunately, although this story has made the rounds of business seminars for more than thirty years, an inquiry to the keeper of the Disney archives brought us a response to the effect that, while the spirit of the story is accurate—employees from top to bottom are involved in providing solutions to problems—the story, itself, is probably apocryphal.

8

Creating Entrepreneurial Structures

The more efficient an organization is, the dumber it is.
—Richard Greene, personal conversation, 1986

INTRODUCTION

It has been suggested that form follows function; the function of a thing should dictate the form it takes. In the same way, structure should follow strategy. Once the Entrepreneurial Manager or the entrepreneurial company has outlined the strategic elements that it wants to pursue or achieve, it moves to the next step of designing structures to articulate with these goals and objectives.

THE JERRY-BUILT STRUCTURE

It should come as no surprise to anyone that the forms of many organizations are outdated with respect to their functions, their desires, their goals, and their strategies. This problem of "badness of fit" leaves many organizations looking as though they had been designed by Rube Goldberg (the man whose name has come to be synomonous with very complex structures used for solving simple problems). We have all seen the occasional building that has passed through numerous hands and that has been added to and changed somewhat by each owner. Lacking elegance is too kind a description. It is a jerry-built structure with gables sticking out here, extra rooms there, a parapet or two, staircases that lead to nowhere, sundry connections to various outbuildings, and so on. In short, it's a mess. And then, some chief executive officer is surprised when the structure doesn't function well.

One problem is the *too complex* organizational structure. Peters and Waterman (1982) speak of structure in their injunction, "simple form, lean staff." Although there are a lot of ways that injunction can be made operational, the general perspective is a good one. Complexity of structures decreases organizational elegance and compounds the difficulties organizations have in accomplishing their goals and solving their problems.

Someone once defined elegance as being equal to the number of variables divided by the simplicity of solution. It is this goal we are trying to achieve in designing organizational structures.

A second problem with jerry-built structures is the complexity of systems that they engender. We focus on systems in the next chapter. Still, it is obviously the case—and it needs to be said now—that the electrical system, the heating system, and so on of the kind of house we described two paragraphs back is convoluted, overlapping, and redundant.[1]

Organizations, therefore, periodically need to go through structural reconfiguration. In a sense at least this perspective justifies some aspects of reorganization that some people find so difficult. Because it is designed to accomplish certain aspects of the organization's goal, each structure retards the accomplishment of other goals. Centralized organization may favor some organizational outcomes over others, whereas decentralization favors others. Reorganization, reconfiguration of structure, or *restructuralization*, therefore, always attempts at minimum to solve those organizational problems that have been generated by and are unattended by the extant structure. However, if that is all reorganization does it is insufficient.

Every reorganization should seek to solve not only those problems left unattended by the current organization, but should also retarget, refocus, and recalibrate organizational efforts toward their markets, suppliers, customers, and so on. We refer to the problem of outdated structures as *structural lag*. We call problems surrounding jerry-built, inelegant structures *Rube Goldberg's Disease*, after our famous friend, Rube Goldberg.

A third structural problem that organizations experience in designing and articulating their operations, is the thought that somehow organizational structure refers only to the organization, itself—that begins with the CEO and ends (probably) with the janitorial service. A related problem is the conceptual frame of reference that suggests that all of the organizational substructures add up to one per unit. As we suggest, some substructures are overlapping and intersecting but, hopefully, not redundant. In general, we suggest that there are three organizational structures that are of particular importance: (1) the macrostructure, (2) the mesostructure, and (3) the microstructure.

The macrostructure refers to the large-scale organizational environment and the impact that that structure has on the organization, itself. Macrolinking structures are those aspects of the organizational structure that have as the chief function articulating with macrostructures. The Board of Directors is an example of a macrolinking structure.

The mesostructure (or the in-between structure) of the organization really refers to what we typically think of as the organization chart. It is the mesostructure that is often changed when reorganization is undertaken. As we suggest, however, shuffling the mesostructure without appropriate adjustments in the macrolink and microlink structures, will not be helpful in achieving the desired organizational goals.

The microstructure refers to the *work space*, work station area. These contain the *individuals* with whom we interact on a daily basis. This the part of the office complex that forms the bulk of our daily routine. Microlinks are those microstructures that serve primarily the organizational job of linking with customers, clients, and markets. In a restaurant business, for example, the owners and their lenders form the macrolinks; those who serve food to the customers form the microlinks. The links are discussed more in the chapter on Creating Entrepreneurial Systems.

We have already spoken to some extent of the linking structures. Microlinks and macrolinks are two types of structures that perform boundary spanning activities; they link the organization to the external environment.

Intramural structures (including legal, financial, office management, and other offices) are those that seek to serve the organizational purpose of keeping parts of the organization informed about what the other parts are doing and/or thinking—what the organization is up to in general. Sometimes, like the Personnel Office, they really service the organization, itself. Other times, like the Customer Relations Office, they provide some microlinking functions and try, as well, to provide intralinks to other parts of the organization based on the information that they receive (properly codified and assembled) from the whole set of customer complaints, queries, and so on.

We discuss macro, meso, and microstructures in some detail. We follow this discussion with an examination of linking structures and evaluation.

THE MACROSTRUCTURE

The macrostructure is really the extraorganizational environment; i.e., those things happening outside the organization that are of importance to and focus on activities of the organization. A constant environmental scanning should be going on to find out "what's out there." The sonar specialist on a submarine performs this kind of function, continually sweeping the sea above, below, and around the submarine to check on what elements are in the environment and to attempt to assess their impact upon the boat.

P-O-E-T (Once again)

The POET scheme, which we mentioned in Chapter 5, is useful here (Remember? Population, Organization, Environment, Technology). The POET elements are the four main macrostructure areas that businesses need to attend to. In the population area, demographics is the name of the game.

But demographics, themselves, are only numbers; and numbers do not speak for themselves terribly well. They require a range of interpretations, proportions and ratios, to focus on potential markets, old markets, their size, and the ratio of market share to other market shares the organization may enjoy. All of these are examples of scanning results. In addition, we are dealing not only with markets for products but also markets for employees— can the organization get the kinds of people and in the numbers and locations that it desires or requires; how long will they stay; what are their characteristics; can they read? These are demographic aspects of population numbers that also become important.

Organizational aspects of the environment include changes in the business beliefs system and climate in general, locations of venture capital, trajectories of governmental support and contracting. These are all extraorganizational structures that affect the organization, itself.

Environment structures refer to physical location of supplies, roads, air, water, toxic waste disposal, and other environmentally related features that are important to the daily functioning of a business or venture.

Technology in this context is in need of constant updating and assessment. Computer technology changes very quickly. There may be other kinds of technology of great importance, as well. Improvement in medical science means people are living longer. Thus, there is an impact on the population sector that may, for example, create a demand for more adequate medical programs, larger payments from the organization for those programs. The average age of the workers, themselves, in the organization may be increasing, which in turn may require special attention to new or altered strategies and structures.

Macroscanning Efforts: Information Development

The key point of macrostructure scanning is to find out what is happening in the structural environment so that better decisions can be made with respect to organizational mission and purpose. Notice that we did not say "adjust" to those changes. Given organizational needs and a knowledge of the environment, an organization has adjustment as an option, but there are two other options that are much more appealing.

Macroscanning Efforts: Securing Support

The first of these is to find those aspects of the environment that are supportive of the organizational goals and dispositions. In other words, we are suggesting that the environment is really not all one piece. For every trend going in one direction, there are trends going in other directions. The organizational context is sufficiently ambiguous so that diverse elements always exist simultaneously. In any organization in particular, any venture or entrepreneurial activity, one does not have to be satisfied with what's "there" because what's "there" is often just what the observer happens to see. A more vigorous search process will produce other aspects of the environment that will be supportive. If the local government is not providing incubator funds, for example, perhaps the state is, or perhaps there is some regional venture that can be tapped. Conversely, if regional ventures don't exist, perhaps local ones do.

Environmental scanning, however, cannot be done on a hit or miss basis. It must be thorough and continuous so that the full sense of the environmental texture and diversity is available for scrutiny and the notion of its diversity and ambiguity is continually reinforced.

Macroscanning Efforts: Developing Commitment

Second, the organization can develop (as opposed to finding), even at a small level, the needed elements within the environment. Firms have always recruited workers from afar, for example, and have brought them to particular locales to work. They have also taken advantage of employees who have been drawn to them. Often, however, these two mechanisms have worked in tandem because the information pathways service those groups simultaneously. If, as a Firm, one finds that there are a limited number of technically trained people in a particular area, then it may be possible to work with a local junior college or community college to provide what is needed. The organization may even sponsor part of the costs of the initial course in order to make it more appealing for the college administration to undertake that desired innovation. If government funding is not available, government funding can be created in response to pressure. One successful example of this in the nonprofit sector is in the area of programs and services for the aging. In many places such programs and services have been lobbied for so successfully that they are now a permanent feature of local tax rolls. Businesses have had their successes, as well, in influencing local government to assist them in the accomplishment of their particular organizational goals and purposes. As a result, they have benefited through tax rebates and credits, tax abatement, assistance in land and equipment acquisition, among other forms of assistance, and so on. Technological changes can be stimulated. Environmental adjustments can be created or negotiated. The key feature here is to attend to it.

A problem also develops the other way. Sometimes there are well-understood changes within the macroenvironment, but the organization is slow to take advantage of them by adjusting the mesostructure. One example stressed through this volume is the aging of society. Although the nonprofit sector has been aging here, business has been less so. This trend is well recognized, and the fact that there are many elderly individuals and many of them are reasonably well to do has not escaped the attention of most social forecasters and analysts. In the case of structural lag, however, most companies (except as noted those in the health care device business and some other aspects of the business of medicine) have been very slow to take advantage of this. The Sears Corporation has been one that has. They've developed a service called "Mature Outlook." It is a membership organization (of modest cost) that allows older consumers special discounts on a range of goods and services especially aimed at that group. Other organizations have developed or are developing similiar foci. Sears' venture is in sharp contrast to that exemplified by other large firms that have done relatively little to link to the older consumer. It is the smaller firms that have tended to take leadership in such areas as senior citizen discounts.

The Board of Directors. One of the most important macrolinks is the Board of Directors. This crucial macrolink deserves a special comment.

There seems to be a general emphasis (Bennis, 1979; Carroll, 1981; Groobey, 1974) evolving that corporate boards are not doing the job they need to be doing in any of the areas we've just discussed. Rather than living up to their names as "directors," members of corporate boards seem more to view their posts as sinecures, rubber stamping much of the material presented to them by the administration in cooperation with the "inside directors."[2] Directors often seem to be the last ones to know about new directions for the organizations rather than being among those groups that initiate periodic organizational review and refurbishment of mission and role (Haft, 1981). The power and influence of inside directors often leads to meetings that express a high degree of self-satisfaction. American business is replete with stories about questionable practices of board members and problems of omission and inattention, as well. The inside-outside dichotomy has, in many cases, led to boards on one hand that know too much about current business and that are overinvolved (through bonuses, for example) in improvements in the quarterly profit statement. On the other hand it has led to boards that don't know much about the organization at all and may thus feel at a loss with respect to strategic and other organizational initiatives (Patton and Baker, 1987). Any change in American productivity needs to focus not only on American workers and American managers, but also on American directors as the models, leaders, and macrolinkers. They are the pattern setters. They are the ones who should be crying "follow me." At present they appear to spend altogether too much time sitting around asking, "What's new?"

Macrostructures, then, perform three functions for most organizations. First, they scan and develop information on what is happening in the environment. Sometimes these activities are formalized, as in the case of an entire research office; sometimes they are very informal, as in the case of a single individual who is assigned to keep up on developments in a particular area. Such individuals are unlikely to think of themselves as macrolinks but, nonetheless, they fulfull that function and perform in that capacity.

Second, macrostructures seek to influence the outside environment. Some aspects of public relations work fall into this category (although much of public relations focuses on developing a good organizational image—influencing the cultural system—rather than seeking political or social impact).

Third, macrostructures seek to influence the organization, itself. That effort is based on what is known about macrostructures. But a look at the middle part of the organization is needed.

THE MESOSTRUCTURE

The mesostructure is the organizational chart. Creating an entrepreneurial climate involves attention to a number of factors.

Think in Terms of Fewer Levels

First among these, as Kanter (1983) points out, is that the long pyramid, the verticle structure with lots of layers, separates the microstructure from the executive core, a very great difficulty in the development and implemenation of new ideas. There are simply too many places for ideas to be rejected, too many places where "questions" can be raised. Think back to our Neanderthal uncle who developed the needle. If he had had to go through seven or eight or ten layers of tribal approval, the likelihood is we would still be waiting for the needle. Whatever the form of the particular organization chart in question, shorter and flatter is better than taller and more narrow.

Encourage the Clash of Ideas

That injunction stems from something else, as well. Firms and ventures that want to encourage the supply of new ideas must also encourage the clash of new ideas. It is in this clash of ideas that problematic aspects of new ideas are uncovered and set aside. Strength does not occur through support. Support permits risk in the first place. The strength of the idea then develops through testing. Most firms understand the concept of *product* testing. A new car, a new drug, a new package is sent to the lab, is jumped on, pounded, torn apart, ripped, and generally abused. Stress reveals flaws, and weaknesses show up very fast.

The same must be true of ideas. One common problem is that idea development is located somewhere off in the corner in its own structure. Important as an idea-generating structure is, it should not allow—as it has in some instances—the rest of the organization to be careless and lackluster about its interest in the development of new approaches, concepts, and services. Activities that seek to reduce organizational hierarchy and encourage both the development and challenging of new ideas are key aspects of Entrepreneurial Management and key elements in the creation of entrepreneurial mesostructure.

Create a Climate of Creativity

The accomplishment of these objectives will move the Firm toward the achievement of a climate of creativity. Some organizations always appear to be bubbling over with new trials, half-baked idea boards, and so on. The creativity may even extend to decorative and structural features of the firm. Other organizations convey the sense that they are not 80 or 100 years old but 1 year old repeated 80 or 100 times over. A climate of creativity is one that tilts in favor of new ideas or approaches on a trial basis and one that has set up structures—including testing and trial structures—to test new ideas. It's a part of the ongoing set of activities that characterize the organization.

Set Aside "Special" Rooms

One technique worth considering is to set aside a special room for idea testing and challenging. There would be a large, sliding, name plate holder on the door. When ideas are to be challenged, the title "Devil's Advocate Session" is listed on the name plate. This identifies the particular session as focusing on Devil's Advocacy. Individuals—the presenter and all others—who come to any meeting in that room know that the purpose of it is to challenge, critique, kick, grind, shake, rattle, and roll the idea to see how it holds up. There's another name plate that may be used on other occasions: "Angel's Advocate." When that sign is in the name holder, the norms are now for support instead of attack. People are required to bend over backwards to see how the idea can be made to work—what's good about it, what are good extensions and side points of it, and so on.

All ideas must go through both advocacy activities. The sequence is also important. At the very beginning of idea evaluation, an Angel Advocate session is scheduled. This is based on the assumption that support is necessary during the birth phases. Too much criticism too early may cause premature rejection. During the more middle phases, Devil's Advocacy comes into play. This is then followed by another Angel session, and finally another Devil's session. This alternation provides both criticism and support. The alternation is crucial. The result of this process is an idea that has support and commitment and fewer problems than usual.

Set Up Idea Departments

Idea departments are important aspects of organizational structures. Even a small organization can have one, though it may be a *role* for a period of time rather than a whole department (i.e., a person assigned to perform this function). The role or department becomes the center for the pulling together of the various relevant new ideas. It also circulates them throughout the organization. A little effort in this department will go a long way and achieve astounding results for most organizations.

Idea departments or roles may also be responsible for holding a Four C's Conference. Such a conference—focusing, you recall, on the Characteristics, Competencies, Conditions, and Contexts needed for entrepreneurial activity—can provide the regularized stimulus for total organizational involvement and growth. The Four C's Conference represents a temporary aspect of the mesostructure. Managers should not believe that all aspects of organizational structure are there forever. A temporary conference, for example, is a good way to reshuffle organizational allegiances and interactions without proposing that such a reshuffling be permanent or fateful.

Use Champions

The Product (or Project) Champion is another example of a temporary role that can be used to good effect. Daft and Bradshaw (1980) pointed out the importance of the Champion concept. The organization should not sit around waiting for a Champion to surface. Rather, to the extent possible, they should identify one or two open slots into which Product Champions can be fit. When an individual has a particularly good idea, then, there is already an existing organizational niche into which they can be placed for a period of time in order to develop their innovation. (If this concept has a familiar ring to it, it should. It is not entirely unlike the notion of a "Fair Witness" that Robert Heinlein conjured in his classic science fiction novel, *Stranger in a Strange Land* [1963]). In an ideal situation, the Champions in an organization should be individuals preselected for their skill in material research and in presentation and to whom the organization accords enormous prestige. Champions should be assigned to promising ideas (and their idea generators) without regard to their personal feelings about those ideas. The task of a Champion is to defend an idea as effectively as possible, in the same way a lawyer defends a client without regard to that client's innocence or guilt. Lots of organizations, particularly very large ones, have something like Champions, though they probably don't recognize them as such. Most large universities, for example, have special offices dedicated to assisting faculty members and research staff to prepare as effective grant proposals as possible without regard to the nature and quality of the idea that generates the proposal.

It is also possible on a temporary basis to engage an organizational design specialist. There are, after all, architects for organizational structure just as there are for physical structure. It would be hazardous for anyone in general and for us in particular, in advance of any particular strategic information, to try to find out, predict, or suggest what would be the most appropriate organizational structure in any particular situation (apart from sharing some general perspectives about the nature and characteristics such a structure might have). An organizational design specialist can assist the organization in reconfiguration. Such individuals draw both on the best of the best organizational design literature and on specific knowledge of strategic goals and objectives.

Mesopreneurs, Macropreneurs, and Micropreneurs

Finally, it is here that the *Intrapreneur* is most likely to function. The Intrapreneur develops new products and services within the organization. Linked to the Intrapreneur, however, is something we might call the *Mesopreneur*. The Mesopreneur is a corollary role or person who specializes in organization reconfiguration, depending on what product or service the Intrapreneur comes up with. Many Intrapreneurs fail only because the organization cannot adjust or adapt to the needs of the particular product or service that they are proposing. Either the product or service introduced experiences failure and dies, or it is rejected in advance. In both cases a great idea may have been lost, not because the idea did not have integrity and validity but, rather, the associated structural features were insufficiently nourished and supported. We can also speak of the *Macropreneur* and the *Micropreneur* as two other organizational roles in which innovation is a key aspect. In the case of the Macropreneur innovation is focused on environmental and boundary scanning activities. In the case of the Micropreneur there is a focus on boundary spanning activities and workplace reconfiguration.

THE MICROSTRUCTURE

Many organizations that spend a lot of time in mesostructure reorganization pay no attention at all to the microstructure of daily work. Whatever the gratifications are in working for a large, prestigious organization, most of one's daily work life is spent within a small confine—one's own office, a suite of local meeting rooms, a cadre of people with whom one spends lots of time. It is most regrettable that more attention is not placed here because, as Kanter (1983) points out, microchanges can ultimately lead to macrochanges. Without microstructure working well, macrostructure will not be able to accomplish *any* of its goals. The exemplary hotel-motel service that so struck Peters and Waterman (1982) in Washington (discussed in their introduction) is an example of a microstructure of the front desk work area. It is *there* where courtesy is or is not extended. It is there where customers' needs are or are not met as they register and check out. For these reasons attention to the microstructure is not only necessary but crucial.

It is within the microstructure that hierarchies can truly be flat. Although limited change may be possible in the overall structure of the organization for a whole host of reasons, within the particular microstructure status differentials can be reduced, power relations eased and tempered, gender differences made moot, and communication channels opened. Relationships can be developed that are mutually supportive but can also have assessment and evaluative aspects. It is within the microstructure context that Quality Circles are instituted—and they, indeed, represent one form of microstructure with which much experimentation is now going on. Whether you may or may not wish to move all the way to Quality Circles is somewhat beside the point. The key element is that there is participation and review. The Staff Meeting takes on new and important dimensions.

Create a Fun Setting

It is within the microstructure that fun and work are most likely to be combined. Some executives think of fun as those rare organizational opportunities such as a picnic or Christmas party when everyone gets together. Most employees do not find these fun. Rather, such activities represent just one more aspect of "work" in which formal relationships are dominant, status recognition is key, and the perils of screwing up are enhanced. What the employer may think of as fun may be in actuality a gut-wrenching, anxiety-generating period for the employee.

The introduction of new ideas and the trying of new approaches, on the other hand, is frequently viewed by workers as "fun." There are some requisites, of course. There has to be some organizational support for the time and energy these activities take. In addition, there has to be sufficient planning and organization. A new idea, dropped on individuals at the last moment, with the injunction "make it work or else" is not what characterizes good Entrepreneurial Management. If other aspects of the organizational microstructure have been set up in the ways suggested here, however, it is unlikely that poor planning will characterize new idea introduction for you. Special rules in Chapters 13 and 14, for example, focus upon future events and mandate "blue skying" as part of the regular activity of the microstructure of meetings.[3]

Use What Your People Know

Microlinks can also serve an important role here, as well. You will recall that microlinks are those individuals who are in regular contact with customers, clients, the marketplace in general. Frequently, they have information that can be helpful. All too often, however, their market information is set aside in favor of more formalized presentations of "market researchers," in shop or out of it. Organizational consultants know that there are rarely surprises when organizational troubles arise. Most of the information about why things have gone wrong is already present within the organizational members. It is simply that that information has not been used. Similarly, and sadly, information and ideas about the solutions to organizational problems are already present. Consultants rarely bring in striking new techniques or unbelievable new diagnoses. Rather, they free up clogged arteries of information flow that prevent information and perspectives on organizational problems and solutions from being used. We'll talk more about the freeing-up process in the next chapter; but from the point of view of organizational microstructure, the problem frequently lies in inappropriately rigid and "status-ified" relationships within that microstructure. The secretary, for example, who meets almost everyone coming into the office area and knows a great deal about the organizational arena, is rarely invited to staff meetings (see McCormack, 1986). As a result her (and, in some cases, his) perspectives on what customers and those hanging around the organization are saying are never used; there is no channel to open up communication to that locus of knowledge. Salesmen and people working on the road are all too often *not* plumbed for their information as an organizational feedback mechanism. Often, the things they hear and need to report are in the domain of some other microstructure. Because they are not members of that microstructure, the "N.I.H." perspective ("Not Invented Here") or, in this case, "not reported by a member of our own microstructure," takes over. One aspect of the organizational microstructure, therefore, has to be a focus upon ways in which the information available from microlinks can be brought into the organizational structure. Lots of good ideas are lost in this transition. Microlink members often do not even understand the role that they, themselves, are playing. As a result, special attention needs to be given to this issue.

It is also important to find ways to "cross ruff" microstructures. Microstructures are small. They represent office and work areas. As such, people from one microstructure may have information pertaining to other microstructures. There needs to be some way, therefore, to link information available from different microstructures.

Decentralize to Work Stations

The microstructure is also a location where supplies, equipment, and other material aspects of doing a job may be located. Here again, the Entrepreneurial Manager can make use of this obvious fact as a way to stimulate innovation. Try to find ways to devolve control of supplies to the local microstructural units. In a small office, this may simply be accomplished by giving the secretary a budget plus permission to make a range of decisions about the kind of supplies, their nature, their storage and distribution, and so on. Allowing people to have control over a certain aspect of their microstructural environment enhances their own feeling of self-worth. It also provides training in the thinking process. When organizational analysts talk about decentralization of decision making and delegation of authority, there is a temptation to think of it in terms of big subunits and major organizational decisions. That can be a focus, of course, but what is often overlooked is that there can be delegation of authority and decision making even within the microstructure itself. The rule of thumb here is that everyone in the microstructure ought to have some realm or area over which they have decision-making power and on which they can report—rather than for which they need to check.

We are not suggesting that these decisions be made in the absence of an overall guiding policy. Quite the contrary. In the context of organizational policy and microstructural policy having been set up—on equipment and supplies, let us say—an individual can then be delegated to proceed and do the job, reporting back and seeking reactions.

The availability of this grant of power is high. Its rewards are incredibly great, both in terms of accomplishing the job, making the task more meaningful, and training people in responsibility and decision making. It is a key aspect of microstructure that should be attended to by all Entrepreneurial Managers.

Reduce Exploitation

One final point about microstructure is important to bear in mind. Exploitation of some members of the microstructure is to be avoided at all costs. We all know the importance of avoiding status differentials that inhibit communication. To some extent the injunction to avoid exploitation falls in that principle. Microstructures are small, organizational work groups. Our experience always tells us that there are people in organizations who work hard, and there are others who do not work so hard. This differential is already the beginning of exploitation potential. Hopefully, in discussions and meetings within the microstructural work group, differences in production trajectories can be discussed at appropriate intervals.

But the problem of exploitation is more serious than this. It involves individuals of lower status being used, coerced, or made to feel guilty for naught; pressured into doing more than they really should for the pay that they are getting. Secretaries often fall within this category, working extra long hours, doing extra typing, filing, and so on for minimal salaries. In this example bosses reap the benefits in terms of the additional free time, and secretaries wind up giving their time for free.

There is a great deal wrong with this. Although it is true that we want to get the most out of everyone, it is the *mechanism* that is important here. The culture of a microstructure is like that of a play staff. Everyone in a high school play works together: the actors, the director, the stage managing crew, the costumer, and so on. It is true that some people have roles that are more prominent than others—the actors for example—but it is very clear to everyone in the production that everyone is needed. Even the small jobs have meaning. Everyone has to do his or her job so that the total play will come off smoothly. When this happens, people will frequently work long and hard to contribute to the common weal. But the stage manager doesn't work harder so that the actor can work less. When that happens, the culture of the work group is soured and poisoned. Although one may coerce larger work efforts out of some individuals through exploitation, the troubled culture saps achievement motivation and engenders overall lackluster performance.

To sum up, then, microstructure is the stuff of daily work life. Strangely, and because of its commonality and familiarity, it has escaped serious attention as a locus of Entrepreneurial Management—or any management at all for that matter. It is in the microstructure context that new ideas are developed. In that context, too, new ideas must be implemented. Hence, for both reasons, it is important to have a well-organized and smoothly functioning microstructure. Without it, few ideas will be generated and almost none will be implemented well.

LINKING STRUCTURES

Given the three types of structures we have mentioned so far—macrostructures, mesostructures, and microstructures—there is the obvious need to provide links among them. The problem, of course, is that there are many and varied types at each level. There are macrostructures, for example, that exist outside the organization. If there are several parts or several divisions of the organization, there are several mesostructures. And there are lots and lots of microstructures.

A second problem is that the subculture and focus of these structures tends to be rather different. These differences complicate the linking process.

Interorganizational Linkages

Linkages between the organization and the other elements in its environment are formally accomplished through macrolinks and microlinks. Macrolinks seek to influence the large-scale elements of the organization's context and environment that affect it. Microlinks are structures that are in daily contact with the suppliers, the customers, and the other contextual elements that the organization needs to function. In general, however, Entrepreneurial Managers need to create structures and/or roles that touch the key elements of the external environment or context. What this principle reflects is the need to have an internal organizational unit specially designed to attend to the key external moments. If government contracts are important, there needs to be a government contracts structure. If securing certain types of employee competencies is crucial, then there needs to be a structure that attends to that, and so on (Hasenfeld and Tropman, 1979).

Organizational strategy is, in essence, a set of rules or predictions that link changes in the environment to changes in the internal organizational structure. What frequently happens, as we have previously noted, is that changes in the environment are recognized by strategy. There are not commensurate internal changes, however, in order to reconfigure and rearticulate the organization to link most effectively with its suppliers, customers, and other units of the context that influence and determine its life course and vitality.

One of the results of the Four C's Conference could be a strategy structure review in which strategic planning is taken as the starting point. We would then look at structure to examine whether there are appropriate structural configurations to accomplish the plan with particular attention to links to the external system.

Intraorganizational Links

The other side of the problem of linking the organization to its environment is the process of internal articulation of parts and elements. In the small or new organization informal patterns of interaction become linking structures in and of themselves. A typical lunch becomes a luncheon meeting. A chat in the parking lot becomes a high-level conference. If there are only a few individuals within the organization, then the structures to link are not terribly difficult to establish. Whether or not these structures accomplish the purpose of linking is another question. For the moment, however, let us focus on the medium to larger size organization.

What is common about the examples in the last paragraph is that they are in some sense "meetings," and meetings are one of the fundamental intraorganizational linking structures. Most organizations have thousands of meetings each year—formal, informal, catch-as-catch-can, and planned well in advance. Unfortunately, most organizations do not understand the importance of the meeting as a fundamental intraorganizational linking device.

Meetings are organized into committees. The very mention of meetings often causes people to shudder. Introducing the word *committee*, or worse, the action phrase, "Let's form a committee," too often adds even more negativism to the concept of group interaction.

In small organizations, meetings will probably suffice. In larger organizations, committees represent extended and orchestrated meetings. Sometimes, in a terminological attempt to escape the inaction often implied by committees, the term *task force* is used. Most organizations of substantial size have dozens to hundreds of committees, task forces, task groups, and so on. These have been created in order to link the various parts of the organization together. At issue is how well they work.

Details and procedures that can assist in the actual meeting acitivity will be discussed in Chapter 13. What we discuss here is the Meeting/Committee Audit, which is the first step in introducing meeting/committee restructure.

The Meeting/Committee Audit as a first step seeks to establish how many and what kinds of meetings are held within the organization, and how many and what kinds of committees exist within the organization. Using rough cost figures of the per hour rate of people in meetings (using averages if necessary), it is possible to establish the cost of a particular meeting. Let's look at an example.

At recently increased rates of senior partners in important law firms around the country ($350 per hour), a one hour staff meeting involving ten senior partners would cost $3,500 for their time alone. This figure does not include any amortized estimate for the meeting room. It does not include staff time for others involved in preparing for the meeting. It does not include the partners' own time involved in preparing for the meeting. For purposes of discussion, let's add $1,500 as an additional amount. Thus, our one-hour meeting probably costs the organization at least $5,000. A two-hour staff meeting with just these individuals would cost $10,000. If these partners got together once a week just to keep current on each other's business for a minimum of one hour, the cost to the firm would be $260,000.

The figures quickly become staggering. The purpose of the Meeting/Committee Audit is to establish how many meetings go on, of what kinds, and then to ask the more serious questions: are these meetings accomplishing their purposes (assuming purposes can be established); are the committees completing their assignments and goals (assuming they have assignments and goals); are any of these meetings in need of restructuring, refocusing, or reconfiguring? It would be the rare organization that would not have a "yes" answer to this last question. Similarly, the whole committee structure—which is nothing more than a permanent string of meetings plus a modest to substantial amount of extra-meeting activity—may, itself, be in need of reconfiguration.

The Entrepreneurial Manager must pay particular attention to committees and meetings, and must develop a formal stategy for doing so (Grove, 1983; Sayles and Chandler, 1971). The first step is the one we have just mentioned: looking at the kind, nature, scope, range of intraorganizational meeting and committee activity and being able to report on this level of activity.

The second step is to examine this segment of organizational activity with respect to organizational strategies, themselves. Certainly, and at the very least, there ought to be committees set up around each organizational strategy and substrategy. You may not wish to reorganize the entire corporation around modest strategic adjustments, but you can certainly reorganize the committee structure and bring together different individuals who are needed to deal with particular issues. Earlier, you may remember, we referred to what Cohen, March, and Olsen (1972) call the "garbage can model of decision making." They argued that organizations are made up of people who know problems of the organization, people who know the solution to organizational problems (but may not know the problems), people who control resources, and decision makers looking for work. Entrepreneurial Managers will seek to bring these four elements together in meetings and committees. If that can be accomplished, the output of group decision making will improve vastly in quality and satisfaction. For each strategic goal, we can ask: what are the problems inherent in it; what are the solutions that we generally might need concerning it; what are the resources that might be involved; and who are the relevant decision makers? Those individuals having been assembled can make great progress. Cohen, March, and Olsen argue that these elements are not usually brought together in a thoughtful way. They use the phrase *garbage can*, because to them these four elements are most often just tossed together. The Entrepreneurial Manager can gain an edge by being sure that all four are carefully assembled together.

In short, the Entrepreneurial Manager can look at the number and focus of organizational meetings and committees and restructure them so that their number is reasonable, their focus is crisp, and their membership is in line with the elements needed to solve the problems or deal with the issues set up by the focus. Larger scale assessments of meetings and committees reconfigure them to address new strategic directions. Effective organizational change agents often introduce organizational change ideas through committee restructuring as an opening ploy. It is a much neglected and potentially very useful arena of intervention.

Committees and meetings are not the only linking structures that Entrepreneurial Managers need to consider. Organizational celebrations are another. Such celebrations, as we noted earlier, have the potential for being negative as sometimes happens with the office party. Such celebrations, however, need not be that way, particularly if they can recognize the efforts and achievements of individuals within the organization and if they can be more frequent rather then less frequent.

Regular celebrations, varied in nature, theme, and celebratory structure, can be enjoyable situations. The inclusion of recognition of organizational achievements allows for mutual sharing of pride and accomplishment.

Celebrations of a party sort are not the only things that the Entrepreneurial Manager can create. Postings and announcements can serve this function as well. Who among us, upon entering a grade school and seeing an entire class's finger paintings attractively displayed has not experienced just a twinge of envy? We all like to see our work displayed, and there are few among us who don't have some aspect of their work that can be displayed for others to see, admire, and learn from. It is paradoxical that organizations will often spend hundreds of thousands of dollars for professional decorators to import an organizational decor that has absolutely nothing to do with the actual achievements and accomplishments of people who work for the organization. So much the better would it be to plan a decor celebrating and displaying the kinds of things that the organization is known for. Such a display could include organizational products, notes of appreciation, photos of famous guests (restaurants often use these), and so on. All this may be a bit hokey if not done with taste and grace, but the underlying purpose should never be forgotten; that is, to create a climate of meaning and genuine membership for those who work for and visit the organization. That creation will be rewarded by a greater effort, attention, fewer mistakes, and higher quality.[4]

There is a range of other activities that the Entrepreneurial Manager can use to create linking structures. Among them are newsletters and announcements, which should feature the achievements and accomplishments of the staff of the organization. Even if the organization is just a small one with a few employees, a little newsletter or series of announcements done periodically is a great reinforcer. A newsletter is a particularly good linking structure because it can list problems that are in need of solution and ideas that people have that might be seeking an application. The newsletter serves to record them, thus avoiding the loss of good ideas. A developing record of organizational progress is automatically generated.

Linking structures are crucial to the functioning of an organization or a system of organization. The April 1987 catalog of the Land's End direct mail merchandising company, contains a quote from a man who runs a laundry business in Chicago, complaining about the lack of linking structures. He said:

You have hit my pet peeve. I can't think of another industry where designers communicate so little with service people. They (shirt manufacturers) taper their shirts so they don't fit our (launderers) presses, then put too much fabric in the collar so it doesn't iron flat. Sometimes they even use a collar liner made of a different fabric so the collar shrinks but the liner doesn't. Or put in nonremovable collar stays that show through the collar when it's ironed. They don't even know enough to cut the sleeve gussets long enough to go over the presses. This shirt can be ironed perfectly. (P. 112)

Land's End did not have this particular problem. That's why they mention it.

The particular example is of an interorganizational system; but, obviously, it would be to everyone's advantage in that business to try to come up with some common definitions, sizes, and procedures. Doubtless, some already exist; but others may be needed. The same kind of story can be echoed in industry after industry, business after business: the widget doesn't fit the flodgette. The caution for the Entrepreneurial Manager is to be ever mindful of linking structures. The following provides support for the need for such attention, and shows the importance of making use of information available from the microstructures—and what can happen if you don't.

A certain, successful, well-known restaurant chain was seeking to combine an evolving taste in Mexican food with a preference for salad. A sort of Mexican combination salad was designed by a central kitchen. It had all the right ingredients but, according to some of those who had to serve it, "it looked god-awful!" It took only a couple of weeks before the product completely bombed, becoming a costly embarrassment to the central kitchen. Lack of communication among relevant organizational substructures led to overcommitment and certainty on the part of the central kitchen. They argued against the usual pretesting on the grounds that they had a winner. (And haven't we all been in the same boat at times?) The extent of the failure was compounded by the fact that the product was then withdrawn completely. Spectacular claims often lead to spectacular defeats. Had both been modulated, the good idea contained in such a combination salad might easily have been salvaged and might eventually have resulted in a prize-winning product.

EVALUATION STRUCTURES

Evaluation structures are extremely important for big and small organizations. The market, itself, is one evaluation structure, as the Mexican combination salad example illustrates. But the market often gives ambiguous messages, and the messages tend to come after the fact. Sometimes the market doesn't know where to give a message. Consider the case of the bad fit of the manufactured shirts cited in the Land's End catalog. The poor fit didn't affect the customer, it affected the launderer; but, when the customer gets a shirt back that is badly ironed, she or he may not know quite how to express disaffection. In short, market information frequently has clear results but unclear meaning.

Evaluation structures try to prevent both Acceptance and Rejection errors (see Chapter 2) and to perform a number of other important organizational equilibrating tasks. Such structures are needed that do more than feed *back*. They must get information in such a way that a feed *forward* system can be introduced. Michael (1980) introduces this concept as a way to anticipate problems and solve them before they affect operations.

Somehow, evaluation, as it is often discussed, is a reactive and sometimes posthumous activity. As such, incidentally, it is not necessarily bad. You can, for example, develop a postproject audit system. Select one or two projects a year that have been completed. Perform an audit/autopsy of them. Review project records, interview project personnel, look at project outcomes and results, and so on. This can prove to be very salutary because the entire organization is informed about the findings, and no doubt some are positive and some are less so. The overall purpose should not be to assess blame but to find out what was good and how it can be repeated and what was bad and how it can be avoided. The difficulty with such a system lies only in its uniqueness. It should, in fact, be only one of a series of evaluative structures that should be set up from an Entrepreneurial Management point of view. But proactive strategies are better still.

In general, there should be four components or substructures to every evaluation structure. They are different in purpose and orientation. They occur with differential frequency, and they have differential fatefulness for the products and services they are looking at. They are: (1) monitoring; (2) oversight; (3) assessment; and (4) appraisal.

Monitoring

The first evaluation structure, and the one on which all others are subsequently based, is monitoring. Monitoring is some type of frequent assessment, designed appropriately for the product or service in question. By frequent, we mean daily or weekly reviews of what is happening. In car manufacturing, for example, daily figures on problems and flaws in car production should be available. In an auto dealership, any sales should be posted and so should daily figures on number of cars repaired, types of repairs, general level of satisfaction, and so on. The monitoring system is the "pulse taking" feature of the organizational evaluation structure. Without the data base that it provides, the remaining evaluative elements—oversight, assessment, and appraisal—cannot go on effectively.

Oversight

Oversight is the second echelon in the evaluation hierarchy. It involves review of daily or weekly service figures, and it seeks to assure that relevant targets, trajectories, and dates are being met. Overseers are able to make adjustment in the system of service or product delivery such that the previously agreed upon targets, trajectories, dates, and so on are more likely to be met. It is anticipated that such oversight reveals essential minor fluctuations in the production/service schedules. Should major departures from such schedules be revealed, emergency meetings may need to be called, and such a situation may indicate other problems, as well. The oversight is simply an organized way of reviewing the data put together by the monitoring system.

Assessment

Assessment may occur at monthly or quarterly intervals and can involve fateful outcomes for the product, service, and people. An assessment review, as opposed to monitoring and oversight review, can generate change *of* the system rather than change *in* the system. Although monitoring reviews descriptive statistics, essentially, assessment begins an intensive analytic process, often using rates, ratios and comparisons. So, for example, the question of car manufacturing errors in an assessment may be proportionalized and then compared to such proportions at other plants, at other times of the year, in other sectors of the same plant, or with external standards or measures known to be valid in the particular case in question.

Similarly, in the car dealership example, the number of new cars sold per day is subjected to some intensive analysis. How many sales were made in proportion to the number of individuals who came in and looked at cars, for example? How does this particular showroom floor compare with others? How many calls of inquiry were made, and how many of these calls resulted in subsequent sales?

The list of proportions and comparisons can go on and on, but the point is made. Assessment can reveal comparative flaws in the system. If the evaluation structure is set up properly and properly linked to other organizational structures, it will be able to initiate changes of the production/service system that will increase the good things that have been discovered and decrease the disappointing and difficult ones. Sometimes additional information is needed in an assessment. If, for example, in the case of the car dealership, there are a low number of sales per visitor, then further information must be sought in order to determine why this might be so. Once reasons are discovered, appropriate changes can be considered.

To put things on a very basic level, using something we have all had experience with, monitoring is the rough equivalent to taking daily attendance in the classroom. Oversight involves periodic testing, such as might be undertaken by pop quizzes and homework review. Assessment represents the midterm and final exams. Appraisal (which we'll talk about in just a moment) involves the summation and judgment of all of these factors taken together in the assignment of a final grade.

Appraisal

Appraisal represents the "final grade." It is the coming together of lots of factors in a final judgment. Judgment is crucial in appraisal and is, finally, what appraisal involves. Like fixing the sale price of a house, it is based on a host of hard data factors, developed during the monitoring, oversight, and assessment processes. In appraisal, however, a final reckoning is accomplished, and this reckoning can be extremely fateful for products, services, and people. Appraisal may involve the judgment of failure and, as a result, product discontinuance and the liquidation of supplies, accounts, equipment, and job positions.

Appraisal is usually done on a yearly or multiyear basis. As in the stock market, time is needed for cycles to express themselves. It is inappropriate to rush in (short of some emergency) and make "crash" appraisals. Often the data are not present for such an undertaking anyway.

Figure 8.1
A Typical Organization Chart

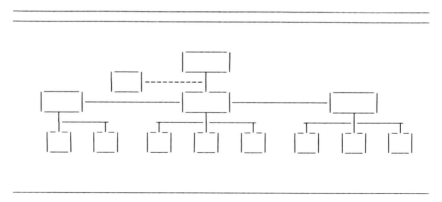

Creating the Evaluation System

In any evaluation system the participation of those who are to be evaluated is important. Such participation starts, as always, with an understanding of what the goals are that are to be achieved. Strategy sets these goals. Then structural elements are put into place that allow those goals to have a chance of being achieved. Evaluation structures are also developed to check on goal achievement progress (monitoring), make course corrections (oversight), change flight paths or trip sequences and routes (assessment), and scrub flights (appraisal). Because different strategic goals will require different evaluation structures, those involved in goal accomplishment should have a hand in designing the elements within each evaluation component.

UNUSUAL ORGANIZATIONAL TOPOLOGIES

An obvious question to ask at this point is: How do all of these things fit together? An obvious answer is: Look at the organization chart, which presumably lays everything out. Let's see if that works.

Envision, if you will, the typical organization chart. An example is outlined in Figure 8.1.

The typical tree-shaped organizational structure revealed in the organization chart is a very common way to think about organizational locations, activities, hierarchies, and so on. Unfortunately, it tends to provide a frame of reference in our mind that emphasizes separation and hierarchy. We're going to ask you to make two alterations in this typical chart and to explore what alterations in your own thinking occur.

Figure 8.2
The Organizational Circle

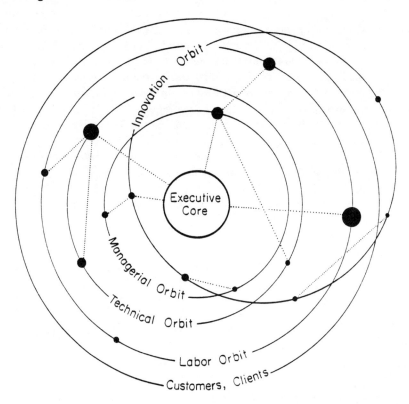

By John E. Tropman

Drawing the Organizational Circle

The first of these involves a mental image. Think of taking the two ends of the bottom row of the chart, one in each hand, stretching them out, bending them around, and attaching them at the top. In other words, create an Organizational Circle. There's no particular reason why an organization chart could not be redrawn as an Organizational Circle. One possible representation of the idea is given in Figure 8.2. Now consider the implications of the Organizational Circle.

To begin with, the hierarchy becomes flat. There is less up and down and a great deal more back and forth. The Organizational Circle concept reframes and refocuses our orientation toward authority. The "higher-ups" no longer exist. Now, the center of the organization is a kind of fulcrum that creates organizational balance and that can redirect its energies as they are needed to various parts of the organization.

A second thing that happens is that contact between the center and second, third, or fourth levels becomes easier. In fact, levels don't really exist anymore because hierarchy has become flattened. They are replaced by orbits. Following Parsons' (1960) ideas, we can distinguish three main orbits: the institutional (executive) (central) orbit, the managerial (second) orbit out, and the technical or operational (third) orbit. We could also add another extraorganizational orbit to represent customers, clients, suppliers, and so on. One can see radii going from the center to the very edge without necessarily going through some of the spheres of activity that exist in the surrounding orbit. The Organizational Circle and its attendant orbital structure tends not to define things as being "beneath" other things (which in and of itself might be sufficient rationale to adopt it).

A third aspect of the organizational circle is that it is possible to locate experimental spheres without necessarily putting them at the "edge" of the organization or having them bumping into other spheres. We call these *incubator programs* (they represent experimental activities being undertaken by the organization that are being watched closely by the central office; they may be expanded to full divisions or other organizational entities, or they may be closed down). Galbraith (1982) calls these *reservations*, but the concept is essentially the same. They are places where new ideas can be tried, and they can be located wherever it's convenient within the Organizational Circle.

Fourth, the Organizational Circle seems to emphasize the unity and interconnectedness of organizational parts rather than their distinctness and their difference. A greater emphasis on blending and oneness seems to emerge. You might find it both fun and enlightening to attempt to present your organization as a circle rather than as a set of boxes.

ROTATING THE ORGANIZATIONAL CIRCLE

The next logical step is to create the Organizational Sphere. This is accomplished by the simple process of drawing an imaginary diameter anywhere on the circle and spinning the circle around that diameter. The result will be a ball or a sphere. In recognition of the dynamic character of organizations, think of it as an Organizational Gyroscope. Orbits are now not only moving out from the center like rings on a plate, they may move in both horizontal and vertical directions—just as they do with a gyroscope.

The Organizational Gyroscope concept further opens up the organizational structure, now allowing for a wide range of placements. Not only can organizational centers or subspheres be located on the orbits, but the orbits, themselves, can be designed in a variety of ways to cut across each other. Centers may exist where orbits cross, and such loci may be sources of innovative ideas as individuals who work in such centers are forced to come to grips with conflicting sets of problems, demands, expectations, and responsibilities.

The point about the Organizational Gyroscope is that it allows us to rethink about the kind of organizational structure we have, to diminish hierarchy, and to emphasize commonality. Furthermore, it provides us a location where we can place fledgling ventures, to allow them to incubate and to develop a bit while having some independence on the one hand and some oversight on the other. From an entrepreneurial point of view, this represents a much better way of thinking about structure than the old tree-and-branch method because of its emphasis on innovational location.

CONCLUSION

Creating organizational structures is an important component of Entrepreneurial Management. Structure flows from strategy.

In this chapter, five important structures were outlined. The first three were (1) macrostructures, (2) mesostructures, (3) microstructures. We also examined how these structures are or might be linked [(4) linking structures] and evaluated [(5) evaluation structures]. Structures are not all separate "parts" of the organization. They represent, rather, crucial variables that affect the organization.

Mesostructure represents the organization, itself. Macrostructure represents the context of the organization; it can be influenced, but changing it is difficult. Microstructure represents compositional elements of the organization. So, too, do linking structures and evaluation structures. Each requires thought and attention so that the organization can develop in a prudent and profitable manner. Each requires reconfiguration from time to time so that each substructure can articulate with other substructures in a way conducive to the accomplishment of organizational strategy.

We then presented a new way of portraying and, therefore, thinking about the mesostructure; namely, the Organizational Sphere/Gyroscope. It reconfigures one's sense of what the organization is and the relationship among organizational elements.

NOTES

1. Though we use the word *redundant*, we want to alert readers to the fact that there are times when redundant systems are needed; e.g., safety measures and computer controls. If a redundant system is generated by design, that's fine. The ones we are referring to occur simply because they are added to the ones already extant.

2. *Inside directors* are those who have appointments within the particular organization and also serve on its board of directors. *Outside Directors* are those who work

elsewhere, who will serve on a particular board for the honor, prestige, or opportunity of influence.

3. "Blue skying" is a name given to that activity in which one "flies" in the blue sky of new ideas. It is designed to be speculative and open-ended and, indeed, mandates fresh approaches. Meetings are a lot more fun when there is an opportunity to do some blue skying because one of the rewards for work groups within the microstructure is the ability to be creative and innovative. All too often, however, the daily or weekly pressures of current events are inimical to this process. It is often said that "daily routine drives out planning." That's what can happen when less specific attention is paid to introducing creative time periods within the ongoing warp and woof of organizational life.

4. An interesting attempt to accomplish this purpose is being undertaken by the Land's End direct mail merchandising specialists (clothes, luggage). In their catalog they have taken to featuring photos of and, in some cases, articles about their staff. The April 1987 catalog, for example, contains a feature by their sport coat buyer discussing sport coats and how he makes his sport coat selections. The same catalog also features photos and endorsements of happy customers on the first two pages. That's a kind of organizational celebration and builds a link between customers and the Firm.

Creating Entrepreneurial
Systems

Peters and Waterman commenting on an exceptional reception at the FOUR
SEASONS in Washington, D.C. "For us, one of the main clues to corporate
excellence has come to be just such incidents of unusual effort on the part
of ordinary employees."

—*In Search of Excellence*, p. xvii

INTRODUCTION

Organizational Systems are those features of an entrepreneurial venture that
link the substructures together and make the organization a whole. Meta-
phorically speaking, they represent the blood and nerves of the organization.
If Structures are boxes or bubbles, then Systems are strings and strands.

THREE SYSTEM PROCESSES

Enterpreneurial Systems are characterized by *flows*: flows of information
from one place to another, flows of authority, and flows of energy and resources.
In thinking about the Organizational Gyroscope, what Systems add are the
threads of interconnections between the nodes and the orbits. This image
can be amplified by considering the threads to be of different colors, indi-
cating different Systems.

Systems allow the entrepreneurial venture to act as a whole. We are all
aware of organizations (especially but not exclusively large ones) in which
the left hand doesn't know what the right hand is doing. Failures of coordination, control, and direction are failures of Systems rather than failures
of Structures. Systems, then, represent the dynamic aspect of organizations.

As opposed to the more static structural features, they represent the process aspects of organizations. And, as in the case of nerves and blood, they not only embody flows but *exchange*: exchange of information, exchange of energy, and exchange of resources.

In this exchange, *transformation*, a third aspect of Systems, occurs. Sometimes information is turned into power and resources are turned into products, just as plants turn sunlight into energy. At other times information is traded for resources, resources for products, and so on.

The Entrepreneur, thus, has three related tasks: establishing Systems, preventing their breakdown, and enhancing their function. In attending to these the Entrepreneurial Manager needs to focus upon flow, exchange, and transformation as three crucial elements.

ESTABLISHING ENTREPRENEURIAL SYSTEMS

Creating and establishing Enterpreneurial Systems is not that different from establishing Systems in general. For every organizational chart, circle, or gyroscope, there is a book of procedures. It is essentially the creation of these organizational procedures that is involved in the establishment of Enterpreneurial Systems.

Procedures involve sets of directions and specifications for the handling of people, ideas, money, material, and so on. Personnel Systems focus on the set of procedures required for the handling of people. Financial Systems focus on the set of procedures required for the handling of money. Materials Handling Systems and other handling Systems focus on the procedures required in the processing of materials. Entrepreneurs will need to establish these sets of procedures. The difference in the Enterpreneurial Systems is that there is special attention paid to the idea handling System. Most organizations do not have a special System for handling, sponsoring, developing, processing, or otherwise generally dealing with ideas. It is here that the Enterpreneurial System distinguishes itself.

ESTABLISHING IDEA PROCESSING SYSTEMS

Entrepreneurial Managers need to pay special attention to two aspects of idea generation. First, they need to be aware that other systems—Personnel Systems, Financial Systems, Information Systems—contain the seeds of new approaches. They may be in the form of problems that need to be resolved and the consequent need for new procedures, Systems, and Structures. They may also be new or different techniques that have become available and that may have fresh and new applications not hitherto considered.

The Entrepreneurial Manager must be sensitive to encouraging the creativity inherent within the existing Systems. This happens through the creation of a supportive culture, to be sure; but it is also enhanced by the creation of an Idea Processing System that is separate from the other major Systems. Through the creation of an Idea Processing System, with the concommitant establishment of an Idea Manager or a Policy Manager (Tropman, 1984) or an Idea Champion, the Entrepreneurial Manager signals and models the importance of new ideas to the venture or enterprise. The Idea Processing System establishes a regularized procedure for all new ideas developed within the organization.

The Idea Processing System may, itself, be a source of new ideas to its own System. In the main, however, the Idea Processing System takes ideas generated from other parts of the organization and begins to move them through a predetermined set of steps. These involve examination, testing, checking, sharing, and ultimate decision making.

A special Idea Processing System is necessary because without it most ideas are either lost at the time they are thought up—like our Neanderthal innovator with the needle—or they have no particular place to go (and so are lost). You'll find it a useful exercise to think about organizations you're involved with, and ask yourself the compound question: "What if I had a new idea? Where would I take it?" When we have asked this question in organizations, the most common answer is "The Boss." For many individuals in moderate to larger organizations, this is not only scary, it is not even totally clear who the relevant "boss" might be. Sub-bosses often resist passing on new ideas on the grounds that it might make them look bad to *their* bosses because they, as sub-bosses, had not thought the ideas up themselves. Similarly, because many people in many organizations have several bosses, it is not always clear which of them is the appropriate one to receive new ideas. These are two of the reasons why ideas become stalled. Doubtless you can add more reasons of your own. In any event, unless we happen to link into an influential sponsor, or unless the idea is just so spectacular on its face that it sweeps away all opposition, the idea is in all probability simply doomed. Therefore, in order to free up what is already present in the organization, the Entrepreneurial Manager needs to establish an Idea Processing System and to set down procedures and steps that guarantee all new ideas will receive attention and careful review.

Many of those new ideas will not pan out. However, don't discard them. You can never tell when an idea that initially appears ridiculous or outlandish may turn out, in whole or in part, to provide a solution to some future problem or become the spark for some new fabulously successful product or service. Every idea, therefore, should go into an organizational inventory, which is, itself, reviewed from time to time. At a later point, components of these older ideas, when combined with still newer innovations may become fantastically profitable. It is this way that the Idea Processing System stimulates a Concept Bank—just like a Staff or a Personnel Bank (the "steno pool," for example) or a Bank Account.

The Idea Processing System, like other Systems, focuses on the flow of ideas from one place to another, the exchange of ideas from one unit to another, and the transformation of ideas, finally, into legitimate and useful products and services. This process goes on informally in many organizations. Like so many other aspects of organizational life, however, once one knows about it, attends to it, and helps it along, its impact is increased a thousand fold.

ESTABLISHING INTELLIGENCE SYSTEMS

Entrepreneurial Managers must also be concerned with the breakdown of various Systems. Breakdowns occur in each of the three areas that are central to the System concept: *flow*, *exchange*, and *transformation*.

Consider first the case of flows. Flows cease or become inadequate—the flow of information is too late, too early, or wrong; the flow of resources and authority may have similar problems. This occurs because flows in organizations become obstructed, or they become uneven, or there are leaks. What is sent out from the front office, for example, may arrive only in small amounts in the field. There are blocks and turns in the flow process that decrease its velocity, force, and timeliness. Although procedures can be set up to work, the question of whether they *do* actually work requires constant scrutiny.

Exchanges can be botched, as well. Even though the flow of information, people, and money arrives at the proper place at the proper time, there may be difficulties in utilization. Sending Structures may not know what to send or how to send it. Receiving Structures may not know what to ask for. The languages and subcultures, even within a small organization, may differ so significantly that communication breaks down. Transmissions may become garbled, and the organization may face the problems of uncertainty absorption and authoritative augmentation. Uncertainty absorption, of course, occurs when certain problems and unknowns that perplex those at the bottom get systematically removed as the information about these problems is passed to the top executives. Similarly, a simple suggestion by a top executive is interpreted authoritatively by individuals lower down, and the negotiation that might occur is thus forestalled.[1]

Finally, the transformation system can work poorly or work when it's not supposed to. Considering this latter point first, sometimes information is transformed when it is just supposed to be exchanged. You recall that when we discussed uncertainty absorption, we described a situation in which uncertain information was "transformed" into certain information as it moved up the hierarchy. You also recall how with authoritative augmentation a query from the top becomes an imperative by the time the request gets to the bottom of the organization pecking order.

Other times transformation does not occur. Many executives complain that they receive undigested "messes" of facts, reports, and "stuff" from subordinates—subordinates who are supposed to process and digest these diverse pieces of information and present syntheses of them to higher ups.

Thus, in addition to an Idea Processing System, Entrepreneurial Managers need to create an Intelligence System. The Intelligence System is that set of procedures, routines, routes, reports, and meetings that bring information in to the Entrepreneurial Manager about how the System is actually functioning. Evaluation Structures will become a crucial formal part of the Intelligence System (see Chapter 8). This is just one way the Entrepreneurial Manager gets information about System functioning. Customer and client complaints and suggestions represent another important way. And it is worthwhile for the Entrepreneurial Manager to pay special attention to these. The old business adage, "The customer is always right," has fallen into disuse and, in some arenas, disrepute.[2] Most of the time, especially for larger organizations, customers have no assurance that their complaints or perspectives get through to the person who needs to know them. The Entrepreneurial Manager, therefore, should set up a set of procedures that require summaries of all complaints and suggestions to be brought to her or his attention on some regular basis. It is especially the pattern of these complaints and suggestions that you will want to look for. If there is repetition involving a particular product or service, that obviously requires attention. If several people make roughly the same suggestion, that is a suggestion worth very careful examination—much more so than the occasional, off-the-wall, "why don't you do this" sort of suggestion that so often passes as a creative thought.[3]

The use of an Intelligence System will serve as a check on the other Systems. As is so often the case, by the time one finds out about System failure, it is usually too late. Hence, proactivity is of the essence. If problems of flow, exchange, or transformation are occuring, the corrective action can be taken at an early point.

REWARD AND MOTIVATIONAL SYSTEMS

Entrepreneurial Managers need to develop Reward and Motivational Structures. Money is usually thought of as the common reward or motivational element. To be sure, money is very important. The questions of how and when and under what conditions money is applied, however, also require considerable attention.

Because the Entrepreneurial Manager is concerned with the development, implementation, and management of new ideas, special monetary rewards should be made available for individuals in groups who meet this goal. New ideas should be rewarded. Both the suggestion and the implementation should be rewarded. Many new ideas need a great amount of energy and attention for implementation to occur. Without these, the idea will not have the kind of impact or profitability associated with it.

Cash income is not the only thing that motivates people. Psychic income is also important. Elements of psychic income include praise, attention, public recognition, and so on. Entrepreneurial Managers should be aware of the different reward needs that different members of their organization have and seek to differentiate among both kinds and amounts of rewards. It is in this context that the phrase *Reward System* is used. The Reward System refers to an interconnected set of motivators, including money, but also including praise, recognition, and all other psychic rewards (Block and Ornati, 1987). Other parts of the Reward System may include things like more flexible work schedules or time off. Because of these different needs, the Entrepreneurial Manager must pay special attention to the kinds of differentiations required. The most successful Entrepreneurial Managers will provide not only constant rewards but differential rewards of cash and other psychic income elements in order to create a climate that is both conducive to and supportive of the introduction of new ideas.

SYSTEM REVIEW: ENHANCING SYSTEM FUNCTIONING

Establishing and maintaining Systems is crucial to the continued good health of an organization. So, too, is upgrading, improving, enhancing those systems. Failure to do so—being content with the status quo—risks letting the Firm fall behind its competitors in the marketplace who are constantly modifying and improving their established Systems for the better. "If it ain't broke, don't fix it," is a popular notion with some politicians and a great many business people. The fact of the matter is, however, that we must constantly "fix" things that aren't broken—in the sense of modifying, upgrading, or replacing them with newer models—in both government and business. What destroyed the American steel industry, once the most successful in the world? In the main it was a failure on the part of the steel companies to invest on a continuing basis in the new plants and new processes. What made such a shambles of the American automobile industry? To a large degree it was insistence by management and union leadership on work rules and practices that were no longer practical for rapidly evolving, high technology manufacturing environments; it was blind adherence to organizational structures that were no longer appropriate; and it was denial by the large car companies of the evidence of their own market research systems.[4]

To improve their existing Systems, Entrepreneurial Managers have several avenues open to them. The first is regular System review—in addition to regular Structure review. Time after time organizations can be observed calling meetings of divisions, departments, and so on. Much more rarely are those individuals who are implicated in systematic procedures called together. Consider it a truism: Organizations are made up of *both* Structures and Systems. It makes as much sense, therefore, to call all of those together who are concerned with a particular process as it does to call those together who are associated with a particular part.

The Process and Procedure Review Meeting is a special kind of meeting that asks about the functions of specific processes within the organization. These may be sales, marketing, finance, customer or public relations, client processing, and so on. Typically, the individuals in those meetings will not know each other well, even in moderate size organizations. This is because Systems are strings that move out over different organizational parts. That's their nature. Rarely, however, do the individuals involved have a chance to get together. The Process and Procedure Review Meeting is a useful technique for accomplishing this, for solving problems, and for making and implementing improvements.

Sometimes systems need to be reconfigured. Certain crucial features may have been left out of the circulating loop that a particular process required. As organizations grow, especially when they grow quickly, the links and coordination provided by Systems may lag. In some ways the rapidly growing organization is like the lanky adolescent whose progress through the day is more characterized by lurch and stumble than by the smoothness of well-greased bearings because the coordination of all the new parts is not yet totally in place.

ESTABLISHING INFORMAL SYSTEMS

System improvement can be attained by the development and use of *Informal* Systems present in all organizations but rarely thought about consciously. Informal Systems are those sets of flows, exchanges, and transformations that occur spontaneously. The classic water cooler provides a good example. Individuals standing around the water cooler (or having a cup of coffee somewhere else) are exchanging information about the organization, its problems and the things that may impede it from achieving its goals. Typical managers are forever chasing people away from these sites on the grounds that they are not being paid to stand around and shoot the breeze. Actually, those people are working and, without knowing it many times, very likely in the best interests of the Firm. They are engaging in information exchange in ways that are most certainly beneficial to the overall organization in both the short and long runs.

For this reason, Entrepreneurial Managers should consider creating Informal Systems, especially those where employees of different ranks, levels, positions, and locations within the organization have a chance to get together. In the smaller organization, the two, three, or four person organization, these kinds of contacts occur automatically. That's the very nature of such small businesses. But as the organization grows to several members with different responsibilities and commitments, it becomes hard to get together to share information, perspectives, and solve problems. It is only necessary to recall the typical family with teenage children and two working spouses to know that even a five or six person organization can have trouble making the linking Structures work.

A variety of other informal activities, therefore, can be helpful, especially when combined with Management By Walking Around (MBWA) (Peters and Waterman, 1982). Through MBWA, Entrepreneurial Managers can get a firsthand look at the actual operating conditions that staff have to deal with. MBWA is much better than getting reports. It can substantiate certain claims and create questions about others. Semiformal or quasi-formal occasions, such as breakfast or lunch with employees, allow at least the conditions to be created for the expressions of views, complaints, and perspectives across all levels of the organization, including going right to the top.

Information garnered through the use of the Informal and Intelligence Systems is unlikely to be able to be totally processed by the Entrepreneurial Manager. It can, however, be turned over to the Idea Processing System for further exploration. Then the Entrepreneurial Manager can get back to whomever it was who raised the issue with a more concrete response.

Part of the Informal System is not only to get employees to talk to the Entrepreneurial Manager but to talk with each other. An organizational celebration, mentioned in Chapter 8, is a good time for this to happen. People have often said about dinner parties, for example, "It's really the chance to get to meet people rather than the actual dinner that I find beneficial." Similar comments often accompany conferences. All too common is the observation that people meet others from the same town, or even from the same organization, at a conference whom they have not seen in a considerable time—"Isn't it amazing, Joe, that we both had to come all the way from Quinter, Kansas in order to get to talk to each other." Promises are made that this won't be permitted to happen again. The promises are inevitably broken because the power and domination of organizational Structure over organizational process tends to recreate the same conditions as before. All-organization activities, at least, do allow people to get together on some regular basis, enjoy themselves, and remind themselves of the work they have to do with other individuals at some future date.

CONCLUSION

The Entrepreneurial Manager, then, is responsible for the establishment of Entrepreneurial Systems, for detecting and correcting problems in them, and for improving the way they function. Particular emphasis was made for Entrepreneurial Managers on several key systems. First was the establishment of an Idea System, so that the ideas within the organization don't get lost and so that there is a common set of procedures for handling suggestions rather than letting the suggestions surface or not depend on the energy of a particular employee at a particular point in time.

Second, Intelligence Systems need to be created by Entrepreneurial Managers. It is through the Intelligence System that System functioning can be assessed and structural problems identified at an early stage. When emergencies occur, when surprises develop—and they will—the question should never be whether it happened or not, only how often. Once is fine. Twice suggests that the real problem is that the Entrepreneurial Manager does not have an adequate Intelligence System. A good one, therefore, needs to be established and made operational.

Third, we suggested the development and enhancement of Informal Systems. These already exist within the organizational framework, but they are frequently viewed negatively and hostilely as occasions of "not-work" or "time wasters." Leaving aside the valuable contributions to organizational culture that informal interaction creates, it becomes a time to reinforce organizational values and to provide nonroutine occasions for people to get together and meet.

Reward and Motivation Systems need to be established. We pointed out that, although money is a key reward element and motivational factor, other, more psychologically focused rewards are often as important—and sometimes are even more important—to individuals. The Reward System developed by Entrepreneurial Managers should identify what these needs might be and seek to provide them.

Finally, we suggested system review, a more formal way of bringing people together: the Process and Procedures Review Meeting. This meeting is designed to bring together individuals from different structures with natural linkage to one another. These people need to know each other to be aware of each other's problems and perspectives. The complaint of the shirt launderer, mentioned in Chapter 8, could have been dealt with by such a meeting.

NOTES

1. Authoritative augmentation is by no means a trivial problem, and in some organizations can have tragic consequences. To illustrate, some years ago, a graduate student in biochemistry, coming in late to a meeting, misinterpreted an offhand remark by his superior, a senior research scientist, concerning the solution of an extremely difficult research problem. The graduate student, believing he was being instructed to solve that problem, and being conscientious in the extreme, worked at it day and night, abandoning every other part of his life until finally, in despair at being unable to solve it, he committed suicide. Apparently, the student did not realize that the research problem had been one that had baffled the best minds in biochemistry for a generation. All the student had heard, as best it could be determined, was the statement by the senior research scientist that the problem "must be solved." What the student had missed were introductory remarks that put that

particular problem in context with a number of others that *at some time in the future* would have to be solved.

2. Often, Firms do not know how to make use of customer information. Suppose you had a great idea for something Sears should do. Where would you take it? Thinking about this problem right now, you would probably be convinced that it would be ignored.

3. But even these shouldn't be totally ignored, nor should one hesitate to make them. The story is told—and, like so many wonderful business stories, it is probably apocryphal—that Coca Cola, at some time during its early years, paid someone a very large sum of money for making a suggestion to the company of just two words: "bottle it."

4. An excellent illustration of this last point occurred in a 1966 interview of an executive of the Buick Division of General Motors. Betty Hansen, who at that time was a reporter for the Saginaw (Michigan) *News*, did the interview and related it to us in a personal communication. According to Hansen, she conducted the interview on the front porch of the executive's home, located in an exclusive, expensive Flint, Michigan subdivision that was populated almost entirely by Buick executives. To the question, "Do you think foreign car manufacturers will ever gain a significant foothold in the American market?," the executive replied in complete sincerity, "No. Never. Americans want American cars. Look up and down this street. Do you see any foreign cars?" She did not. In fact, in almost every driveway there was a Buick. This sort of self-delusion still plagues the American automobile industry, even as its share of its own market continues to dwindle. Tom Peters made a similar point about General Motors' insularity in an interview with the Detroit *Free Press*, September 7, 1987, p. 1 (O'Connor, 1987, p. 1).

10

Creating Entrepreneurial Staff

#1: "I can do it all." Clark Kent in a speech before the KLS (Kryptonite Lovers Society).

#2: Lone Ranger: "Tonto! We are surrounded by Indians."

Tonto: "What do you mean, 'WE,' paleface?"

#3: "If everyone who reports to you is not smarter than you, you're in deep trouble."

—CEO (anonymous), 1986.

INTRODUCTION

The completion of entrepreneurial responsibilities in the areas of Strategy, Structure, and Systems moves us now to the "soft S" group—the less focused, less well-defined, less well-understood areas of Staffing, Style, and Skills (although aspects of Systems are at least semi-soft). For all of the fuzziness that may surround them, the Entrepreneur cannot ignore these soft S areas.

THE NEED FOR OTHERS

Let us begin our exploration of these somewhat murky waters with an observation that will seem ridiculously simple on its face, yet from which will emerge complexity and convolution: the Entrepreneur needs *Others*. It's the wagon train. Not only is this true for the initial stages of entrepreneurial activity but also in the growth and maturing stages. In any of our achievements, in fact, Others play a crucial and (frequently) seldom recognized role.

A familiar illustration of this is the typical Academy Award "Thank You" speech. Almost without exception (an especially brilliant actress to the contrary and nothwithstanding—"I did it all myself") not only do the recipients accept their awards on behalf of themselves but on behalf of a long (sometimes an interminably long) list of others, all of whom made some contribution. For most of us involved in complex projects, those kinds of "thank you's" are entirely appropriate. We recognize at once the essential correctness of the statement, "I couldn't have done it without: (check one or more) you; the team; the coach; my family; my staff, etc."

Unfortunately, the most dominant American values, focusing on independence and "macho boss" orientations, tend to work against the interdependence frequently needed to achieve results. Still, results *have* been achieved in the past, and there are several answers to this apparent paradox.

One of the most important of these answers, as we've already mentioned, lies in the subordination of talent and credit. The Lois Lanes, the Tontos, the Bumsteads all play crucial roles in the development of the enterprises of their bosses and masters. Yet they rarely get the recognition they deserve. In fact, it is easy to think of the concept of "side kick" as a sort of nonessential, tag-a-long person. That may be true in some instances, but it is far more likely the case that side kicks are essential partners in the accomplishment of entrepreneurial purpose.

Entrepreneurial Management, then, requires that the entrepreneurial venture be staffed with the appropriate individuals. It also means recognizing what is required and both seeking the kinds of people who are needed from outside the Firm and developing those who are already employees of the Firm. All Staff must then have the opportunity for advancing with the development of the Firm. Without an adequate Staff, no Strategy, no Structure, no System will work at all.

There are eight elements, then, that Entrepreneurial Managers need to attend to when thinking about their Staff:

1. *Recognizing* the need for others;
2. *Recognizing* the kinds of Staff conditions that are relevant;
3. *Recruiting* the appropriate Staff;
4. *Inspiriting* new and old staff, which almost always must include their family members to some degree;
5. *Rewarding* performance;
6. Offering opportunities for *Advancement*;
7. *Training* the Staff;
8. *Evaluating* the Staff.

Let's now take a detailed look at each of these eight elements that must occupy the attention of the Entrepreneurial Manager in the Staff area.

RECOGNIZING THE NEED FOR OTHERS

An initial step in the staff development process is a recognition that staff are crucial, and that it is the totality of people working together that makes the enterprise successful. There is a story about the organizational researcher illustrating the absence of this recognition. The researcher was asking individuals in a many-layered company the following question, "If technology permitted it, at what level do you think this company could, really, be automated?" The answer was the same from every level of the organization. "Below me." Each respondent was convinced of her or his own importance, and viewed those below as "merely" technical. It is this kind of attitude that has brought the productivity problems to us that we experience today.

RECOGNIZING RELEVANT STAFF CONDITIONS

The second step in the Staff development process is recognizing the crucial nature of Staff and taking inventory of the current staff. In a small organization this won't take long. In a larger organization more time will be needed. This process is called *profiling Staff demographics*. It deals with the degrees and backgrounds of Staff. It also deals, to the extent it is possible to know, with interests, goals, and so on. If you depend on a group of individuals to assist you in carrying out your venture, then it is important to know who they are and what they are like. This demographic profile, alone, allows some questions to begin to be asked: "Do we have the kind of Staff that is going to meet the needs that we are going to be facing?" "Do we have the kind of Staff capable of dealing with the Strategies and tactics that we are developing?" Negative answers to these questions do not automatically mean that you must fire everyone. Instead, you must now begin to ask still further questions about how the current Staff can be brought to the level or area of competence that is needed. This is what Grove (1983) calls *task relevant maturity*.

A crucial point of recognition is that jobs today are much more complex and multifaceted. This is especially true in the existing entrepreneurial venture and *very* much the case in the new entrepreneurial venture. There, everyone is doing everything. Specialization and focus are out the window (if they ever came in the door). People do what has to be done. Job descriptions are ambiguous, if they exist at all. It is this complexity that makes individuals difficult to replace.

The Entrepreneurial Manager, therefore, takes inventory of the Staff available. He or she recognizes that members of the Staff are valuable, contributing members of the venture.

RECRUITING THE APPROPRIATE STAFF

As the entrepreneurial venture begins to get under way, Entrepreneurial Managers need to select Staff. Few processes are as crucial. There is limited venture capital available. Some of that will go to pay to the Staff you select. How should you proceed?

First, you—and all Entrepreneurial Managers—should keep a private list of individuals they know, with whom they have worked, and with whom they would like to work again at some time. These people may be anyone from persons who do cleaning, persons who do accounting or effective sales people to company pilots and so on. This list should consist of individuals who have impressed you, who represent a sort of fantasy team. As you contemplate starting a new venture, you begin with a list of a number of individuals whom you have observed work and produce and who are available to start. Obviously, you probably won't get all of them. You might not even get any of them, but the list provides a place to begin. And frequently, individuals whom you appreciate and admire know other individuals whose work you might also appreciate and admire. Those on your list, then, can be an invaluable source of recruitment leads. And, as you talk about your idea with them, you receive good advice.

The emphasis we place here on personal observation and the actual carrying out of tasks represents the central kind of criterion for hiring Staff. Individuals who have produced in the past can be expected to produce in the future.

Implied in this suggestion is a de-emphasis on the interview process for hiring employees. The interview process is one fraught with difficulties. It is a tense time both for the interviewer and the interviewee at which neither may be at their best. It often does not ask the interviewee to actually perform the tasks for which the interviewee might be hired. Rather, the prospective employee is invited to talk about the kind of performance that might be involved. The test, therefore, is indirect at best. Instead, you should seek work samples and attempt to judge as much by the past as possible.

Entrepreneurial Managers should also seek varied backgrounds and boundary crossing activities. The very kinds of things that are often discounted in a resume or record, from an Entrepreneurial Manager's point of view, are likely to be pluses. Individuals who have done different things have a range of perspectives. They are likely to be more adaptive, more flexible, more willing to try new things than those with more singular backgrounds. Those who have been involved in boundary crossing activities in particular would be especially good at Systems design and implementation as they have had the experience of different business cultures and the impacts that these different cultures have on work styles and interpretations.

As you hire, you should not only look at people, but also at roles. The entrepreneurial organization needs different roles to keep it functioning. It needs Idea Generator roles to be filled (Galbraith, 1982). It needs Champion roles to be filled. Indeed, Entrepreneurial Managers need to be sensitive to the whole range of Competencies when thinking about filling any particular slot.

If you are looking for innovative individuals in particular, some of the best advice comes from Galbraith (1982), who says:

The best idea sponsors and idea reservation managers ... are people who have experienced innovation early within careers and are comfortable with it. They will have been exposed to (the) risk, uncertainty, parallel experiences, (and) repeated failures that led to learning, coupling rather than assembly line thinking, long time frames, and personal control systems based on people and ideas not numbers and budget variances. (P. 23)

As Galbraith points out, they can be either recruited, or they can be developed from the inside. In either case some inspiriting is necessary.

INSPIRITING NEW AND OLD STAFF

The inspiriting process encompasses the ways in which Entrepreneurial Managers get individuals to do the will of the organization. In some respects the problem is a simple one because there are only three Strategies available: *force*, *inducement*, and *commitment*. These are broad, general Strategies that completely encompass the available techniques to secure compliance. In force, individuals are simply ordered to undertake certain tasks. Force is the backbone of the Theory X Manager. (See Chapter 11 for a Theory X definition.) The problem with force is that it generates resentment and does not invite employees to think of ways they might independently and innovatively contribute to organizational mission and purpose.

Inducement, the classic economic cash reward, suggests that if one accomplishes a particular task, one will be paid. Unfortunately, this Reward System tends to develop commitment to the reward rather than the organization. Thus, if another organization comes along and offers a larger reward, the very Reward System teaches the individual to jump ship and move to the more lucrative location.

The third area, commitment, centers on the inspiriting process. The Entrepreneurial Manager will use command (force) and consensus (commitment). Because of the uncertain nature of the venture, however, and the possibility or actuality of rapid growth, commitment of individuals to the venture is needed if stability is to be achieved and if a marketable service or product is to be provided.

Commitment is built through interpersonal interaction and support. The Entrepreneurial Manager, therefore, must first model the kinds of behaviors that he or she expects from staff. If long hours are part of what is to be important here, then the Entrepreneurial Manager must model that kind of commitment. Hence, modelling is the first step in the inspiriting process.

Coaching is a second step. It is often difficult for those individuals who, in a particular case, know what to do to let others do it. Asking one's child to help around the house with some task is a good example. One arrives on the scene, finds the tasks half done, and jumps in to finish up. Unfortunately, when this happens, the child never learns to complete the task. The same is true for the employee who starts but is not allowed to complete an assignment. That employee feels the anger and disappointment of not finishing but never the satisfaction of completion. For sports teams, the role of the coach is crucial in most cases for determining how well the individual players and the team as a whole play and, to a large extent, whether the team wins or loses. A coach cannot jump into the game and play it. Whatever playing is to be done must be done by the players. In many respects this analogy translates well into the business enterprise. Lots of business tasks must be done by the employees. The Entrepreneurial Manager cannot run around delivering pizzas, making Big Macs, installing circuit boards, or licking envelopes. It is the *employee* who is the fundamental actor. Recognition of this fact gives meaning and value to the coaching concept.

A third step in the inspiriting process is to explain strategic direction and to provide tactical directives. To be sure, the overall organization has a Strategy. It is often unclear to an individual employee how what she or he might be doing in a particular case relates to that overall Strategy. This interpretation needs to be made by the Entrepreneurial Manager and reinforced continually. This reinforcing is especially important where the tasks do not seem terribly meaningful in and of themselves. Washing dishes in a restaurant, for example, must seem like a terribly unimportant task until the dishwasher fully understands the health implications of dirty dishes, the restaurant's commitment to quality, as evidenced by the cleanest possible dishes, and the devastating public relations impact on a restaurant's reputation when a customer receives a dirty dish. Such concepts need to be bolstered periodically.

In relation to Strategic interpretation, there needs to be tactical direction. In the case of a restaurant, for example, tactical direction refers to the way the restaurant's commitment to excellence is translated into reality through the kinds of things done by each employee. This reinforcement must be provided on an ongoing basis by the Entrepreneurial Manager.

REWARDING PERFORMANCE

As we already noted in Chapter 9 rewards play a crucial role in the Staff process and, indeed, in the whole entrepreneurial venture. It is crucial that there be a Reward System in place—and we've already talked about this in

Chapter 9. Similarly, the process of reward allocation must work smoothly, getting rewards to those individuals for whom they are designed. We took that point up when we talked about the Reward System. What we need to do now is pull two points together and add a few more.

To restate the obvious once again, Staff require financial compensation. Before we move from the idea of financial compensation, it is important to consider the various ways compensation can be offered. Salary, of course, is a direct way. In addition, bonuses, individual and collective, can be a very effective incentive. Individual bonuses are those that accrue to some particular individual for his performance. Collective bonuses, somewhat less common but very effective when used, accrue to groups, committees, task forces, action teams, and so on for outstanding collective performance. Especially as Firms are moving into the use of groups, the group bonus concept is one that is worth thinking about.

Increments can be in dollars or in percentages of a base salary. Dollar increments benefit those with lower salary, because they wind up being a greater percent of base salary, relatively speaking. Percentage increments tend to benefit those in the higher ranks, giving as they do higher dollar amounts. Often Entrepreneurial Managers seek some combination of dollar and percentage bonus systems, in order to balance the competing tendencies of the two systems. Furthermore, you can divide increments between allocations to the base and yearly bonuses. Naturally, allocations to the base would stay and become part of the employee's salary. Bonuses can be involved in special recognition as a sort of "re-ward" for work accomplished. Again, both of these systems are useful.

The concept of re-ward, however, is a re-active one, providing income to someone after a particular task has been accomplished. Rewards are often cash, but part of the reward is the public recognition that an employee has accomplished something. You may wish to consider, however, whether or not the reward is an effective motivator or as effective as something else. You might want to make use of a pre-ward in combination with a reward. A pre-ward represents an investment in an individual. The reward says that a particular goal has been accomplished in an outstanding way. The preward says that in order to accomplish a particular goal, effort beyond that normally to be expected will be required. Coming as it does at the beginning of the effort rather than at the end, the pre-ward is more likely to be an effective stimulus. It involves the recipient individual in a sense of obligation and commitment much more than a reward. It also allows the Entrepreneurial Manager to focus the effort of Staff more directly. Thus, it is a concept worth considering.

Even though money is varied in the way it can be applied, there are a whole range of other rewards and prewards; that is, goods that can be drawn from the workplace and that can be used by the Entrepreneurial Manager to recognize talent and to encourage motivation. One of the very important ones—and increasingly recognized as such—is time. Especially today, when more women are in the labor force and where both men and women are undertaking child care responsibilities, the flexibility of time may be an almost incalculable benefit. You may very well want to look at your enterprise from the point of view of enhancing its flexibility. Many of us work from nine to five simply out of habit, and we tend to think that employees should do the same. What is really important, however, is getting a total effort out of an employee and trying to arrange the job so that it can be done by the employee. Although some situations don't have the flexibility that would allow for differing blocks of time, many jobs increasingly do. All Entrepreneurial Managers should be alert to this possibility.

Other kinds of gratifications that workers get from an employment situation are less tangible but no less important. Colleagueship—"the people I work with"—is a very important reward in and of itself. This is another reason for an emphasis on recruitment. New employees should not only please the Boss, they should also please other people with whom they have to work. In some respects that may be even more important, as they are less likely to work with the Boss to the same extent as with the other employees. Once individuals become committed to an enterprise, their willingness to become involved depends in part on how involved everyone else is. It's at this point where hard work and team effort become fun—because of the interpersonal enjoyment each of us gets out of being involved in a key enterprise.

Whether freshly started or operating sectors within existing businesses, Entrepreneurial efforts are, by their nature, new efforts. Participating in something new, something challenging, is inherently a reward for some individuals. The recruitment phase, therefore, needs to search out those for whom the new is also the exciting. The venture, itself, and the opportunity to participate in it can be a significant reward that should not be overlooked.

Finally, equity, both financial and psychological, is something that people in the entrepreneurial area need to be aware of and develop. Individuals who participate in the development of something new and something different, whether it is an idea, product or service, like to have some recognition of their involvement, some credit for their participation. Part of this is simple recognition: the announcement that they were involved— putting their name on a product, procedure, or service, for example. Individuals love to have planets and stars named after them, new species of plants and animals, and so on. This kind of wish is very powerful and very important. In addition to credit, financial equity to be realized later, is also worth considering.

The whole point of rewarding the Staff is to recognize that there is a large range of rewards available and to try to find that mix that is both healthy for the venture and healthy for the employees. That search will be well rewarded in terms of commitment, cooperation, and production.

OFFERING OPPORTUNITIES FOR ADVANCEMENT

It is certainly possible to think of the concept of employee advancement as part of the Reward System. Upward mobility, with its attendant psychic and financial rewards may well be the best package of all. For whatever reason, the wish for upward mobility seems to be a central American value. For this reason, Entrepreneurial Managers need to try to provide ways in which individuals can advance.

Providing advancement is difficult for a number of reasons. Many entrepreneurial ventures are small with few positions to advance into. A second interrelated difficulty is that Entrepreneurs often seek to protect their own positions. All of the things that the Entrepreneurial Manager does are done, in part at least, for himself or herself. For this reason, upward mobility can be threatening to the Entrepreneurial Manager.

The first way out of these dilemmas is to recognize that all employees wish to get ahead. That's part of the reason that they are interested in new ideas, new developments, new products, and new services. Ways must be found, therefore, to encourage this powerful motivation in employees.

In addition, the Entrepreneurial Manager must not be threatened by others' wishes to advance. This is almost easier done than said. It involves only a slight modification of perspective. The Entrepreneurial Manager is the coach. No matter how good the players get, they are never going to replace the coach. By the same token, no matter how good the coach gets, the coach is not going to play in the game. The rule of thumb for you to follow as an Entrepreneurial Manager, therefore, should always be to have people more talented than yourself working for you. This not only pushes you to some extent, but it creates the kind of product or service performance or production that will work to your credit in the end.

Aaron Wildavsky (1960) says that he once saw three churches of the same denomination in a town so small that it struck him one would have served quite nicely. But, he observed that if there were three churches, there were also three presidents of the church boards, three sets of church boards, three vice-presidents of church boards, and so on. In other words, Entrepreneurial Managers can create niches, titles, assignments that gratify employees' cravings for special recognition and upward mobility on the one hand and on the other, help the organization by further specifying and locating the work to be done. In no sense is the creation and development of the positions and assignments fake. Rather, they represent attempts to focus the work and to provide recognition for it.

TRAINING THE STAFF

Of all the things that Entrepreneurial Managers pay attention to, the one that may have the most value, and is frequently the least well thought out, is the whole issue of employee training and development. This is especially necessary in the area of Entrepreneurial Management. Manager and employee are at the cutting edge of activity in the particular product or service field. For this reason, the opportunity to learn more about the particular product or service and to work through some of the relevant ideas is absolutely essential. Without such development and training the products will not develop. Notwithstanding that fact, it is axiomatic that the better prepared the employee, the better the contribution that employee is likely to make. Regular opportunities for employee training and development, therefore, should be provided.

In part, the training and development of employees is for the employer's own benefit. In part, however, it's for the employee's own benefit. This latter is a sticking point with some employers, because they fear that the money spent training and developing an employee may ultimately redound to the benefit of some other company (Morita, 1986). Although the concern has some validity, it is nevertheless part of the risk that Entrepreneurial Managers must take. It is quite true that after receiving additional training, an employee may bolt. The action to take, however, is not to stop training but to find out what it is about your company or division or department or business that was sufficiently unattractive that it allowed for other organizations to make better bids.

Typically, organizations that have based their entire compensation on cash experience these kinds of problems more than others. Cash is easy to increase. New colleagues, a rewarding and gratifying work environment, a chance to be centrally involved in a developing project of great importance—these kinds of compensation packages—are harder to replicate.

EVALUATING THE STAFF

To complete the attention to Staff, a System of evaluation must be present, as well. It is difficult to apply some of the other elements mentioned here (rewarding or advancing, for example) if you do not know the past level of performance. There are lots of ways Staff can be evaluated, and an adaptation of the Structure for organizational evaluation (monitoring, oversight, assessment, and appraisal) can be used here—although the first two might be a bit much for many Staff. Still, whatever the System/Structure, several points need to be kept in mind.

First, understand that some System is necessary. All Firms, in fact, have Evaluation Systems. Some people get ahead and some don't. The real questions are whether the System is the right one and whether it has the right results; people who are talented and who contribute are the ones who get rewarded. Specifying the System means that you and the Staff can look at it.

Second, apply the System across the board. Often there are two (or more) Evaluation Systems—those that are announced and those that are operative. For Entrepreneurial Managers, it is crucial that those who contribute innovatively will be evaluated well. This is good for the individuals, but it is also good for the organization.

Third, let the individuals have some participation in the design of the System and the actual, yearly evaluation. This involvement yields great gains when troublesome findings come up.

Fourth, be proactive. Rather than evaluation *after* the year ends, work with the Staff to set goals *first*. Then ask the Staff to evaluate at year's end how they did. This also serves to alert the Entrepreneurial Manager to resources that need to be produced if specified goals are to be met. In addition, it is always easier to do a monitoring check in June if goals have been specified in January.

CONCLUSION

In no sense have all of the elements that an Entrepreneurial Manager needs to attend to with Staff been touched upon here. The main categories do provide a sort of checklist that you may wish to use in order to see if you are covering some of the most crucial bases.

Management is often thought of as "productivity through people." The people are the Staff, the team, the employees, the colleagues. Without them the venture will not succeed. Only through them can goals be reached. The first step in understanding this process is understanding thoughts and truth. Without that recognition very little else that you do will make a great deal of difference. With it, attending to matters of recognizing, recruiting, inspiriting, rewarding, advancing, and training staff will pay great dividends.

11

Creating Entrepreneurial Style

As in all important aspects of life, style is everything.

—Anonymous

INTRODUCTION

At most management meetings, a lot of time is spent discussing the issue of management Style: what Styles are preferred, what Styles are disliked, what is positive Style, what is negative Style. It is also true that employees in more informal settings talk a great deal about the Style of their bosses. Yet, few concepts are as elusive and hard to pin down in any concrete way as this matter of Style.

Style seems to be the *way* an individual goes about doing the job rather than the specific techniques used. Style is best thought of as the distinctive pattern of behaviors and actions that characterize a particular manager, a group of managers, or a particular organization. For that reason, we divide this discussion into two categories: personal Style as an Entrepreneurial Manager and organizational Style.

PERSONAL STYLE

Reams of material have been written on Style. Bass (1981) provides a particularly good summary. There have been discussions beyond counting of people-oriented managers and product-oriented managers, Theory X managers and Theory Y managers—and now, of course, Theory Z managers.[1] Tests are available to find out if individuals have "Entrepreneurial Style" or fit the entrepreneurial mode. Individuals agonize over whether they have the right Style or the wrong Style.

The first thing that needs to be said about these ruminations is that there does not appear to be one Style that is always effective and always leads to success. Entrepreneurial Managers, therefore, might just as well relax a bit in their pursuit of the perfect Style. There isn't one. Several factors account for this fact.

To begin with, conditions differ. A Style that might be successful under one set of circumstances might fail in another.

Second, there are antecedent and consequent conditions to a particular episode of managing with a particular Style that cause it to be successful or not.

Third, people differ in their response to particular Styles. An open Style that emphasizes closeness and intimacy may work well with some employees and be rejected as inappropriate by others.

The main conclusion we can draw from all of these is that a Style repertoire is the best. If Style is, as Erving Goffman (1959) suggests, "the presentation of self in everyday life," then it is quite possible for Entrepreneurial Managers to vary the kinds of presentations of self that they make, at least within some range. These variations can occur in different situations, with different people, and as the conditions under which one works change. In point of fact, we probably do this anyway. Most of us act differently when we are "out with the girls" or "out with the guys" than we do at home. What the Entrepreneurial Manager must particularly avoid, however, is to get into a stylistic rut in which she or he is always the same—or always appears to be the same—regardless of the conditions and situations. In Chapter 12 we talk about an "observing ego" and the way in which one tries to observe oneself adjust. That concept can be usefully applied here, as well, in terms of the development of differing Styles. Think of yourself as an actor on a stage, playing different roles. Sometimes you may need a tougher, more directive role. At other times you may need a more understanding role. Although it may not be possible for individuals who are oriented in the "directive" direction to shift into an "understanding" direction very easily, there might be times and situations when this new Style could be tried out.

In sum, then, there appears to be no consensus on *the* effective Style. Rather, a variety of Styles seem to be associated with success and with failure. The ability to have a range of Styles available, then, and to seek to select Styles as the situation calls for them appears to be the most solid step to take right now.

CHARACTER AND LEVEL OF STYLE

There are two key aspects of Style: *character* and *level*. The character of a Style refers to certain choices about approaches that an individual Entrepreneur might make. There are Participative vs. Directive Styles, Autocratic vs. Democratic Styles, Task-Oriented vs. People-Oriented Styles, Fixed Styles vs. Situational Styles. These are among the most important divisions, though it is certainly possible to identify others. As you will come to understand when you finish our chapter on Styles, you do not want to have a single Style. Instead, you will want to have a role repertoire that allows for a number of comfortable Styles to be available for selection.

You can also think of Style as the level of performance, regardless of the particular character of any particular Style. When someone says, "He has a great deal of style," the reference is to level rather than to character. You can have an Authoritarian Style and still carry it off with aplomb. You can also have a wooden and jerky Authoritarian Style. The same is true of each of the others. The five-stage hierarchy of leadership competence that Dreyfus and Dreyfus (1986) suggest fits in well here. They identify: (1) the Novice Stage; (2) the Advanced Beginner Stage; (3) the Competence Stage; (4) the Proficiency Stage; and (5) the Expert (or Master) Stage. These serve as generalized, developmental foci through which we all progress, whether the focus is on entrepreneurship, tennis, chess, or fly fishing.

The following are types or characters of Style:

1. *Participative.* A Participative Style is one that involves a wide range of organizational members in setting the direction or purpose of the organizational System.

2. *Directive.* A Directive Style centers the responsibilities for these tasks in a small executive cadre or, even more restrictively, with a particular individual (often the CEO or "boss").

3. *Autocratic.* An Autocratic Style may be linked to the Directive Style in many instances, but it tends to emphasize a shorter, more crude, and less sophisticated mode of interaction than the Directive Style. A Directive Style can emerge from Competence and knowledge. An Autocratic Style tends to emerge from superior position. There are, of course, times when the Autocratic Style does not involve the knowledge implicit in the Directive Style. This makes the Autocratic Style all the more difficult to tolerate.

4. *Democratic.* A Democratic Style, on the other hand—like a Participative Style—involves many individuals in decision making; but the involvement tends to be on the basis of prior decisions about entitlements rather than relevance and appropriateness, which are implicit in the participative mode.

5. *Task-Centered.* A Task-Centered Style focuses on the accomplishment of organizational purposes, often specified in very specific terms; e.g., "the bottom line." Organizational Strategies, Structures, and Systems are assessed in terms of their established contribution to task accomplishment.

6. *People-Oriented.* A People-Oriented Style, in contrast, assesses organizational activities in terms of the personal impacts on Staff, customers, clients, and local communities. Allegedly narrow and mechanical definitions of organizational purpose and measures of that purpose are rejected.

7. *Fixed*. A Fixed Style is one that is invariant and repetitive regardless of the particular Conditions.

8. *Situational*. A Situational Style is one that may vary considerably with those same Conditions. A situational Entrepreneur, therefore, might be Autocratic and Democratic, Participative and Directive, and relatively untroubled by the apparent conflict among these various Styles.

Level of Skill Performance

Like character, the level of Skill performance is also an aspect of Style. Regardless of what you may know in the intellectual or interpersonal area, you must somehow give expression to your knowledge. Futhermore, it's not only a matter of giving expression to your competencies, you've got to do it reasonably well. It is always true that stylistic assessments involve not only describing what one has chosen ("she plays badminton better than tennis"), but how well the game is played ("and she plays tennis outstandingly well").

The distinction between character of Style and level of Style is an important one. It may help to clarify that distinction to think of character as a kind of horizontal measure of Style, and level as a kind of vertical measure of Style. By using something like the five-step assessment form of Dreyfus and Dreyfus (1986) mentioned earlier, it's possible to get a pretty good idea about where one fits on both dimensions. The Expert or Master, for example, is able to understand all cues, handle all developments, and do so in the same way a gold medal roller skating champion does, with apparent ease and unconcern. The Novices, like individuals who are just beginning to learn to dance on skates, are still counting, aloud or in their minds, "one, two, three; one, two, three." Their focus is on skate wheels and elementary form, not on grace, aesthetics, and the special nuances of performance.

THE "ELEMENTS OF STYLE"

Whatever Style you adopt, there are some common elements that Entrepreneurial Managers should seek to infuse in that Style, elements that seem to be more likely than not to be associated with the production of new ideas for products and services and their implementation in the work force.

People Enhancing

The first element is to adopt (or try to) a people enhancing posture. There are many ways that this can be done. Supporting people does not mean that you are a wimp. There are different ways of communicating encouragement and backing. There are tough coaches who are hostile and negative, and there are tough coaches who are supportive and positive. There are laid back individuals who provide support directly, and there are laid back individuals who provide support more distantly and removed. Because the Entrepreneurial Manager depends on people for ideas, it is imperative that he or she adopt a people enhancing, people supportive Style in order to permit new ideas to be developed and shared.

Creativity

The Entrepreneurial Manager needs to exemplify and model creativity as an aspect of her or his Style. This means physically doing different things in the organization. Staff take messages from a wide range of sources; and if the Entrepreneurial Manager asserts new things, new ideas, new products and services, but never gives any evidence of trying anything new, that is construed as a double message. Usually, in a double message situation, individuals select the message that is potentially least harmful. In this case, not doing anything seems closest to the winning strategy. Creativity also needs to become an ongoing part of the Entrepreneurial Manager's life. Thus, attempting to be creative in some comparable area (such as an artistic or sports arena) keeps the creative juices flowing and keeps the problems and difficulties of creativity squarely before the Entrepreneurial Manager. If an Entrepreneurial Manager can demonstrate creativity, this will attract others who are also creative and liberate the quasi-creativity in the rest.

Optimism

The Entrepreneurial Manager needs to bring in a certain optimism into his or her Style. The reason for this is straight forward. In the new idea, product, or service game, everything is uncertain or ambiguous and looks odd. Discouragement, defeat, and withdrawal always seem just a step away. When an individual is proceeding into the unknown, Staff need hope: hope that the idea will work, hope that the new product or service will be successful, hope that others will see the possibilities. It is this impetus that the Entrepreneurial Manager needs to provide.

The provision of hope is not blind, however. The Entrepreneurial Manager is continually questioning the new idea, putting it in different contexts, and seeing how it might work under varying conditions. But these are positive tests that any new idea initiator expects and accepts. If the new idea for a product or a service does not meet these tests, then hope of a different sort must be provided: hope that the next idea will be successful or hope that this idea, when certain other developments have matured and can be combined with it, might at that later time be successful.

Hope is a great stimulus and should be a part of the Style Repertoire of any Entrepreneurial Manager. It involves focusing on the possible while planning around the potentially problematic.

The Ability to Doubt

As important as the ability to hope is, it is no more important than the ability to doubt. Hope tends to be expressed toward the *new* product or service. Doubt tends to be expressed toward the *existing* product or service. The reasons for the latter are the inverse of those for the former. In the new area we tend to look for the possibilities. We stress these while keeping the problems in view. But we don't permit problems to be completely determining. We already know the possibilities for the existing product or service. Therefore, doubt, questions, or wondering about whether or not that particular product or service is actually doing all that it possibly can should take precedence.

A second element of doubt has to do with established wisdom. It would be too strong to say that Entrepreneurial Managers should reject established wisdom. It is also fair to say, however, that breakthroughs have occurred over history in exactly the areas where what people said couldn't be done, was done. The Entrepreneurial Manager, therefore, must keep working at an open-minded approach. It is helpful to remember that most things we are now certain can't be improved upon, will be improved upon shortly.

It follows, then, that the Entrepreneurial Manager must give permission readily to question established wisdom. It is in this easy grant of permission to question that doubt has its most effective stylistic impact. Picture yourself in a marketing meeting of some sort. A new Staff member suggests that a new and different (from the Firm's point of view) market segment be targeted for the Firm's product or service. The other Staff members in the meeting— old hands with your organization—say something like, "We've already tried to crack that group and failed. It cost us a bundle before. It would just be pouring money down a rathole now. Everyone knows that 'they' (whoever 'they' are) aren't going to buy our electric fork."

Now's your chance to prove what a solid Entrepreneurial Manager you are. You can certainly agree with the established wisdom. That will close a potential line of inquiry, and there are times when that is the right thing to do. This is especially true if recent studies of the market have just been done and the data are fresh and persuasive. There are also times when going with the flow of established wisdom is not the appropriate course. Indeed, more often than we care to admit in situations like this, the hard data is old and stale—or worse, there is no hard data, only lore. Conviction is high that the old situation still prevails but evidence is slim. When that is true, you should adopt a somewhat different scenario in your Entrepreneurial Manager role; namely, hedge your bets. In other words, adopt the prime directive of bureaucracy: When in doubt, equivocate. Respond with something like, "Well, it's been a long time since we've looked into this. There's a lot of change going on. Maybe it would be worth taking a look at. If we were to take another look at it, what are the kinds of things we ought to keep in

mind?" This is an opening, freeing the kind of response that doesn't necessarily agree with the new employee's proposals but does validate the idea
of the proposal and gives permission for the group to begin to think about
it. That's the power of doubt.

Be Curious

The last aspect of Style to be mentioned here is curiosity. Curiosity involves asking questions: Why is that? How can we explain this result? What
do you suppose was going on there? These simple questions, especially in
a group context, are enormously powerful. They become yet another way
to cut through established wisdom.

As humans, we are always simplifying and short-cutting causal relationships
in our environment—this causes that; gods are bowling and cause thunder;
lightening is the spear of the gods, and so on. Throughout history, quickie
explanations of this sort have been the staple of many. A more select few,
however, have asked additional questions. Some have even gone so far as
to fly a kite in the rain, to see whether or not electricity would come down
the wire attached to the kite.

Curiosity, as an aspect of Style, is so very important because, like doubt,
it is liberating. It opens things up for investigation. It suspends prejudgment
and, thus, allows new ideas, new procedures, and new approaches to enter
the System.

Listen

One of the most important aspects of leadership, as Robert Bolton says
in his book, *People Skills* (1979), is the ability to listen. McCormack (1986)
agrees. All too often managers find themselves directing rather than receiving, instructing rather than absorbing, commanding rather than consulting.
Entrepreneurial Managers in particular need to listen. All too frequently we
miss the key points that others are sharing with us because we are already
preparing our reply. Listening involves focused attention on the speaker. It
involves setting aside one's own thoughts, wishes, desires to get into the
conversation, desires to put the speaker down. It requires interaction but of
a very special sort. Some listeners use greatly specified and highly detailed
questions as an apparent listening device when, in fact, it is an attacking
device. Questions are important to clarify, to probe, to reformulate but not
to trap or to corner speakers. If you listen, you not only gain the ideas that
are being shared in the exchange but an extra positive benefit, as well. That
is the interpersonal respect that arises toward the listener from the speaker.

Think, for a moment, about the last time someone really listened to you.
It was probably a terrific and memorable experience. Whatever the Style

that the Entrepreneurial Manager uses, or whatever range of Styles are selected, listening should be an extremely important part.

ORGANIZATIONAL STYLE

Organizational Style does not require a great deal of attention here because it is really derived from, and is an expression of, organizational culture. One way to think of the matter overall, however, is to compare Japanese and American organizations in toto, to derive a sense of the overall differences in emphasis and approach. In any such comparison it should be understood that we are dealing with what Max Weber called *ideal types* (Lockwood, 1964). When looked at in any real detail, there are lots of variations within each. Furthermore, whatever is dominant in one culture is certainly sub-dominant in the other. Thus, Japanese characteristics can be found in all American organizations, though they are usually not as prominent. Conversely, American characteristics are to be found to some degree in all Japanese organizations.[2] Nevertheless, it is possible to get a sense of stylistic difference from such an overall comparison.

To begin to understand the difference between Japanese and American organizations is to look at Japanese and American rice. If you have eaten both kinds of rice, you will instantly recognize the important differences. Japanese rice sticks together in big clumps. It's quite possible to eat it with chopsticks because it packs together so well. You might say (though not too loudly) that Japanese rice has a collective orientation. American rice is just the opposite. Each grain fights for its own independence. A fork full of American rice has most of the rice falling back into the bowl. As a metaphor for the different orientations of the two countries, rice paints a picture as well as any: collectivism vs. individualism.

A second aspect of culture can be seen in the contrast between the bonsai and the burger. The bonsai tree is one that requires meticulous care and a long length of time to produce. The burger, in contrast, is the center of our fast food industry—made within seconds and often consumed even more quickly. These contrasting elements express long-term orientation of Japan relative to the short-term orientation of America.

A third point of difference is in the mode of expression. The alphabet used by Americans is, in its way, a marvel of economy. All of our words are made using combinations, and some of those letters are used only rarely. All languages are not this way, including Japanese. Japanese uses three separate writing systems including a large number of borrowed Chinese characters to communicate. Thus, to be moderately well-educated in Japan, one needs to know about 1,200 of these separate characters; to read the paper, about 2,000; and to be literate, a good deal more than that. There are, to be sure, some commonly used characters. But these number in the hundreds. The implications of these differences are stunning. One of these

Table 11.1
Ouchi's Summary of Japanese/American Organizational Differences

Japanese Organizations	North American Organizations
1. Lifetime Employment	Short Term Employment
2. Slow Evaluation and Promotion	Rapid Evaluation and Promotion
3. No Specialized Career Paths	Specialized Career Paths
4. Implicit Control Mechanisms	Explicit Control Mechanisms
5. Collective Decision Making	Individual Decision Making
6. Collective Responsibility/	Individual Responsibility
7. Wholistic Concern	Segmented Concern

Ouchi, 1982, pp.48-49.

is that there are no typewriters capable of handling the entire range of the written language. No keyboard is extensive enough to hold even the common characters.[3] Given such a system, interpersonal communication in great detail is almost a necessity.

These cultural differences are the springboard for some organizational differences. They are best summarized by Ouchi (1982, pp. 48–49) in Table 11.1.

Naturally, these distinctions are oversimplified, but they do provide a sense of the way in which Japanese organizations may differ from American organizations. It may well be that a combination of these two rather opposing Styles would be most productive. Ouchi comments that:

In a Type Z company, the explicit and the implicit seem to exist in a state of balance. While decisions weigh the complete analysis of facts, they are also shaped by serious attention to questions of whether or not this decision is "suitable," whether or not it "fits" the company. A company that isolates subspecialities is hardly capable of achieving such fine grained forms of understanding. Perhaps the underlying cause is the loss of the ability for disparate departments within a single organization to communicate effectively with one another. They communicate in the sparse, inadequate language of numbers because numbers are the only language all can understand in a reasonably symmetrical fashion. (P. 61)

What Ouchi is suggesting is, in effect, what we discussed in Chapter 6 on Subculture. There are competing orientations, competing Styles. Emphasis on a single Style is likely to become problematic. The very best Entrepreneurial Managers are able to produce combinations of Styles within their organization that meet evolving needs. A mix of Japanese and American Styles may be one step in this direction, but other combinations—including more autocratic vs. more democratic—may also be appropriate.

CONCLUSION

Style remains an elusive concept. Although all seem to understand that it is the way organizations and individuals go about achieving their goals, the very concept of Style seems to have resisted attempts to provide a complete list of Style alternatives. It may be that the elusiveness of the concept itself accounts for the fact that rather different Styles are found to be both successes and failures, depending on a range of antecedent and subsequent conditions and, possibly, the skill of the individual person in displaying the Style. The conclusion suggested here is that, rather than seeking *a* successful Style, Entrepreneurial Managers should cultivate a *range* of Styles or a range of ways in which they can present themselves that will vary, depending on the situations in which they find themselves. Given that difference, however, some common elements of Style, aimed specifically at the encouragement of new ideas for products and services, have been suggested.

Organizational Style evolves from and links to organizational culture. That, in turn, links to national culture. Contrasts between Japanese and American Styles can be seen as examples of different approaches that could be combined in different ways, depending on the particular time, location, employee mix, and other variables.

NOTES

1. These popular initials refer to different orientations toward people. Theory X managers assume that individuals do not wish to work, have to be watched, pushed, and checked. A Theory Y manager believes people want to work and need to be directed and guided. A Theory Z manager (Ouchi, 1982) is some combination of them. For a complete list of alternative Styles, see Bass (1981), p. 289. For a sample assessment chart developed by Likert, see Bass (1981), p. 304.

2. There are a number of ways that this commonality can be productively exploited, and it is not necessary that the activities connected with doing so be dull and uninteresting. Rather, they can be directed at the fun aspect of work. You might, for example, consider showing a film like *Gung Ho*, which starred Michael Keaton, and is available at many video outlets. It is a rather accurate portrayal of many Japanese management practices and orientations. The story is about a Japanese auto firm that locates in a small American town and tries to establish a production facility. The conflicts that ensue might provide rich fodder for discussions. Whatever the special celebrations and recognitions, they should help create and reinforce a culture of acceptance of new ideas.

3. This is in the process of change through the use of computers and light emitting diode (LED's) keyboards. Machines are now being designed that store the symbol systems in memory batches that are brought up and displayed on an LED keyboard. This makes it possible to bring up the whole symbol system in batches. Though not quite as convenient as a typewriter, it is moving in that direction.

12

Creating Entrepreneurial Skills

Almost everything improves if you think about it.

—John Tropman

INTRODUCTION

A set of reasonably specific Skills represents yet another of the competencies that an Entrepreneurial Manager must have. In many ways this list of Skills is not all that different from other such lists that managers, leaders, and so on would find helpful. That is in part because there is not as much difference between the Entrepreneurial Manager and the Excellent Manager as one might think. What is different is that the Entrepreneurial Manager has the central responsibility for looking for and finding new ideas.

INTRODUCING NEW IDEAS

Entrepreneurial Management, among other important things, involves the introduction of new and fresh possibilities and the excision of bad ideas and constraining cultures. Although almost everyone would agree that the introduction of new ideas is important and worthwhile, the actual process of introducing new ideas—the actual things one might do and points one might consider—becomes substantially more vague. New ideas require work; and the Entrepreneurial Manager needs intellectual, interpersonal, and organizational Skills to speed their introduction. The individual who has all three sets of Skills personally or in concert with others will be more successful than the individual who does not have them all.

The problem is not a new one, as *Scientific American* points out in a March

1987 review of its own history. The magazine quotes from its March 1887 issue as follows:

Inventors often complain of the experience in inducing capitalists in joining them in their enterprises. Not infrequently the blame rests as much with the inventor as with the man with money. The capitalist is often blamed for not seeing into the advantages of an enterprise when the fact is it has never been presented to him in the right light. Every man, therefore, who would seek the aid of capital in furthering his plans for introducing an invention should first be prepared to show the whole state of the art covered by such an invention and wherein the improvement lies. Second, he should, if possible, show what particular market needs to be supplied by such an improvement, and something approximating, too, the returns which reasonably may be expected. Third, he should have some well settled plan of introducing a new product or furthering the new scheme. If his invention is worth pushing, in nine cases out of ten there will be little trouble in procuring financial help if the proper methods be employed. (P. 10)

So, the new idea is needed. But that is not enough. What is also required are ways to introduce that idea into the ongoing systems and structures so that it is acceptable and not rejected. Intellectual and interpersonal skills are needed, as well as organizational ones.

INTELLECTUAL SKILLS

Intellectual skills involve dealing with ideas—their structure, their parts, their wholes.

Creative Conditioning and Practice

The first point about intellectual Skills is to establish the realization that top-level intellectual performance, like top-level physical performance, requires conditioning and practice. You cannot wait around until new ideas strike (Argyris, 1982). Rather, you must actively seek them, beginning with yourself in day-to-day work. The Entrepreneurial Manager can engage in, and encourage others to engage in, innovation assessment. Considering family life, work life, relationships with colleagues and children, ask yourself, "What is new? What is different that I am doing in the approach to the problems and concerns that I have? Have I tried different approaches?" If you are unlikely to introduce anything new into your own household, you are similarly unlikely to introduce anything new into your own work place. A pattern of innovation receptivity and awareness of the risks associated with innovation needs to be established and cultivated. Set specific goals in the various sectors important to you. Set goals aimed at the introduction of new approaches, new prespectives, and, in the work place, new products, services, plans, and programs.

Seek to improve your own thought processes, your own creative approaches. To do this, consider following the example of James Rumsey "the most original" inventor in American history. Edwin T. Leyton, Jr. (1987) describes Rumsey as "a remarkable American inventor" whose role lay in "changing the very process of invention," itself (p. 50). Leyton comments:

Rumsey's methods have been incorporated into modern engineering design technique, usually as aids to creativity. First, he would gain an abstract understanding of the elements of the machine then he would manipulate these elements by mental operations similar to those employed by scientists in considering the spacial relations of geometric figures or the interactions of material bodies. That is, HE WOULD COMBINE MECHANICAL ELEMENTS, SEPARATE THEM, REVERSE THEIR ROLES, CHANGE THEIR SPACIAL RELATIONSHIPS (e.g., move an object from vertical to horizontal, turn it upside down, etc., reverse the direction of motion or flow, or reverse the motion of an entire machine; that is, imagine it running backwards).

Reverseability has proved an especially powerful analytical tool for technologists, and Rumsey was one of the first to use it systematically. He apparently realized that just about any machine, if reversed, will result in another machine. (P. 54, emphasis in original)

The essential techniques of personal creativity are neither new nor impossible to achieve. We have deliberately sought an example from a historical figure to illustrate that the principles of thinking about new ideas, making new combinations, introducing new approaches is not something that depends on new technologies, microcomputers, laser beams, or pies in the sky. Rather, it depends on the mental work of combination, recombination, inversion, and taking an overall fresh look. Rumsey's approaches are as valid today as they were years ago. Rumsey was an Entrepreneur. He failed because, like Maxim, he lacked certain competencies involved in negotiating the system within which his inventions would take place and from which they (and he) could prosper. But, as we think today about how we can introduce creativity and new approaches into our lives or into our own Firms, his kinds of questions are as sensible now as they were then.

If a product has been sold routinely to the customer, consider bringing the customer to the product. Play with the implications in that particular approach.

If a product has been aimed at a youth-oriented market, consider aiming it at an older market, as well.

The point of all this is to engage systematically in explorations that challenge conventional assumptions and postulates. You might decide that those conventional assumptions and postulates retain their vitality. Such a decision will have validity only if it comes after rigorous investigation and testing rather than being based on easy agreement. The kinds of things that Rumsey speaks of are sometimes called *assumptions audits*. The point of an assumptions audit is not to necessarily change anything but to have a systematic practice through which questions about traditional, usual, regular approaches can be asked. This audit can be part of the other audits already undertaken in the Four-C's Conference and the Concert of Components Conference (see Chapter 1). The technique is intellectual and requires certain interpersonal Skills and organizational structures for this to occur. But you must begin with your own self.

Environmental Scan

We have already mentioned the innovation inventory and techniques to increase creativity. It is vitally important to make sure that your own supply of new ideas is, itself, adequate. It is very difficult to introduce new ideas into other systems if you have none yourself. We are not speaking necessarily of earthshaking, Nobel Prize winning technologies and ideas, although these certainly may be possible. Rather, we are referring to the regular, ongoing set of procedures and processes that each person must engage in if he or she is to be reasonably current. Inventory techniques, assumption audit techniques, or creativity techniques won't help if there is not a sufficient body of information to use them on. Entrepreneurial Managers, therefore, need to be information gatherers and garnerers.

The procedures for doing this are not terribly difficult. As an Entrepreneur, you already know a lot. You must simply add to your existing knowledge base. Begin with newspaper reading. All Entrepreneurial Managers—and those who wish to structure entrepreneurial systems—should read at least three newspapers daily: one national newspaper, one local newspaper, and one trade or professional journal. Keep current on new books. If there is not time available to read the whole book then subscribe to a service that provides summaries or listen to them on tapes. It's not necessary to become a scholar, but it is necessary to be aware of and alert to the different topics that are capturing the attention of writers and readers, not only the substantive material but the number of times it is mentioned, the depth of coverage, and the scope of reader interests. These things will alert you to new trends, new possibilities to be explored, and problems to avoid.

This injunction seems very simple and yet it is among the hardest to follow. As we all know, "daily routine drives out planning." There tends to be little time in most people's busy day for anything more than the most cursory look at semirelevant or not yet relevant materials. But that's the whole point. You do not yet know the relevance until you expose yourself to the printed materials available to you.

The printed word is not the only place where new ideas come from. You also get them from other people. Entrepreneurial Managers should spend a good bit of time just listening to people. That is taking advantage of the situation. We all meet people throughout the course of our day: colleagues, people on planes, people in airports, family members, and so on. We should seek to use these opportunities both as sources of new ideas and as testing grounds and reaction points for new approaches, new products, and new services.

One Entrepreneur we know about claimed he got all his information from people in airplanes. He felt that they were completely neutral, knew nothing about him or his enterprise, and could thus give a completely unbiased view of the kind of problem and the potential solution that might be helpful. Another Entrepreneur we know of used to fly out to places and get a firsthand look at new or competing modes of production and marketing (Wicther, 1987). All of these Entrepreneurs said approximately the same thing: without a great deal of input from diverse sources, they were not confident they would obtain important information about changes that might affect them. They all have Staffs who can do these things, but there is March and Simon's (1959) *Principle of Uncertainty Absorption*. We've referred to this before, but let's review once again. That principle states: "Uncertainty absorption takes place when inferences are drawn from a body of evidence; and the inferences, instead of the evidence itself, are then communicated" (p. 165). With respect to these particular Entrepreneurs, editing removes precisely the "uncertainties" and "ambiguities" that might be relevant to the development of new products and markets. To a considerable extent, then, some part of the environmental scanning must be done by you, personally.

These intellectual techniques are primarily appropriate for developing your own capacity for coming up with new approaches. They do not really deal with the issue of implementing them.

Implementation Techniques

Simply having a good idea is not enough. Ideas do not implement themselves. There are a number of techniques to deal with the whole implementation process including PERT (Program Evaulation Review Technique), flow charting, various kinds of project flow monitoring, oversight techniques, and so on (see Allen, 1978). But none of these work without the stimulus of the fresh thought, the fresh insight: the energy of thought.

Technical Business Knowledge

It is imperative for the Entrepreneurial Manager to have the standard business knowledge that is required of all business persons. Marketing, financial analysis, business planning, and so on are simply taken for granted. In addition, specific knowledge about the product, service, or area—substantive knowledge—is also important. Knowledge of the product or service without technical business knowledge leads to as much trouble as general business knowledge does when a person has no knowledge of the particular product or service area.

Writing

Entrepreneurial Managers need to be able to convey their thoughts in written form. The memo is an especially important document, yet it is one that most of us spend little time on and frequently do badly. One of the best sources available for memo writing is the book *Send Me a Memo* (1984) by Dianna Booker. She not only goes through a range of ways to develop memos, she also provides a whole series of strong and weak examples. All Entrepreneurial Managers should read this book and practice its precepts with and for profit.

Failure Analysis

America's preoccupation with success often leaves us unable to learn from our failures, as a special section of the December 15, 1986 *Wall Street Journal* points out. According to the *WSJ* of that date, in 1986 a total of 250,456 new concerns were started.

But we don't hear much about the 56,067 outfits that went belly up during the same period, more than half of them less than five years old. We don't hear much about the highest rate of business busts since the Great Depression. Failure is clearly not getting the attention it deserves. (P. 25)

All too frequently, though, we do not really analyze what went wrong. Instead, we seek quickly to blame it on some individual and get rid of that person, or we paper the whole thing over and forget it ever happened. Both of these approaches are means of denial. They don't really come to grips with the fact that the failure occurred. In fact, for too many Entrepreneurs, failure is not a concept they use a lot. It's too bogus, too general. They tend to dwell on particular deals that fell through rather than examining the Strategies and tactics that led to the failure and finding in such examination lessons for future success.

If one establishes the climate where failure—at least some failure—is both acceptable and expected, then individuals will be much less up tight about looking at it. When people go bowling, after all (or golfing or playing tennis or engage in any of the myriad popular games or sports), they spend endless hours discussing their game, what went wrong, where the problems were, and so on. It is perfectly all right to make mistakes in these areas, to discuss those mistakes, and to learn from them. It is not generally all right in most organizations. It must become so. Some level of mistake, some level of error must be tolerable in an effective Entrepreneurial Management System.

Once acceptability of at least some mistakes is established, then, regular failure analysis sessions need to be set up. There is no particular format for such sessions. What is important and crucial is the scheduling of it and the doing of it.

Thought Orientation

Given the action orientation that characterizes American business, we all too frequently act first and clean up the mess later. The successful Entrepreneurial Manager needs to have a combination of action *and* thought orientation. Thought orientation is what one Entrepreneur calls "simple logic." It involves thinking through the problem, considering alternative solutions to the problem, and avoiding the trap of stereotypic answers. New thoughts and ideas come before new products and services. Without new ideas, the products remain old and tired; the services remain routine and humdrum.

Awareness of Idea Stages and the Entrepreneurial Staircase

Ideas go through a series of developmental steps. If you are in the business of introducing new ideas—whether in the idea form, itself, or as a product or service resulting from an idea—awareness of the life cycle of ideas is useful in developing support and overcoming resistance. Similarly, as we have stated previously, organizations go through stages. We have called these the Entrepreneurial Staircase. Knowledge of these stages and the opportunities and perils presented at each stage is crucially important in advancing your ideas and mastering challenge and avoiding defeat. It is imperative that in your role as Entrepreneurial Manager you know the stages and phases that the organization is going through and the meld of skills and competencies that might be needed at each stage. You must also know the problems that are likely to be encountered (see Chapter 4). Without this knowledge the wrong troops can be assembled and the wrong battles are apt to be fought.

INTERPERSONAL SKILLS

Introducing new ideas into an organization requires that you have them in the first place. But the Entrepreneurial Manager has to get others to accept them. The heavy use of interpersonal Skills is one of the reasons for Acceptance Errors, which we first introduced in Chapter 2. Entrepreneurs must pay special attention to their presentations and must seek to acquire Skills that will enhance the receptivity of ideas they offer while avoiding Acceptance Errors and Erroneous Rejection.

Role Repertoire

As we mentioned before, in his book, *The Presentation of Self in Everyday Life* (1959), Erving Goffman talks about this very point. He asks us to think of life as a theatrical play (which Shakespeare said it was, anyway) and to think of the roles we play as similar to theatrical roles. Our presentation of self to family, to colleagues, to co-workers, then, can be thought of as a series of roles. That total constellation of roles that we have available to pick from can be called a *role repertoire*. Any given role performance involving one or more of our roles with the roles of others can be called a *role ensemble*.

Most of us are aware of the fact that the performance of others is affected by our own performance, that the roles of others are dependent in part on the roles we play. Most of us, however, fail to exploit this general knowledge in any immediate personal or practical way. We occupy ourselves with pointing out to ourselves what others are doing wrong. Implicitly, this approach suggests that, if "they" would change, things would be better. Because the Entrepreneurial Manager is in a business of influencing people, the place to start is with herself or himself. No one has greater control over you than you do. One way to produce the desired behaviors in others, therefore, is to *change your own presentation of self*; that is, vary your own role repertoire. Change may be too strong a word. What we have in mind is adding a variety of personal styles so that you can enhance the likelihood that the new ideas you wish to introduce will be accepted and that the system within which you are working will be productive and creative of new ideas.

Observing Ego

Self-analysis is the first step in understanding and then expanding your role repertoire. You need to develop what some therapists call *observing ego*. An observing ego is that portion of us that allows us to observe our own behavior. It allows us to comment on it to ourselves, to modify it, to moderate it, or to adjust it, depending on the nature of the situation.

An observing ego is a fairly objective, fairly *external* observer of ourselves. Naturally, none of us can be completely independent or completely objective. But some individuals *are* able to see themselves almost as well as others see them, to place themselves outside their own interaction and watch themselves perform. Most of us become so involved, so enmeshed in our own needs and wants that we lose all objectivity. Goffman (1959) concluded that your role performance will be better if you understand that it *is* a role. Overinvolvement leads to role malperformance. The development of an observing ego will give you greater role flexibility. It will help you to develop greater Skill in using self deferentially in interactions to achieve the kinds of deals that you wish to make.

The development of an observing ego will lessen the impact of personal ego on deals. Sam Zell (1986) says that ego gets in the way of more deals than anything else he knows about. By ego he is referring to the relative uncontrollability some have for displaying all of their assets, wealth, power, influence and so on in particular situations. What they actually *need* to display is only the amount of influence, money, and persuasiveness to do the particular deal in question, to influence the particular persons necessary.

The development of an observing ego, then, is one of the first interpersonal Skills necessary for the successful Entrepreneur. In essence it is the cultivation of greater objectivity with respect to oneself and one's interactions with self. Such objectivity allows more chances for varying self as one seeks to implement new ideas or to make new deals.

The Analyst vs. the Partisan

An interpersonal Skill that is an offshoot of the objective ego is the ability to distinguish between the roles of analyst and partisan in the introduction of new ideas and in the doing of deals. Objectivity with self will assist in the development of objectivity with situations. The converse is also true. As we go about our lives, most of us are both analysts *and* partisans in the events in which we participate. In introducing new ideas, for example, one can look at a situation from the point of view of what we want, personally—what we would like to see, what we hope would happen—versus how this situation may look to an outsider. Many individuals are unable to disentangle their analyst role from their partisan role. As a result, the facts they see or the analyses they undertake are always colored by their particular wishes and views. It is extremely important for the Entrepreneurial Manager to keep the nature of the situation and the options available in the situation separate from her or his own wishes in the situation. Once others believe that you're only a partisan, interested in introducing your own ideas, they will begin to suspect your objectivity (and rightly so). Even if you are right, the suspicion may keep you from being successful.

External Mentor

How can you develop these competencies? First, recognize that they are needed and that they require work. Recognize, too, that the high degree of self-involvement in what is being corrected makes it extremely difficult to do this entirely by yourself. It is for this reason that the development of an *external* mentor relationship is very important. Identify and seek out some individual who is not associated with your Firm, your family, or your daily life routine. This should be an individual with whom you meet on a regular basis—once a week, once a month, once a quarter, but regularly. The purpose of such meetings is to review your current situation and to invite this external observer to comment both on your own performance and on the kinds of dynamics and problems that might be developing within that situation.

Some may argue that such an outside person cannot be helpful because he or she doesn't know enough about the details of what is going on inside.[1] My experience, and that of a great many successful individuals, argues quite the contrary. First, it is precisely *because* of this independence that your mentor's views will be useful. Second, organizational situations and problems are much more common than one might think. To be sure, there are individual details that are unique to this or that situation. But, in general, an experienced organizational consultant/mentor has heard it before and is able to ask the kinds of questions that you might not think of. This beginning step in the development of observing ego, then, suggests that you start from the outside. After a period of regular meetings and discussions with this individual, you will be able to pick up the perspectives, the style, and some of the Skills of your mentor, in effect taking that person into yourself and making his or her views and styles a part of yourself. As that begins to occur, you must be careful not to delude yourself into believing that your external mentor is no longer needed. Other issues, other perspectives, other problems will come up on which conversation will be helpful.

The mentor concept I'm introducing here is different from the traditional mentor role. In the traditional approach, the mentor is someone within the organization who will sponsor a new or younger individual. It assumes that the older, more experienced individual does not need a mentor. Inherent in the concept too often is the notion that an entrepreneurial individual who is working in a small group or alone doesn't need a mentor to help find his or her way around the garage. One who accepts such a proposition is like the tennis player who agrees to take on all comers with his hands tied behind his back.

Although securing a mentor from inside the organization can be a powerful force in helping you to advance, there is an important caution for you to keep in mind. Always remember that mentors have their own axes to grind. They are not necessarily independent and selflessly interested in the advance of their colleague. They can and do have their own agendas with respect to the organization of which you are completely unaware. We believe, therefore, that the external mentor is more desirable.

Recognize that, in addition to developing an observing ego, introducing new ideas into a system requires additional interpersonal competencies. First, you must generate an idea-permissive climate. Think of it as establishing a climate in which both intellectual and financial risk are permissible.

Permissive Atmosphere

Discussions of Entrepreneurs focus heavily on the ideas of risk and their willingness to accept it. Implicitly and explicitly these risk discussions center mainly on financial risk—the willingness to "put your money where your mouth is." Substantially less attention has been given to intellectual risk; that is, the willingness of individuals to come up with crazy ideas and to say to others (who are certainly likely to be suspicious), "Hey, what about this?"

Entrepreneurs and Entrepreneurial Managers need to create a climate of intellectual permission in which it is okay to advance new and fresh ideas and in which it is recognized that most of these new and fresh ideas will be crazy and *won't work*. The problem with new ideas is that you never know in advance which ones will be the most productive. Hence, one has to have a tolerant, permissive atmosphere in order to get as many ideas as possible out on the table for examination. If people who suggest new ideas are going to be subject to derision or made fun of or kicked around emotionally, they'll just keep their mouths shut. This is a loss because you never know what it would have been like if they had made the suggestion the environment discouraged them from making.

The *Scientific American* previously quoted from (March 1987), also comments on one spectacular case of missing the boat. Again, quoting from their March 1887 issue:

When the last census was taken, to wit 1880, the census man did not consider the electric lighting investment of sufficient magnitude to warrant him collecting the data. Today (1887) the investment is worth one hundred seven million dollars; that is, $107,000,000. And how long has it taken for this vast sum to be attracted to the electric lighting field? Only six years! (P. 10)

Permissive here does not mean anything goes. Rather, it is a matter of "if it makes sense, it's worth bringing up."

Modelling

Modelling is another important interpersonal Skill. As we've already noted, Entrepreneurs need to show others in the organization—and outside of it— that they are willing to place themselves at risk in the area of new idea introduction. Paradoxically, the fact that an Entrepreneur has a history of some failures as well as some successes strengthens, rather than weakens, his or her value as a model. Nobody is right all the time. Those who have failed, who have not done well in some instances but have done well in others, have learned how to deal with rejection, and how to cope with lack of success. One's own lack of success makes it possible for others to be successful.

Cooling Out

But there is, as we already noted, a dark side to all of this. Entrepreneurs are often talented and imaginative individuals who like to be right. When the *desire* to be right becomes displaced by a *need* to be right, the scene is set for potential disaster. When the need to be right becomes a need to be right *all the time*, ultimate failure is almost a foregone conclusion. Rather than energizing the system, it is not uncommon for entrepreneurs to destroy it. It is not that Entrepreneurs intend for this result to occur. Rather, as deVries (1985) points out, the very energy that can be creative can also be destructive. Hence, the Entrepreneurial Manager needs in some instances to reverse or invert the techniques in order to "cool out" or "cool down" an Entrepreneur who has such excessive energy that an organization simply cannot process the new ideas, techniques, and approaches. The very characteristics that Entrepreneurs value—tolerance of ambiguity, for example—may be anathema to a number of other individuals in the organization. They can tolerate some ambiguity, but there may be levels that become too much.

For this reason the Entrepreneurial Manager must find ways to refocus, rechannel, or otherwise deflect overabundant entrepreneurial energy that may sometimes come up. This can be handled in a variety of ways. Among these are sending the Entrepreneur on assignment, focusing on some particular project away from the others, separating development activities from operating ones, and so on. None of these techniques are terribly difficult to implement. The problem is recognizing that an individual who contributes can also harm. The harm that such an individual does is not lessened by the value of earlier contributions. The only thing that is lessened is a willingness by the Entrepreneurial Manager to intervene. As a result, more harm occurs than is necessary.

MIXED SKILLS

Mixed skills are those that involve both the mind and the heart—intellectual and interpersonal elements. Network building, for example, involves both recognizing in someone else conceptual similarities to what you, as an Entrepreneurial Manager, are doing and being able to effect a link that creates a sharing atmosphere. Meetings and group management represent areas of mixed skills where both are needed.

Network Building

One mixed Skill that an Entrepreneurial Manager needs is that of network building. The need for others was stressed in the chapters (9 and 10) on Systems and Staff. Network building requires the understanding that other Entrepreneurial Managers are doubtless facing problems similar to the ones you, in particular, are facing. We frequently run into individuals at a meeting or some session, and in the course of a casual conversation we each recognize that the other is dealing with problems similar to our own. As we mentioned earlier, comments like "we'll have to get together" are made, and that's the last anyone ever hears of it.

This lapse is extremely unfortunate because, in addition to the external mentor, the network provides a valuable source of sharing, support, advice, and so on. On a highly selective basis, therefore, Entrepreneurial Managers should identify and note such individuals and take the initiative of getting together with them. In fact, if the interpersonal aspects of such meetings work out all right, they could become regular things. We are aware of groups of managers who get together just to read some current book or article and discuss it. There is no particular agenda except for this; and, in almost all instances, fascinating discussions, linking current problems to new readings in literature, are brought to the fore.

Speaking/Oral Presentation

Entrepreneurs need to be persuasive. The very idea of entrepreneurship, as referred to almost everywhere, means working up hill, against the time, and needing to convince and persuade. Sometimes you can persuade through written presentation. There are other times when you let the "target" persuade himself or herself through creative listening. But there are times, too, when you must go to a venture capitalist or a boss or a CEO or someone in a special power relationship with you and *sell* an idea. Sam Zell talks about this process in his own shop (Equity Financial Management of Chicago) as crucial. "If my staff can't sell me on an idea," he says, "it will never go anywhere."

Speaking in public—and these kinds of presentations *are* public speaking—is frightening for most of us. We fumble. We are inarticulate. We speak with all of the involvement and excitement of a wax dummy. We make fools of ourselves.[2] Professional speech teachers and public speaking coaches, in fact, often compare the fear of public speaking to the fear of death. There is only one way to conquer the fear: practice in front of an audience. That practice comes easiest in a supportive environment such as that provided by speech courses offered by community colleges, university extension services, organizations such as Toastmasters, or any of the excellent specialty seminars offered by publicly-funded institutions or privately-operated business education companies. However you go about gaining the necessary experience, take heart in the knowledge that the fear *does* diminish with practice. Of all business skills, the one without which success may be the most difficult, may well be the ability to behave as though you were reasonably comfortable in any sort of public speaking situation (even though your stomach may be churning). It is far better to gain the poise you require in such situations in less crucial situations (as in a public speaking course) than in the actual give and take of everyday business, where oral clumsiness can destroy you.

Orchestrating People and Information

The Entrepreneur needs to be able to work with people and information. Orchestration here means getting the right information to the right people and the right people to the right information sources. It involves team building and the shaping of assignments to fit teams. And, it involves the construction of teams to fit assignment needs.

Bargaining/Coaching

As Sayles and Chandler point out in their book *Managing Large Systems* (1971), individuals filling that role are frequently in a position that involves orchestrating or directing new ventures within larger organizations. As a result, they are required to configure new developments from old organizational parts. Frequently, they do not have all the authority needed for the responsibility they have been asked to assume. Sayles and Chandler felt that bargaining and coaching are among the key Skills needed by individuals in these developmental spots. We believe this is the perfect description of the Entrepreneurial Manager (though these authors do not use this title). Entrepreneurs are always involved in configuring new elements from old parts, in bringing together people and ideas. Almost never do they have the authority, money, or clout that is needed to do the job they have set out to do fully. That is almost the definition of a new product or service. In these kinds of ambiguous situations, the notion of ordering, directing, bossing is much less a dominant theme than coaching and bargaining. One needs to bargain for resources. One needs to coach others to do the job. Coaching is especially important in the growth of entrepreneurial ventures because it is during growth that other people need to take the ball and run with it.

ORGANIZATIONAL SKILLS

So, intellectual and interpersonal competencies are needed if ideas are to be successfully introduced and maintained over time. But certain organizational competencies are also needed. Features of the organzation need to be structured so that the energy of thought can be released. In the new venture these kinds of organizational features can be (and should be) built in. In the mature venture, they need to be introduced so that they can contribute to organizational renewals.

Create Entrepreneurial Ad Hocracies

Think of these competencies as unusual kinds of organizational forms. Typical of such unusual forms is the *Crazy Idea Group*. The Crazy Idea Group specializes in introducing weird or half-baked ideas for further consideration. The group's title acts as the legitimizing factor, giving permission for people to bring ideas that are not fully formulated—and that's the whole idea: to get ideas in the early, developmental stage before the system has the chance to reject them. One particularly useful norm for the Crazy Idea Group is to prohibit negative comments (the same rule that is applied to brainstorming sessions). People do not need to begin defending their idea at the same time they are trying to get it out. The idea is simply presented to the group by anyone, and it may not be criticized. This group can make special use of the Devil's Advocate/Angel's Advocate room we talked about in Chapter 8.

A second organizational form is the *Weird Idea Board*. This is a bulletin board on which individuals are invited to post crazy, unusual, surprising, weird, or striking clippings from papers, magazines, personal letters, or any other source. These would be items that might be amusing, interesting, or shocking to others in their organization or work station area. Their purpose is to act as a constant source of stimulus to people and involve them in looking for things to post themselves.

Group Management Techniques

We talk about meeting management techniques in Chapter 13, but it is an important organizational Skill and needs to be mentioned here. Entrepreneurial Managers will spend a considerable amount of time in meetings. Whether that time is productive or wasted or whether the ideas that come from meetings are enhanced, embellished, and made better than when the meeting began is a function of meeting management. It is because of the importance of this topic that we devote two entire chapters (Chapters 13 and 14) to it.

CONCLUSION

Entrepreneurial competencies are not a great deal different from the competencies that every manager needs. There is a special focus on the aspect of idea generation, on the exploring of new ideas, and on the problems and difficulties of getting new ideas implemented. There is also a special focus—as in failure analysis—in looking very carefully at ideas that did not make it so that we can learn as much as possible from them. Finally, there is an emphasis on the intellectual, interpersonal, and organizational competencies. None of these is sufficient by itself.

NOTES

1. This is a principle borrowed from the practice of clinical counselling. All clinical counsellors of quality have other counsellors to whom they turn on a regular basis

for a sort of supervision. In this context supervision does not refer to direction. Rather, it recognizes that in ongoing, day-to-day life, individuals are likely to become overinvolved with clients and fail to recognize that involvement. The teaching or supervising therapist points out these potentials and actualities to the counsellee. Entrepreneurs face a similar danger and thus need structured objective outside inputs.

2. Mark McCormack (1985) speaks of making a presentation to John Z. DeLorean, then of G.M.'s Pontiac Division, about some creative advertising that could be done with the Pontiac Chieftain symbol. At the end, DeLorean pointed out that Pontiac had just spent several million dollars to get rid of the symbol!

THE ENTREPRENEURIAL ENSEMBLE: ORCHESTRATING ENTREPRENEURIAL PERFORMANCE

In this volume we have emphasized the Four C's—Characteristics, Competencies, Conditions, and Contexts—and the ten S's—Self, Skill, Style, Staff, Subculture, Structure, System, Strategy, Superordinate Values, and Superordinate Culture—as the focal elements for the Entrepreneurial Manager. Each of these has been discussed in some specific detail. In addition, we introduced the concept of the Entrepreneurial Staircase, and we discussed and considered specific problems and difficulties at each level. Taken together, it's a lot for an individual to keep in mind all at once. But the task is not over. These things we have been discussing represent the players in the entrepreneurial orchestra. What is really needed in terms of the dynamic entrepreneurial function is for the Entrepreneurial Manager to put these all together in some kind of simultaneous, dynamic format.

In most modern contexts that format is going to be the meeting. It is for this reason that we now focus a section of this book on meeting management.

A number of authors (Grove, 1983; Jay, 1976; Ouchi, 1982; Tropman, 1984) emphasize the importance of meetings to high quality decision making and entrepreneurial success. In spite of this, there is a great lack of attention in the literature to meetings as a focus of intervention and a tool of management. Instead, meetings seem to be viewed as a passing irritant.

That is deplorable. The mistake it represents is an extremely grievous one. The very best meetings represent the collective wisdom and experience of all the members in the meeting. They are able to spot problems and avoid errors that might well be committed by a single person.

On the other hand, when run badly, they can exhibit, as Irving Janis (1971) suggested, "group think." In short, meetings, like any human institution—marriage, schools, hospitals, business concerns—can either improve the people and products or diminish them. The latter lessening effect has become so common that it has almost become synonymous with the concept of meeting or committee. The committee concept in particular is such a joke that people will frequently announce that they are going to form a committee as a way of getting a laugh.

How sad this is, especially in the entrepreneurial area where new ideas are often presented half formed with holes here and problems there. An effective group process can be—and almost always *is* (the Japanese understand this)—exactly what is needed to make that product or service outstanding. But, as in the case of our Neanderthal inventor of the needle, negativistic stand-pat-ism is too often the rule. Myth, misunderstanding, and outright ignorance about the group decision-making process are obstacles that must be overcome if the entrepreneurial venture is to give itself the maximum opportunity to succeed. Fortunately, such obstacles can be overcome and with relative ease. This is the subject of Chapters 13 and 14.

13

Entrepreneurial Power Groups: Achieving High Quality Decisions in Meetings

Similarly, group dynamics was perceived as old fashioned, a field that had seen its hey day in the gestalt encounter groups and corporate brainstorming procedures of the early 1970s, but now is dated and passe.

Norman, himself, could not comprehend this. It seemed to him that American society was one in which people worked in groups, not alone; rugged individualism was not replaced by endless corporate meetings and group decisions. In this new society, group behavior seemed to him more important, not less.

—Michael Crichton, *Sphere* (p. 12)

INTRODUCTION

In 1976 Anthony Jay published "How to Run a Meeting" in the *Harvard Business Review*. That article is now regarded as something of a classic. Nevertheless, though the structure and dynamics of meetings have attracted much attention since the publication of Jay's piece, meetings are still widely regarded as some sort of resented, necessary evil of organizational life. In this chapter we review some of the reasons why things go wrong in meetings. We present seven important principles that underlie the meeting process. We also propose twelve "rules" for making meetings go right. A thorough understanding of these principles and diligent application of these rules will inevitably lead Entrepreneurial Managers to conduct more effective meetings with higher quality group decisions. Our experience—and that of others who have dealt extensively with the power of group problem solving—demonstrates that higher quality decisions will come even in the face of recurring problems of personality in meetings.

MEETINGS ARE CRUCIAL

Meetings and committees are crucial to the American way of business, and they are utterly indispensible to entrepreneurial ventures. Important business decisions are almost never made in isolation. Almost always, in fact, those decisions are the direct or indirect product of some group, meeting in committee. In spite of the fact that a good many people have many negative attitudes and orientations toward them, meetings remain *the* primary mechanism through which American business decision making is accomplished.

We do love our myths about business leadership and the captains of industry. So long as they are harmless, they can be highly entertaining. We can all recount endless apocryphal tales of some hardheaded CEO, closeting himself alone for days while he wrestles with some potentially cataclysmic problem, emerging, finally, sweat covered and exhausted, with the solution. The fact that it seldom happens this way doesn't seem to bother us particularly.

Some business myths are not harmless, however. Some can lead, in fact, to real catastrophe for a company or an organization that refuses to shed them in spite of strong evidence to the contrary. Among the more dangerous are those we perpetuate about committees and the meeting process: "a committee is a group that takes minutes to waste hours"; "a camel is a horse designed by a committee"; "If you want to be certain nothing gets done about a problem, turn it over to a committee." Reality is quite different.

Almost no important business decision is made entirely outside the meeting context, without some shaping by the meeting process, without some review by other committees. Meetings and group decisions are powerful and essential elements in any organizational enterprise. Successful business cannot function without them.

In the abstract, meetings don't deserve their bad press. In the abstract, a meeting is like an elegant, cleverly structured, intricate, action game. In our society, it is a game everyone must play at one time or another. In business, it is a game played without end. The problem is that almost everyone plays it badly. Unlike baseball (another game the elegance of which is axiomatic), there is no organized learning system for meetings, a system that begins in grade school, continues through high school, moves to the sand lots, then on to the minor leagues, and finally to the majors. Chris Schenkel does not broadcast the World Series of Meetings. As a result, very few of us ever get to see the game played well.

To be sure, there are a handful of meeting "major leaguers" around. Unfortunately, most of us have never seen them perform. If by chance we do run across one, we view him or her as a "natural" with inborn skills that we are sure *we* cannot possibly learn. That is another harmful myth and because of it, we allow ourselves to be thrown into the game without proper training, without a knowledge of the rules, with little concept of effective game strategy and tactics, and without a clear understanding of which position (role) we are being expected to play. Our only role models for the meeting game are poor players like ourselves. So, we condemn the game when our real problem is the ineptitude of the players.

The experience of most of us with meetings leaves us wanting to get back to something that at least has the appearance of being productive. Although meetings, ideally, may be places where decisions *should* be made, all too frequently they are exercises in inefficiency.

For most organizations, then, worries about the inefficiencies of group decision making are appropriate and well targeted. The solutions, however—avoiding meetings, reducing their number, getting rid of committees—are, flat out, wrong! For the entrepreneurial venture in the innovation or growth stages in particular, such solutions are a clear invitation to failure. Downplaying or attempting to eliminate meetings and committees must inevitably lessen the quality of decisions presently being made, because it truncates the base of wisdom, knowledge, and experience available for decision making.

The best solution—the only real solution—lies in learning to play the meetings game with skill. The first step in that learning process is understanding why things go wrong.

WHY THINGS GO WRONG

To prescribe a suitable remedy, we must first have a proper diagnosis. We begin with a series of questions: Why are meetings generally viewed with such negativity? Why don't meetings accomplish what they should accomplish? Why do so many view meetings as a waste of time? In short, why *do* things go wrong? There are many answers.

Values

Group decision making—most group activity, in fact—runs counter to the popular view most Entrepreneurs hold of themselves as fierce individualists. We believe that things run better if we do them ourselves, on our own, without having to rely on others. "I can't get any work done if I have to be in meetings all the time." The implicit assumption here is that meetings are the antithesis of work, that work is something we do alone in our offices.

Not only is work viewed as best being done alone, but credit for work is seen as an individual reward. In our arts and in our industry we glorify the individual and deprecate the group. Every day must be a replay of *High Noon*. Things go wrong in meetings because, too often, the committee room is a coliseum of conflict instead of a center of cooperation.

Hidden Functions

Meetings and committees perform a number of hidden functions on behalf of society. These can confound and confuse decision making. Social purpose, for example, is embedded in the meeting process that is related to American traditions of representative democracy and pluralism. In our society we recognize that individuals have both a need and a right to have their say on important issues. This has extended itself into the political system of American business where the committee has become a way in which diverse factions are allowed to argue their various points of view. It gives those who would lose out in a simple majority vote a chance to be heard.

Lack of Training

Playing the meetings game effectively requires a certain amount of skill that can only be achieved through expert training. Although we provide ample opportunities for practice (everyone participates in meetings), such practice is without guidance and focus. As important as the group decision-making process is to every aspect of business life, our society devotes little time and almost none of its resources to teaching the rules of the meetings game and training individuals in the application of those rules. Things go wrong in meetings because the participants simply have no idea how to make them go right.

The Self-Fulfilling Prophecy

Because we have no "good meeting" referent, much of our experience with meetings is negative. Out of that experience base have come strong negative expectations about meetings and the effectiveness of the group decision-making process. We expect meetings to be time wasters, and we engage in behavior that proves them to be time wasters. Things go wrong in meetings because we expect them to go wrong.

HOW TO MAKE THINGS GO RIGHT: SEVEN GENERAL PRINCIPLES OF THE MEETINGS GAME

Meetings and group decision making can be improved. Learning and then applying a few simple rules (prescriptions, if you will, for curing the ailing meeting process) will quickly yield dramatic improvements in both the quality of meetings and the quality of the decisions that emerge from them. A few broad principles form the basis for these rules. Examining those principles will help to place the twelve rules in proper perspective.

An important caveat must precede that examination. Principles and rules go only part of the way toward improving business meetings and the decisions that come from them. People are people. Potential conflict between us and among us exists whenever and wherever two or more of us gather. Yet, there are places—a courtroom, a ballgame, a play, an orchestra performance— where the very existence of rules makes for better performance possibilities. Still, rules (and the principles that underlie them) do not of themselves guarantee outstanding performance in meetings. (Neither do they guarantee it in courts, ballgames, plays, or orchestra performances.) What they do accomplish is to give groups more of a fighting chance by preventing some bad things from happening.

There are many principles involved in the meetings game. The list that follows is not exhaustive. These seven, however, are seen by meetings major leaguers as being among the most important (Tropman and Morningstar, 1984).

The Role Principle

Just as there are roles in a play that various actors are fit into, there are various meeting roles; and these are as well-defined as the parts in a play. At the very least, these include the role of Chair and the role of Member. There is usually a Recorder role, as well, and often a Staffer role. Sometimes there are also specialized roles such as Advisor.

Everyone connected with a meeting casts himself or herself (or is cast by someone else) into one of those roles. As long as each participant plays the assigned role—speaking lines and presenting behaviors appropriate to that role—meetings run as smoothly as a well-oiled machine. Problems arise when the actors attempt to expand their parts in a conscious or unconscious effort to usurp the role of someone else (usually the Chair, but all too frequently Chairs have been known to take on the Member role).

One of the main reasons for why things go wrong, Entrepreneurs often say, is "mental illness"; i.e., "all the people on my committee but me are crazy." Although that may be overstating the case a bit, aberrant or inappropriate behavior on the part of committee members is often the root cause of some major meeting problems. These are common occurrences: a committee member voices constant anger, making other members uncomfortable, and the Chair seems incapable of firm control; one member dominates discussion to such a degree that other members get up and leave; one member gets so involved in minutia (harping on Minutes, for example) that the productive work of the committee goes unaccomplished.

Such disruptive behavior causes us to focus on personalities. The real problems, however, have very little to do with personalities. Rather, difficulties arise when individuals depart from their assigned and defined roles within the meeting context.

Once we recognize that our focus should be on the roles participants must play in the meeting and *not* on the personalities they bring to their parts, we move away from the negative affect that inevitably accompanies a focus on individual personalities. We can then begin to consider the dynamics of the group more rationally and with more reason.

The Orchestra Principle

In considering the dynamics of the group, consider how an orchestra works—there are a *lot* of similarities. The orchestra has a score to perform (something like an agenda). There are the rehearsals before the performance (as there is some degree of preparation for any well-planned meeting). There is a conductor to lead the orchestra through the performance (as there is a Chair to guide the meeting). The musicians, each with his or her own contribution to make to the totality, come together as a body on a preplanned basis to make music (just as meeting participants should always be brought together on a preplanned basis to make decisions).

We would find it surpassingly odd if we attended an orchestra concert, at the outset of which the oboe player stepped forward and played all of his notes in a Beethoven symphony and then left with the explanation, "I'm feeling a little pressed, and I've got to duck out early." That this kind of behavior happens routinely in meetings sheds still further light on why the meeting experience is so frequently unsatisfying.

The Content Principle

This principle is closely related to the Orchestra Principle. *Excellent* meetings are organized by *content*. *Poor* meetings are structured by *person*. ("We will now have the Treasurer's report.") In poor meetings, individual participants are allowed (encouraged, required) to present all of the material specifically related to them, all at one time, without regard to the possibility that this material might be of many different kinds and relate to many different items with which the meeting is concerned. Thus, when the Treasurer gets up to give the report the Chair has just called for, it is just like our oboe player giving us all of his notes at once. At best, meetings organized by person result in a great deal of repetition that fosters inefficiency and lengthens meetings unnecessarily. At worst, such organization reinforces the focus on personalities and works to the detriment of good meetings.

The Three-Characters Principle

Matters before decision groups have one of three characters: they are informational, decisional, or discussional. Each is distinctly different. In the well-played meetings game, these are separated before the meeting begins and organized together so that the group can deal with all the information items at once, all of the decision items at once, and all of the discussion items at once. This is what we mean when we talk about organizing meetings by *content*. This kind of organization leads to dramatic increases in the efficient use of meeting time and resources. More importantly, even, it leads to better decision making by the group.

Such organization may (and usually does) require some individuals to appear more than once on the agenda. This is no more odd than our peripatetic oboe player doing his or her thing as the score requires throughout the symphony.

The No-More-Reports Principle

Reports are a major enemy of meetings. This is true for two reasons. First, they involve one individual heavily and all others only passively. That is not the reason the group was brought together. Second, they tend to be organized by persons rather than by content (again, the ever popular "Treasurer's report" or any other "reports" where individuals get up and report on all matters pertaining to their departments, regardless of the character of the information presented).

Reports make it difficult for groups to cope with their expected tasks. This is true because reports generally require the participants to move rapidly back and forth among items of different character, that have differing requisites, and that make differing demands. The informational content of the usual Treasurer's Report should, in fact, be allocated across the agenda items and presented whenever, wherever, and only to the extent that it is relevant. The information contained in any individual's report should emerge as a natural part of the decision or discussion processes.

The No-New-Business Principle

The introduction and discussion of New Business is a meeting enemy even more formidable than reports. It achieves this status not because there is no need for new business. Rather, introducing new business at the meeting disrupts the orderly flow of the meeting process.

New Business is, by definition, that about which little is known. The ability of the group to process New Business is severely limited. Neither the quality of any discussion about it nor any decisions made concerning it are likely to be of high quality. Injecting New Business into a meeting is roughly equivalent to a football coach introducing a new play into a critical situation of a football game, a play that not only has never been practiced but is one with which the players are not even familiar. In the well-played meetings game, what might be called "New Business" is introduced at the end of the meeting, *without discussion*, as a kind of preview of some subsequent meeting.

The Proactivity Principle

Most groups spend most of their time reacting to issues. This fosters the appearance of items on an agenda that are already at some crisis point. The reactive position is always structurally weaker than the proactive one. It is therefore in the interests of good meeting process to reach out for issues, to garner them before they require crisis management. Small problems are easier to solve than big ones. Small decisions requiring minimal discomfort are easier to make than large decisions involving great pain.

TWELVE RULES FOR HIGH QUALITY DECISIONS

The goal of the meetings game is high quality decisions. Well-played meetings games have nothing to do with making people happier in groups (although that will happen because some of the problematic activities will no longer be present or will have changed). For the most part, the feelings of the players are of only minimal concern. The real focus of the game is on the output of the group over time. That output needs to be assessed on a constant basis to provide effective feedback to the players on how well they are playing the game. What follows now are twelve rules for making things go right in meetings. The last of these rules provides one possible mechanism for conducting this ongoing assessment.

The following are twelve rules that need to become a part of the operating strategies for every Entrepreneurial Manager. As you will discover, when you apply them things will go right in meetings. When you ignore them, things will go wrong. These rules focus on both the substance of information and on the procedures for presenting it. They are concerned both with meeting items and with the kinds of considerations that are desired from those items. This latter is particularly important because it is from such consideration that Staff come to know the kinds of things expected of them.

Some of these rules deal with the meeting, itself. Others deal with the preplanning and preparation that go into the meetings. It is extremely important to keep in mind that the rules apply whether you meet once a year or twice a day, and they apply regardless of the kind of meeting you think you are calling—morning staff meeting, sales meeting, directors' meeting, whatever.

The Rule of Halves

Identify the halfway point that lies between the end of the last meeting and the beginning of the next. During the first half of that period gather information about the kinds of items that are to be considered at the upcoming meeting.

End the item gathering at the halfway point. At that point examine all of the items that have been gathered. Remove all of those that can be handled on a one-to-one basis in people's offices. If something does not need group attention (and our guess is that about 40% of all items that generally come before meetings don't and should never be there), don't put it on the Agenda. Removing such nongroup items permits more intensive focus on the remaining items.

For each potential meeting item, assess what people, information and/or resources are needed and arrange for their presence at the upcoming meeting. If the appropriate information, individuals, or resources are not available, eliminate the item from the meeting. It makes very little sense to waste the group's valuable time discussing them.

Sort the candidate items into three groups: information items, decision items, and discussion items. Meeting participants not only want substantive information about what they are discussing, they want that information given to them in a procedural context. ("Are we just hearing about this? Are we deciding it? Or are we just noodling around?")

Information that once would have been presented in a single Report (such as the Treasurer's Report) should be examined for each of its informational, decisional, and discussional components and scheduled appropriately.

The Rule of Sixths

As the final Agenda is taking form, inspect the meeting items and seek to find those that flow in about the following proportions: (1) about one-sixth should be items from the past, historical items that have not yet been completed; (2) About four-sixths should be, relatively speaking, here-and-now type items; (3) About one-sixth should be future-oriented, "blue sky" type items about which the meeting participants can do some proactive, plan-ahead type thinking.

The virtue of this system is not only that good ideas are generated, but a certain amount of affect, especially around controversial items, is allowed to be expressed in a nonthreatening situation. Individuals are allowed to express their creativity in a context where creativity may be expected to have some impact. This becomes "psychic income" that meeting planners can provide for the group. It is more likely to keep individuals more pleased, happier, and willing to return for additional meetings. This is a side benefit of proactivity that reaps great rewards.

The Two-Meeting Rule

As this system gets under way, in the meeting planning phase, look for controversial items and seek to schedule them according to the Rule of Sixths. At the very least, controversial items should be discussed at least *twice*; in other words, in at least two different meetings. The first discussion should be just that: a discussion. This process allows for affect to be expressed and for new ideas to be introduced about how the difficult items might be approached. The next time such issues come up it can be for decision.

For very controversial items, three or even four periods of discussion may be appropriate before a decision is taken. All too frequently our hesitancy to deal with controversial matters encourages us to delay them, taking them up only at the last possible moment under severe constraints of pressure and time. Separating the discussion process from the decision process for such items greatly reduces equivocation and enhances action.

The Rule of Three-Fourths

By the three-fourths point in the time period between meetings, the Agenda should be in its final form. Send it to the individuals attending the meeting so that they have time to review it and to read any accompanying materials. Usually the meeting packet contains three items: the Agenda, Minutes of the last meeting, and Reports of various kinds. Each of these will require some specific attention before the meeting takes place.

The Rule of the Agenda

Agendas should look like a *menu*. Most Agendas, unfortunately, are simply lists of topics that regularly pass up opportunities for structuring the decision-making context in a helpful fashion. With a menu-type Agenda items are segregated into their information, decision, and discussion groups. Instead of simply "the PDQ Report," for example, the Agenda might say something like "Information about the PDQ Report" or "Decisions concerning the PDQ Report" or "Discuss the PDQ Report."

Below each Agenda item, the "dish" on the menu, provide a one or two sentence summary of the key elements of the item so that individuals scanning the Agenda can have a full sense of what is involved.

As part of the item itself or in parentheses next to it use one of the three key words (*information*, *decision*, or *discussion*). This allows the meeting participants to understand the context of the item.

Finally, on the right-hand side of the Agenda, where price might be on a menu, put a running clock with differential amounts of time allocated to the different items. This tells the meeting participants when the meeting will start, when it will end, and how much time in the meeting roughly is being allocated for each item. Figure 13.1 presents an example of how a well-constructed agenda might look.

The Minutes Rule

Provide *Content focused* Minutes that give brief summaries of the main points of discussion. Skip a line and, in capital letters, put in the decision

Figure 13.1
A Sample Meeting Agenda

AGENDA

Tropstar Corporation Unlimited, Ltd.
Weekly Staff Meeting
1 - 3 p.m.

Item #	Item	Item Action	Item Time
1.	Minutes	Decision	1:00 - 1:10
2.	Announcements: a. New ID cards out b. New Elevator times	Information	1:10 - 1:25
3.	New Supply Disbursment System The new policy for issuing desk supplies has been revised, taking your current needs into account. (See Attachment A)	Decision	1:25 - 1:35
4.	Sick Time Reimbursement Issues A proposal to let employees "cash out" 1/2 of unused sick time. (See Attachment B)	Decision	1:35 - 1:50
5.	Bonus Payment Plan A proposal to pay this year's increases as a bonus at the end of the year. (See Attachment C)	Decision	1:50 - 2:30
6.	Christmas Vacation Some employees wish to have Christmas Week (between Christmas and New Year's) off without pay. Others do not.	Discussion	2:30 - 2:55
7.	Adjournment	Decision	2:55 - 3:00

---

or action. It is here that names are mentioned, times are given, and responsibilities are assigned. This cures the frequent problem of meeting attendees being unable to remember from one meeting to the next precisely what was decided. It also tends to prevent descriptions of decisions that are so vague no one later knows what they meant—"Take appropriate action," for example.

Meeting Minutes are almost always taken in the wrong way. They get set down as descriptions of the meeting process, with long litanies of "he said" and "she said." These, not surprisingly, are called *Process Minutes*. Not only do they fail to convey fully the extent of meeting work that went on, but they focus on individuals (which you now know is absolutely the wrong thing to do). Where such individuals perceive the Minutes placing them in a bad light, it is not uncommon to engage in protracted discussions of the Minutes in order to improve their positions retrospectively. Content Minutes will cure this problem.

The Rule of Reports

Use the Executive Summary technique and the Option Memo technique for all Reports to be presented at a meeting.

Most meeting planners send out too much information. Too much information often becomes disinformation—the potential meeting participant looks at the huge packet of material sent to her or him as preparation for the next meeting, and puts it aside. "I'll look at this when I can really devote the appropriate amount of time to it." That time never comes, the packet of preparatory material was worthless, and the meeting participant attends the meeting completely unprepared (and invariably concludes, "Boy, are these meetings a waste of time").

The Executive Summary technique is the answer. Reduce all Reports to no more than two pages. If an attendee wants or needs more information, it is available on request.

Options Memos go hand-in-glove with Executive Summaries. Option Memos are designed to enhance discussion and to prevent it from getting off the track, one of the most common problems in groups. The technique presents all Reports, written or oral, in three steps: (1) a problem statement, (2) a set of options that reasonable people might consider to handle the problem, and (3) a set of recommendations for action based on a selection from the option set.

Options Memos encourage the work of the group and discourage rubber stamping the work of a single individual or subcommittee (the "O.K., here's the problem, and here's what I think should be done about it" presentation). It virtually eliminates the problem of the group focusing on whether to accept or reject a proffered solution. Instead it leads the group into looking at the proposal, itself, as a basis for discussion and improvement.

Options Memos present information that the group wants and needs. They answer latent questions and stimulate the process of discussion to begin. The act of discussing options often leads to the discovery of still other alternatives and may also uncover hidden difficulties. The final result is a decision on which the full force of the group has been focused. That decision is almost always a good one with difficulties removed or diminished and positive features added.

The Rule of Two-Thirds

All meetings are divided into three parts: (1) a "git-go" part at the beginning, (2) a heavy work part in the middle, and (3) a decompression part at

Figure 13.2
The Agenda Bell

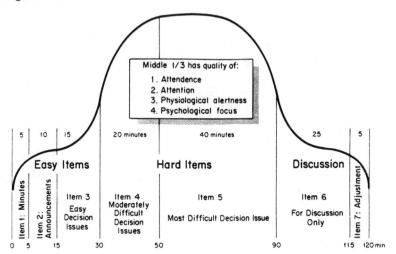

the end. Allocate information items and simple decisions to the first third of the meeting. Process difficult items in the middle third. Deal with discussion items in the last third.

Groups need a little time to get going. Key items, therefore, do not belong at the beginning of a meeting. Toward the middle of the meeting maximum attendance has been achieved. Energy, both physical and psychological, is at its high point. This is the time to handle the toughest items.

The decision making that occurs in the group under this model *does* tear at the fabric of group cohesion. This cohesion needs to be rebuilt whether the group is a group of strangers or is made up of people who work together on a daily basis. Discussion provides a way to continue group work, on the one hand, while allowing for group rebonding on the other.

The Rule of the Agenda Bell

Orchestrate meetings so that the emotional component follows a bell shaped curve. Figure 13.2 demonstrates how this might be done.

Item 1 is always the Minutes. If there are not enough people there to approve the Minutes "officially," they can be reapproved at a later point.

Item 2 is always made up of information items. These may take no more than about 10% of the total meeting time. This will prevent the meeting from becoming simply an oral newsletter.

Item 3 (a, b, c, etc.) contains decision items of only modest difficulty. Short, easy decision items allow the group to get going.

Item 4 (a, b, c, etc.) matters are the more difficult decision items. These and the Item 3 items represent a moderate and then strenuous warm-up for what is now to follow.

Item 5 is always the single most difficult item on the Agenda for that particular meeting. It should occupy space between the 40% and 60% points, allowing for optimum group attention and energy. Because of its difficulty, this item will almost always follow the Two-Meeting Rule. That means that this will be at least the second time in the history of the group that this item is being considered.

By the completion of Item 5, with one minor exception, all of the decision items have been handled. Item 6 (a, b, c, etc.) is composed of discussion items. These are items where thought is needed but where final resolution is not yet appropriate or is not yet in the purview of this particular group.

Item 7 is a short, easy decision item on which all can agree. Usually this will be an item that appears to be substantially trivial in content. It is not at all trivial, however, in its importance to the meetings game. Such an item allows the meeting to end on time and on a psychological note of agreement and accomplishment ("Well, at least we got *something* done").

The Rule of Temporal Integrity

Start on time. End on time. Keep to the rough internal time order. Carefully planned meetings combined with properly prepared meeting attendees should almost never require more than an hour and a half.

The Rule of Agenda Integrity

Deal with *all* of the items on the Agenda. Do *not* deal with any items *not on the Agenda*. Individuals make attendance decisions based in part upon what they are informed will be covered. They invest time in reviewing meeting materials. Maintaining the integrity of the Agenda reinforces the decision to attend and provides a substantial return on the time investment.

Nothing short of an act of God justifies changing the Agenda at the last moment. Nothing whatsoever justifies wandering from the Agenda during the meeting.

The Rule of Decision Audit and Decision Autopsy

For important groups, go back on a year to a year and a half basis and look at some of the key decisions made by the groups. Any evaluation can be used. Here is one that has been proven effective.

Take a sample of past decisions. For each decision, rate it "A" if it was an all-win situation; everyone benefitted though not necessarily equally. Rate it "B" if the decision had some winners and some losers but on balance had a positive result. Give it a "C" if a decision was made but nothing happened. A "D" rating is the inverse of "B," both winners and losers but on balance the result was negative. An "F," also known as the "Nuclear War Decision," is an all lose decision.[1]

Calculate a grade point average for the sample and feed it back to the groups. Whatever rating mechanism is used is purely a matter of choice. What is crucial is going back and looking at decisions in an effort to assess where strengths and weaknesses lie in the decision-making process.

This assessment leads to the autopsy. In any such review, take the very best decisions and the very worst ones, and take them apart. Answer, to the extent possible, the questions, what went right and why, what went wrong and why. It is imperative that both good and bad decisions be linked together in the autopsy process. Using only bad decisions in the autopsy generates group defensiveness and fault avoidance behavior.

CONCLUSION

The mechanics of meeting orchestration provide one of the most important areas of influence for the Entrepreneurial Manager. Although an actual invention or innovation may not be thought up right there in the meeting (though many are!), meetings are crucial to creating the climate in which ideas flourish. They are the forum in which ideas are shared (or not shared). Meetings act as the mechanism through which ideas can be improved and linked with other ideas to make a total innovation package. Finally, meetings are the decision gate through which ideas must pass. For these reasons, entrepreneurial management or idea management pays special attention to meetings and seeks, always, to come to high quality decisions.

NOTES

1. IBM's system for "Process Quality Management" uses a grading system, as well. See Hardacer and White, 1987, p. 188.

14

Entrepreneurial Power Group Roles: The Meeting Scenario

Chair: "Will you please shut up!"

Member: "Why should I shut up? I've had this meeting up to here!"

Chair: "Because I'm the Chair, and I told you to shut up."

Upon discussing this incident later, the Chair says, "Well, I stayed in charge." and a commentator says, "Yes, but what you were in charge of was a non-meeting."

—From *More Bloody Meetings*, Xicom Films.

INTRODUCTION

In the game of football it is not enough to know the rules to play the game well. It is also important to understand what is required of each position on the team—what the quarterback does, what the center does, what the line-backer does, and so on. The same is true of the meetings game. To play it well, it is important to understand what is required of the various positions on the meeting team because, over the course of time, we will each play all of the positions.

THE CHAIR ROLE

The Chair is one of the key meeting roles. Entrepreneurial Managers spend a lot of time Chairing meetings. In spite of that fact, most of us have never learned to Chair a meeting properly. For most people, indeed, the decision to accept the responsibilities of a meeting Chair is a fairly casual matter. They make the decision without regard to much more than whether they have the extra time available that is always assumed to go with Chairing a committee. Although that assumption is usually correct, the time involved in Chairing a meeting does not have to be appreciably more than that of any other meeting role. Everything depends on the meeting being conducted properly—at the very least according to the rules we've outlined for you.

Being an effective Chair requires you to make certain of several things. First, the group that will be meeting must have the necessary and sufficient resources to do the kinds of things that it is being asked to do—the necessary money, if money is required; the necessary staff, if extra staff is required; and so on. If this condition is not met, the group should not meet, and you should refuse to Chair the meeting if it does meet.

Second, to be an effective Chair you should have a feel for the politics of the group. Are they something you can work with; and, if so, how? A careful political assessment done in advance can save many future problems. If you can't figure out what's going on, or if you sense that there are murky hidden Agendas on the part of some or all of the members, decline the Chair and forgo the meeting.

Third, if you really want to get good at the meetings game—and you should for it can place enormous power and capabilities for accomplishment in your hands—it will be necessary for you to engage in a certain amount of self-assessment in connection with Chairing a meeting. You must ask yourself questions like, "What does it mean for me to be Chair of this group? What kinds of signals does my reputation in the business convey? How will others react?" Others will be reacting to you on the basis of these signals. If you are aware of what you symbolize, you can avoid being trapped by the perceptions of others.

Fourth, you must understand thoroughly the purpose of the group you are expected to Chair. If the Chair is to be the custodian of this purpose, it should be written down and provided to the other Members. This is true even for the simplest staff meetings held on a frequent, regular basis. If someone else is the custodian of the mandate, then that individual should be asked for it in writing. During the crafting period, negotiations about the nature of mandate, the scope, and the resources can be undertaken.

Fifth, and most importantly, in undertaking the role of the Chair you need to ask yourself whether it is possible for you to move from the role of partisan to the role of statesman. Many Chairs feel that once they assume the Chair, they will be able to get their own way. Unfortunately, as Anthony Jay (1976) pointed out, self-indulgence is one of the great problems groups face. It is necessary to assume the posture of a statesman if the meeting process is to be successful, facilitating the product of the group rather than promoting one's own wishes and desires.

The role of the Chair falls, basically, into the two skills areas we discussed previously: intellectual and interpersonal. Intellectually, the Chair needs to *blend* the ideas of those in the meeting. At key points, often after a round of discussion when everyone has had the opportunity to contribute, the Chair should summarize, suggesting to the group where it is at that moment, bracketing those areas of agreement and setting them aside, refocusing the discussion on those items that remain. This process is really the decision process with individuals (often the Chair but not always), summarizing, building, refocusing, until the entire decision stands before the group in a way that no individual would have anticipated.

In this process the Chair uses an interrogative rather than a declarative mode of interaction. Instead of saying, "That's a dumb idea," or "that's a terrific idea," the Chair raises questions of a "what if" nature. This is especially true of weak or bad ideas. The individual who offers a poor concept might well be the genius who provides the key to the solution of the next problem. Squelching that individual may cause him or her to retreat and contribute no further. The idea is to guide the contributing process in a way that invites the individual to confront some of the problems of the poor idea but, yet, receive support for the basic effort of suggesting and trying.

Jay (1976) points out that there is a sequence to the discussion process that facilitates that process if it is followed. First, there is the discussion of the problem. Second, there is discussion of evidence and points of view about the problem. Third, there is an agreement about what the evidence and perspectives mean. Fourth, there is a decision. Fifth, there is action.

In so far as possible, it is your job, as the Chair, to keep the discussion moving through these stages, seeing that each one is resolved before the next one is begun. Throughout, the Chair maintains equality for persons but equity for issues; people are all treated equally but issues are not. More attention is lavished on some issues than on others in order to achieve the appropriate and necessary group results.

With respect to interpersonal activities, the Chair must try to protect the weak participants and temper the strong in order to allow for an evenness of group participation. Those individuals who do not participate need to be invited to share their views. (They are often the ones who will protest most vocally in the restaurant after the meeting.) Feelings and affect need to be diffused. This is best accomplished by direct recognition: "Jim, you seem to feel strongly about this." We deal with the Jims directly instead of watching them glower in the corner.

The Chair supports the clash and conflict of ideas. At the same time the Chair seeks to find aspects from different types of suggestions that may become part of an overall solution.

Throughout, you as the Chair have overall responsibility for the group product, not for getting your own way. The Chair exercises influence by asking questions, by directing the discussion, by structuring and shaping the Agenda, and through the preparation and supervision of Options Memos.

The Chair's influence, then, is more indirect than direct. But this is appropriate. After all, if an issue is so clear cut that the Chair can decide it, it shouldn't be before the group in the first place.

THE MEMBER ROLE

The popular view is that the Member's role is a passive one with nothing to do and nothing special to know. ("There's nothing to it. All I have to do is show up and doze off.") Like so many popular views relative to meetings, this one is also wrong.

To begin with there is the matter of preparation. No procedural problems loom larger in poor meeting practice than those caused by the unprepared Member. Without proper preparation, discussion becomes prattle. The unprepared participant presents the worst of all possible role models for other Members. It is almost a truism that the unprepared Members of a group will attempt to cover their lack of preparation with bluster, rancor, sarcasm, and general negativity. So, preparation is the first responsibility of the Member.

Knowledge of how the meetings game is played is a second Member responsibility. This not only means a thorough understanding of good meeting procedures in general (such as the meeting rules presented here), but a complete knowledge of the specific rules of the committee upon which the Member sits. (Although the rules of some groups are more formal than for others, all group decision-making bodies have specific rules of their own.) It is the Member's responsibility throughout the life of the group to cooperate in the enforcement of committee rules. At the very least this includes such things as coming on time, coming prepared, and requiring the meeting planners to provide a straightforward Agenda.

Third, the Member needs constantly to monitor his or her level of participation in the meeting, contributing at a level that is appropriate for this particular group decision-making activity. Some groups are high participation groups; others, low participation. Within either context it is the Member's responsibility both to contribute at the appropriate level and to aid the Chair in seeing to it that all other Members likewise contribute appropriately.

Fourth, although issue crystalization and decision focus is generally the Chair's responsibility, it does not always have to be the Chair's actions that accomplish it. The Member should be constantly alert for opportunities to provide summative reflections at various points and to assist in the crystalization of ideas.

The Member should be equally alert to other Members who have a tendency to dump on the group; those who raise problems then sit back with arms folded as if to defy the group to provide solutions. It is both correct and useful when one has a problem with a particular proposal or line of thinking to share that perspective, provided such sharing is accompanied by good faith attempts to seek solutions. It is incorrect, unfair, and harmful for a Member to raise an issue without making it clear to the other Members where one is at with respect to that issue. It forces the group to shift its focus away from the issue and into a mode where it must probe to see what makes the recalcitrant Member happy.

Finally, Members owe loyalty to the group outside of the group. This means supporting group decisions that one opposed. It also means not knocking the group, its Members, or its Chair in other meetings, at cocktail parties, or anywhere else.

THE RECORDER ROLE

The individual who is taking the meeting record (using the Rule of Minutes, of course) is in a unique position to facilitate and focus the group discussion. This role is especially important for the Entrepreneurial Manager because meetings become a source of ideas for the Concept Bank. As the new meeting format involves not only a summarizing of discussion but also a brief statement of the actual resolution, the Recorder should use both of these to assist group functioning. As discussion is beginning to come to a close, for example, a Recorder can say something like, "Well, for the record, let me see if I understand the various points we have been discussing." A skilled Recorder can actually craft a summary on the spot and, in doing so, may uncover more or fewer areas of agreement than hitherto thought. In either case, it is to the advantage of the group. Similarly, the Recorder can shape the summative statement, itself. "As I understand it, here is what we have concluded." This helps to focus and crystalize group activity and to build support for group decisions.

THE STAFFER ROLE

A Staffer is an individual who is paid or assigned to assist a group in carrying out its functions. This individual is different from other participants because the Staffer is *not* a Member of the group. This point is extremely important. All groups know who are and who are not Members, even if everyone is well acquainted with one another, as is the case for most businesses.

The Staffer performs five kinds of functions for most committees. First, the Staffer is a researcher, providing various types of information for the group (political, historical, economic, scientific, items of program history, and so on).

Second, the Staffer is a knowledge synthesizer. It is not enough simply to present a range of information to a group (though some use it as a procedure for dumping on the group). Rather, the information should be organized, synthesized, and integrated. This function is an important one for the Staffer to perform. For a committee considering executive compensation, for example, the Staffer might say something like, "Here is a list of other companies and the compensation packages they provide their executives. They seem to fall into the following groups, based on what appear to me to be the following kinds of criteria and linked in the following ways to corporate income, and so forth."

Third, the Staffer is a writer and a documentor. The role may involve taking Minutes and recording. It usually involves the preparation of Reports, preparing Executive Summaries, and generally doing the "leg work" of the committee.

Fourth, the Staffer is an aide to the Chair. In meetings this usually involves sitting close by the Chair in a kind of dead zone that diminishes the physical position of the Staffer and emphasizes her or his "assisting" rather than "membering" function. The Staffer does not participate directly in discussions or decision making in the sense of giving her or his opinion on this matter or that.

Fifth, the Staffer is an administrator. In part this relates to the function of aiding the Chair, and this may involve many things. The Staffer may get out the Minutes, may assist in preparing the Agenda, may review meeting strategy with the Chair, may arrange for the meeting room, and so on. This "Stage Manager" activity is not especially dramatic, but it needs to be done if the setting for the meeting is to facilitate the meeting process rather than hamper it.

CONCLUSION

Meetings can be improved. Therefore, meetings should be improved. Improvement means that the output of meetings—decisions—should be of the highest possible quality. In moving toward high-quality decisions, we have presented procedures that shorten time, focus discussion, and generally make meetings less painful. But, it is important for you to understand that it is *not* removing pain from the meeting that is our goal. Rather, it is making the pain pay off.

As individuals experience meetings that are productive, that invite and involve their participation, a process of reinforcement will begin that will ultimately reverse the negative aspects of the self-fulfilling prophecy and use that mechanism for improvement and achievement.

15

Entrepreneurial Leadership: The Thing That Makes It Work

> Some people are born to be leaders. Others simply stumble into leadership. But most leaders are manufactured with surprising care and precision over a long period of time by the processes and social mechanisms—call them social machines—that make society work.
>
> —Gersh Morningstar

In this book we have been concerned primarily with the idea of Entrepreneurial Management and you, as the Entrepreneurial Manager. We have not focused particularly on starting a new business, though there is ample guidance here if you choose to do so. Neither have we been overly concerned with being in business for yourself—but again, there is much in these pages that can help you reduce your business risks. What we've really been centering on throughout our effort here is the importance of the new, the innovative, the creative.

Without an adequate supply of new ideas, the American organizational community—whether it's business or government or some nonprofit undertaking—is doomed to ever decreasing productivity and to ever increasing disappointments and failures in the world competitive community. The tragedy of this situation is twofold. First, it occurs. The tragedy should end there; but it doesn't because, second, it is completely *unnecessary*. All we have to do is look around us to see the abundance of creative and interesting ideas in our shops (our organizations, our Firms, our agencies, our offices, our bureaus). The concept and process of Entrepreneurial *Management* rests heavily on the need to develop or orchestrate or promote or follow-up on or implement—use whatever terms you prefer—these ideas so that some kind of organizational and behavioral change results from them. There can be no more important issue before this society. Those who are able to achieve progress toward this goal will have achieved Entrepreneurial Leadership.

Entrepreneurial Leadership differs from Entrepreneurial Management in that the Leadership component involves envisioning and enabling in ways that Management often does not achieve. The Entrepreneurial Leader is the one who *develops* and *implements* new ideas repeatedly and who *enables* others to do so, as well.

Entrepreneurial Leadership is desperately needed today in our three major organizational systems: business, government, and the nonprofit sector. A look at the erosion of the American competitive position in the world today ought to be sufficient evidence that such leadership is badly deficient at the present time.

The current problems of American business don't need retelling here. We're all familiar with them.

The problems of government activities and programs are also well-known, especially at the federal level. At least at the state and local levels some successes have been paired with the failures. (Assisting businesses and start-ups is one important area of such success.)

Our education system seems to be working very poorly. The criminal justice systems seems, if anything, to be counter productive. The nonprofit system seems replete with crises, from adoption agencies to symphony orchestras.

And these by no means exhaust the list.

Entrepreneurial Leadership encompasses Entrepreneurial Management, but it goes far beyond it, extending Entrepreneurial Management concepts to other spheres, other arenas. The Entrepreneurial Leader, in effect, spreads the word. Where Entrepreneurial Management harnesses and directs good ideas, Entrepreneurial Leadership extends, expands, and interlinks them. It is this capacity that must be recaptured in American enterprise, and it is this capacity that will reenergize the Systems where it is applied.

Bibliography

Abegglen, J. C. *The Strategy of Japanese Business* (Cambridge: Ballinger Publishing Company, 1984).

Allen, T. H. *New Methods in Social Science Research* (New York: Praeger, 1978).

Allison, D. *The R&D Game: Technical Men, Technical Managers and Research Productivity* (Boston: MIT Press, 1969).

Argyris, C. "Individual Actualization in Complex Organizations." In F. D. Carver and T. J. Sergiovanni (Eds.), *Organizations and Human Behavior: Focus on Schools* (New York: McGraw-Hill, 1969).

Argyris, C. *Reasoning, Learning and Action: Individual and Organizational* (San Franciso: Jossey-Bass, 1982).

Bass, B. M. (Ed.). *Stogdill's Handbook of Leadership* (New York: The Free Press, 1981).

Begley, T. M., and Boyd, D. "Psychological Characteristics Associated with Performance in Entrepreneurial Forms and Smaller Businesses." *Journal of Business Venturing*, 2, 1 (Winter 1987), pp. 79–93.

Bennis, W. G. "RX for Corporate Boards." *Technology Review*, 81, 3 (December 1978/January 1979), pp. 12ff.

Berry, W. "Beyond Strategic Planning." *Managerial Planning*, 29, 5 (March/April, 1981), pp. 12–15.

Bischoff, D. *The Manhattan Project* (New York: Avon, 1986).

Block, Z., and Ornati, O. "Compensating Corporate Venture Managers." *Journal of Business Venturing*, 2, 1 (Winter 1987), pp. 41–52.

Blustein, P. "Top Treasury Aide's Criticism May Trigger Debate on U.S. Productivity." *The Wall Street Journal*, November 10, 1986, p. 4.

Bok, D. *Higher Learning* (Cambridge, MA: Harvard University Press, 1986).

Bolton, R. H. *People Skills* (Englewood Cliffs, N J: Prentice-Hall, 1979).

Booker, D. *Send Me a Memo* (New York: Facts on File, 1984).

Boorstin, D. *The Americans—The Colonial Experience* (New York: Random House, 1958).

Boorstin, D. *The Americans—The National Experience* (New York: Random House, 1965).

Boorstin, D. *The Americans—The Democratic Experience* (New York: Random House, 1973).

Bramson, R. M. *Coping with Difficult People* (New York: Doubleday, 1981).

Brandt, S. *Entrepreneuring in Established Companies* (Homewood, IL: Dow-Jones Irwin, 1985).

Brooks, H., Liebman, L., and Shelling, C. S. (Eds.). *Public and Private Partnership: New Opportunities for Meeting Social Needs* (Cambridge, MA: Ballinger Publishing Company, 1984).

Brown, D. S. *Managing the Large Organization* (Mt. Airy, MD: Lomond, 1982).

Burch, J. G. *Entrepreneurship* (New York: Wiley, 1986).

Burgelman, R., and Sayles, L. *Inside Corporate Innovation: Strategy, Structure, and Managerial Skills* (New York: The Free Press, 1986).

Butlin, N. G., Barnard, A., and Pinkus, J. J. *Government and Capitalism: Public and Private Choice in Twentieth Century Australia* (Sidney, Australia: Allen and Unwin, 1982).

Carroll, D. T. "From the Boardroom." *Harvard Business Review*, 59, 5 (September/October 1981), pp. 62–66.

Charnes, A., and Cooper, W. W. *Creative and Innovative Management* (Cambridge, MA: Ballinger Publishing Company, 1984).

Checkoway, B. *Strategic Perspectives on Planning Practice* (Lexington, MA: Lexington Books, 1986).

Chochran, T. "Entrepreneurship." In D. L. Sills (Ed.), *The International Encyclopedia of Social Sciences* (New York: MacMillan/Free Press, 1968).

Churchill, N. C., and Lewis, V. L. "Growing Concerns." *Harvard Business Review*, 61, 3 (May/June 1983), pp. 31ff.

Cohen, M., March, J., and Olsen, J. P. "A Garbage Can Model of Organizational Choice." *Administrative Science Quarterly*, 17, 1 (March 1972), pp. 1–25.

Collins, B., and Guetzkow, H. *A Social Psychology of Group Processes for Decision Making* (New York: Wiley, 1964).

Cox, A. *The Cox Report on the American Corporation* (New York: Delacorte, 1982).

Crichton, M. *Sphere* (New York: Knopf, 1987).

Crosby, L. B. "The Just-in-Time Manufacturing Process: Control of Quality and Quantity." *Journal of the American Production and Inventory Control Society*, 26, 4 (Fourth Quarter 1985), pp. 94–100.

Daft, R. L., and Bradshaw, P. J. "The Process of Horizontal, Differentiation: Two Models." *Administrative Science Quarterly*, 25, 3 (September 1980), pp. 441–456.

Davis, S. M. *Managing Corporate Culture* (Cambridge, MA: Ballinger, 1984).

DeHartog, J. *The Peaceable Kingdom* (New York: Fawcett, 1971).

Delbecq, A., and Van de Ven, A. "A Group Process Model for Problem Identification and Program Planning." *Journal of Applied Behavioral Science*, 7 (September 1971), pp. 466–492.

deVries, M. "The Dark Side of Entrepreneurship." *Harvard Business Review*, 63, 6 (November/December, 1985), pp. 160–167.

Dreyfus, H., and Dreyfus, S. *Mind Over Machine: The Power of Human Intuition and Expertise in the Era of the Computer* (New York: The Free Press, 1986).

Drucker, P. *Innovation and Entrepreneurship* (New York: Harper and Row, 1985).

Dyer, W. *Pulling Your Own Strings* (New York: T. Y. Crowell, 1978).

Fiedler, F. E., et al. "Organizational Stress and the Use and Misuse of Managerial Intelligence and Experience." *Journal of Applied Psychology*, 64, 6 (December 1979), pp 635–647.

Filho, P. "Strategic Planning: A New Approach." *Managerial Planning*, 30, 5 (March/April, 1982), pp. 12–20.

Fischer, D. *Growing Old in America* (New York: Oxford, 1978).

Fisher, B., and Ury, W. *Getting to Yes* (New York: Houghton Mifflin, 1981).

Fitzgerald, T. Lecture. (October, 1987).

Flamholtz, E. G. *How to Make the Transition from an Entrepreneurship to a Professionally Managed Firm* (San Francisco: Jossey-Bass, 1986).

Ford, C. H. "Manage by Decisions, Not by Objectives." *Business Horizons*, 23, 1 (February 1980), pp. 7–18.

Frohman, A. L., and Ober, S. P. "Establishing Leaderships: How to Analyze and Deal with the Basic Issues." *Management Review*, 69, 4 (April 1980), pp. 46–54.

Fucini, J., and Fucini, S. *Entrepreneurs: The Men and Women Behind Famous Brand Names and How They Made It* (Boston: Gaven K. Hall, 1985).

Galambos, L., and Spence, B. *The Public Image of Big Business in America 1880–1940: A Quantitative Study in Social Change* (Baltimore, MD: Johns Hopkins University Press, 1975).

Galbraith, J. R. "Designing the Innovating Organization." *Organizational Dynamics* (Winter 1982), pp. 5–25.

Gartner, W. B. "A Conceptual Framework for Describing the Phenomenon of New Venture Creation." *Academy of Management Review*, 10, 4 (1985), pp. 696–706.

Garvin, D. "Competing on the Eight Divisions of Quality." *Harvard Business Review*, 65, 6 (November/December, 1987), pp. 101–109.

Garwood, R. D. "Explaining JIP, MRP II, Kanban." *P&IM Review* (October 1968), pp. 66ff.

Gevirtz, D. *The New Entrepreneurs* (New York: Penguin, 1984).

Giermak, E. A. "Individualism vs. the Committee Process." *Advanced Management*, 25, 12 (December 1960), pp. 16–19.

Greene, R. Personal Communication (1986).

Goffman, I. *The Presentation of Self in Everyday Life* (Garden, City: Doubleday/Anchor, 1959).

Gordon, W. J. J. *Synectics: The Development of Creative Capacity* (New York: Collier, 1961).

Griffiths, D. E. "Administration as Decision-Making." In F. D. Carver and T. J. Sergiovanni (Eds.), *Organizations and Human Behavior: Focus on Schools* (New York: McGraw-Hill 1969).

Groobey, J. "Making the Board of Directors More Effective." *California Management Review*, 16, 3 (Spring 1974), pp. 25–34.

Grove, A. *High Output Management* (New York: Random House, 1983).

Gwe, F. "Push, Pull, Z1, JIT Production Methods: A Perspective." *Proceedings of the American Production Control Society*, Twenty-Eighth Annual International Conference, Toronto, 1985, pp. 116–119.

Haft, R. "Business Decisions by the New Board." *Michigan Law Review*, 80 (November 1981), pp. 1–67.

Hamby, R. "Gender and Sex-Role Behavior in Problem Solving Groups." *Sociological Focus*, 11, 3 (August 1978), pp. 211–219.

Hardacer, M., and White, B. K. "How to Make a Team Work." *Harvard Business Review*, 65, 6 (November/December, 1987), pp. 112–120.

Harrigan, B. L. *Games Your Mother Never Taught You* (New York: Warner, 1978).

Hasenfeld, Y., and Tropman, J. E. "Interorganizational Relations." In F. Cox, et al. (Eds.), *Strategies of Community Organization* (Itasca, IL.: F. E. Peacock, 1979).

Hauser, P. "Aging and World-Wide Population Change." In R. Binstock and E. Shanas (Eds.). *Handbook of Aging and the Social Sciences* (New York: Van Nostrand Reinhold, 1976).

Hawkins, K. L., and Turla, P. H. *Test Your Entrepreneurial I.Q.* (New York: Berkley Books, 1986).

Heinlein, R. *Stranger in a Strange Land* (New York: Putnam, 1963).

Heskett, J. L. *Managing in the Service Economy* (Cambridge, MA: Harvard Business School, 1986).

Hirokawa, R. Y., and Poole, M. S. (Eds.). *Communication and Group Decision Making* (Beverly Hills: Sage Publications, 1985).

Hirshman, A. O. *Shifting Involvements* (Princeton, NJ: Princeton University Press, 1981).

Hisrich, R. D. *Entrepreneurship, Intrapreneurship and Venture Capital* (Boston: Lexington Books, 1986).

Holcombe, M., and Stein, J. *Writing for Decision Makers, Memos and Reports with a Competitive Edge* (Belmont, CA: Wadsworth, 1981).

Holloman, C. R., and Hendrick, H. W. "Adequacy of Group Decisions as a Function of the Decision Making Process." *Academy of Management Journal*, 15, 2 (June 1972), pp. 175–184.

Hoselitz, B. "The Early History of Entrepreneurial Theory." *Explorations in Entrepreneurial History*, 3 (1951), pp. 193–220.

Hosmer, L. "Entrepreneurship: What Is It?" Unpublished paper, University of Michigan, 1985.

Hosmer, L. T., Cooper, A. C., and Vesper, K. H. *The Entrepreneurial Function* (Englewood Cliffs, NJ: Prentice-Hall, 1977).

Janis, I. L. "Groupthink." *Psychology Today*, 5, 6 (November 1971), pp. 43–53.

Janis, I., and Mann, L. *Decision Making* (New York: The Free Press, 1977).

Jay, A. *Corporation Man* (New York: Random House, 1971).

Jay, A. "How to Run a Meeting." *Harvard Business Review*, 54, 2 (March/April, 1976), pp. 43–57.

Jones, C. "If I Knew then . . . " (A personal essay on committees and public policy). *Policy Analysis*, 5, 4 (Fall 1979), pp. 473–479.

Kanter, R. *The Change Masters* (New York: Touchstone Books, 1983).

Kaufman, H. *Time, Chance, and Organizations: Natural Selection in a Perilous Environment* (Chatham, NJ: Chatham House, 1985).

Kidder, T. *The Soul of a New Machine* (New York: Avon, 1981).

Kirkland, C. "Just in Time Manufacturing: What You Need to Know and Why." *Plastics Technology* (August 1984), pp. 63–68.

Kuhn, R. L. *Frontiers in Creative and Innovative Management* (Cambridge, MA: Ballinger, 1985).

Land's End Catalog, v. 23, 4 (1987), p. 112.

LaPorte, T. R., Ed. *Organized Social Complexity* (Princeton, NJ: Princeton University Press, 1975).

Lawton, M. P. "Environment and Other Determinants of Well Being in Older People." *The Gerontologist*, 23 (1983), pp. 349–357.

Levinson, H. *The Great Jackass Fallacy* (Boston: Division of Research Graduate School of Business Administration, 1973).

Leyton, E. T., Jr. "The Most Original." *The American Heritage of Invention and Technology*, 2, 3 (Spring 1987), pp. 50–56.

Libnick, F., *Wall Street Journal* (September 22, 1986), p. 16.

Liles, P. *New Business Ventures and the Entrepreneur* (Homewood, IL: Irwin, 1975).

Lippitt, R., Watson, G., and Westley, B. *The Dynamics of Planned Change: A Comparative Study of Principles and Techniques* (New York: Harcourt Brace and World, 1958).

Lipset, S. M. *The First New Nation* (New York: Basic Books, 1963).

Lipset, S. M., and Schneider, W. *The Confidence Gap* (New York: The Free Press, 1983).

Lockwood, P. "Ideal-Type Analysis." In J. Gould and W. Kolb (Eds.), *A Dictionary of the Social Sciences* (New York: The Free Press, 1964).

Lundstedt, S. B., and Colglazier, E. W., Jr. *Managing Innovation: The Social Dimensions of Creativity, Invention and Technology* (New York: Pergamon Press, 1982).

Lynd, Robert. *Knowledge for What* (Princeton: Princeton University Press, 1939).

Maidique, M. "Entrepreneurs, Champions, and Technological Innovations." *Sloan Management Review*, 21, 2 (Winter 1980), pp. 59–76.

Malinowski, B. *Magic, Science and Religion* (New York: Doubleday, 1954).

March, J. G. (Ed.). *The Handbook of Organizations* (Chicago: Rand McNally, 1965).

March, J. G., and Wessinger-Baylon, R. *Ambiguity and Command* (Marshfield, MA: Pittman Publishing, 1986).

March, J. G., and Simon, H. *Organizations* (New York: Wiley, 1958).

Mason, D. E. *Voluntary Nonprofit Enterprise Managements* (New York: Plenum, 1985).

Mazzolini, R. "How Strategic Decisions Are Made." *Long Range Planning*, 14, 3, (1981), pp. 85–96.

McCormack, M. *What They Don't Teach You at the Harvard Business School* (New York: Bantam, 1986).

McCoy, C. S. *Management of Values* (Boston: Ballinger, 1985).

McGregor, D. *The Human Side of Enterprise* (New York: McGraw-Hill, 1960).

Merton, R. K. *Social Theory and Social Structure*, rev. ed. (Glencoe: The Free Press, 1957).

Michael, S. R. "Feedforward vs. Feedback Controls in Central Planning." *Managerial Planning*, 29, 4 (November/December 1980), pp. 34–38.

Miles, R., et al. "Organizational Strategy, Structure, and Process." *Academy of Management Review*, 3, 3 (July 1978), pp. 546–562.

Miller, L. *American Spirit* (New York: Morrow, 1984).

Mintzberg, H., and Waters, J. A. "Tracking Strategy in an Entrepreneurial Firm." *Academy of Management Journal*, 25, 3 (1982) pp. 465–499.

Monden, Y. *Toyota Production Systems* (Norcross, GA: Industrial Engineering and Management Press, 1983).

Moore, C. "Understanding Entrepreneurial Behavior." Paper given at the Academy of Management, Chicago, 1986.

Morita, A. *Made in Japan* (New York: E. P. Dutton, 1986).

Morris, I. *On the Nobility of Failure* (New York: Holt, Rinehart, and Winston, 1975).

Naisbitt, J. *Megatrends* (New York: Warner, 1983).

O'Connor, L. "Business Warned: Change Now or Die." *Detroit Free Press*, September 7, 1987, p. 1.

O'Toole, P. *Corporate Messiah* (New York: NAL, 1985).

Ouchi, W. *Theory Z* (New York: Avon, 1982).

Parmalee, R. "JIT Implementation by the Numbers." *Proceedings of American Production and Inventory Control Society*, Twenty-Eighth Annual International Conference, Toronto, October 1985, pp. 457–461.

Parsons, T. *The Structure of Social Action* (Glencoe: The Free Press, 1949).

Parsons, T. *The Social System* (Glencoe: The Free Press of Glencoe, 1951).

Parsons, T. *Structure and Process in Modern Societies* (Glencoe: The Free Press of Glencoe, 1960).

Parsons, T. "Suggestions for a Sociological Approach to the Theory of Organizations." In A. Etzioni (Ed.), *Complex Organizations: A Sociological Reader* (New York: Holt, Rinehart, and Winston, 1961).

Pascale, R. T., and Athos, A. *The Art of Japanese Management* (New York: Warner, 1982).

Patton, A., & Baker, J. C. "Why Won't Directors Rock the Boat?" *Harvard Business Review*, 65, 6 (November/December, 1987), pp. 10–18.

Peter, L. J. *The Peter Principal* (New York: Bantam, 1970).

Peter, L. J. *The Peter Prescription* (New York: Bantam, 1972).

Peters, T., and Waterman, R. *In Search of Excellence* (New York: Harper and Row, 1982).

Pfeiffer, J. E. "Early Man Stages a Summit Meeting in New York City." *Smithsonian*, 15, 5 (August 1984), pp. 50–57.

Pfeiffer, J. E. "Cro-Magnon Hunters Were Really Us, Working Out Strategies for Survival." *Smithsonian*, 17, 7 (October 1986), pp. 75–84.

Pinchot, G. *Entrepreneuring* (New York: Harper and Row, 1984).

Popcorn, F. "Comfort and Indulgence Among Trends." *Entrepreneur*, 14, 10 (October 1986), p. 10.

Quinn, J. B. "Technological Innovation, Entrepreneurship and Strategy." *Sloan Management Review*, 20, 3 (Spring 1979) pp. 19–30.

Quinn, R. *Beyond Rational Management* (San Franciso: Jossey-Bass, forthcoming).

Reich, R. B. *The Next American Frontier* (New York: Times Books, 1983).

Riggs, H. *Managing High-Technology Companies* (Belmont, CA: Lifetime Learning Publications, 1983).

Ronstadt, R. C. *Entrepreneurship* (Dover, MA: Lord Publishing, 1985).

Rosovsky, H. "Deaning." *Harvard Magazine*, 89, 3 (January/February, 1987), pp. 34–40.

Rotter, J. "Generalized Expectancies for Internal Versus External Control of Reinforcement," *Psychological Monographs*, 80, 1 (Whole #609) (1966).

Sargent, A. *The Androgynous Manager* (New York: Amacom, 1981).

Sayles, L., and Chandler, M. *Managing Large Systems* (New York: Harper and Row, 1971).

Schein, E. *Organizational Culture and Leadership* (San Francisco: Jossey-Bass, 1985).

Scientific American, 256, 3 (March, 1987), quoting from the March 1887 issue of *Scientific American*.

Setterberg, F., and Schulman, K. *Beyond Profit: Everything You Need to Manage the Non-Profit Organization* (New York: Harper and Row, 1985).

Sexton, D. L., and Van Haken, P. *Experiences in Entrepreneurship and Small Business Management* (Englewood Cliffs, NJ: Prentice-Hall, 1982).

Sexton, D. L., and Simlor, R. W. (Eds.). *The Art and Science of Entrepreneurship* (Cambridge, MA: Ballinger, 1985).

Silver, A. D. *The Entrepreneurial Life* (New York: Wiley, 1983).

Simon, H., Smithburg, D., and Thompson, V. *Public Administration* (New York: Knopf, 1956).

Slade, J. W. "The Man Behind the Killing Machine." *The American Heritage of Invention and Technology*, 2, 2 (Fall 1986), pp. 18–25.

Sprague, R. H., Jr., and Watson, H. J. (Eds.). *Decision Support Systems* (Englewood Cliffs, NJ: Prentice Hall, 1986).

Stack, C. *All Our Kin* (New York: Harper, 1975).

Stinchcomb, A. "Social Structure and Organizations." In J. G. March (Ed.), *Handbook of Organizations* (Chicago: Rand McNally, 1965).

Taylor, C. "Do You Have What It Takes (to be an entrepreneur?)." *B & F Review* (July 1985), pp. 3–5.

Tichy, N. M., and Devanna, M. A. *The Transformational Leader* (New York: Wiley, 1986).

Towers, F. Personal communication, 1986.

Tropman, E. J., and Tropman, J. E. "Voluntary Agencies." *18th Edition of the Encyclopedia of Social Work*. 1987.

Tropman, J. E. *Policy Management in the Human Services* (New York: Columbia University Press, 1984).

Tropman, J. E. *Public Policy Opinion and the Elderly* (Westport, CT: Greenwood, 1987).

Tropman, J. E. (with Gersh Morningstar). *Meetings: How to Make Them Work for You* (New York: Van Nostrand, 1984).

Tuchman, B. *March of Folly* (New York: Knopf, 1984).

Vesper, K. H. *New Venture Strategies* (Englewood Cliffs, NJ: Prentice Hall, 1980).

Vinter, R. *Budgeting for Nonprofits* (New York: The Free Press, 1984).

Vroom, V. H., and Yetton, P. W. *Leadership and Decision-Making* (Pittsburgh: University of Pittsburgh Press, 1976).

Wall Street Journal, December 12, 1986. Allen Michael's comments on the prelude to the failure of his firm, Convergent Technologies, Inc.

Wholey, J. S., Abramson, M. A., and Bellavita, C. *Performance and Credibility: Developing Excellence in Public and Nonprofit Organizations* (Lexington, MA: Lexington Books, 1985).

Whyte, W. H. *The Organization Man* (New York: Simon and Schuster, 1957).

Wicther, S. K. "How One Economist Tries to Keep Abreast of Third World Trends." *Wall Street Journal*, January 2, 1987, p. 1.

Wildavsky, A. Personal communication. 1960.

Wissema, J., Van der Pol, H., and Messer, H. "Strategic Management Archetypes."
    Strategic Management Journal (January/March, 1980), pp. 37–47.
Wolfe, T. *The Right Stuff* (New York: Bantam, 1984).
Wooden, J. "On Staying Power." *New York Times Magazine—The Business World*, Part
    2 (June 8, 1986).
Yankee Magazine (September, 1986).
Yankelovich, D. *New Rules* (New York: Random House, 1981).
Yinger, J. M. *Countercultures* (New York: The Free Press, 1982).
Zander, A. *Making Groups Effective* (San Francisco: Jossey-Bass. 1982).
Zell, S. Personal communication, 1986.
Ziller, R. C. "Four Techniques of Group Decisionmaking Under Uncertainty."
    Journal of Applied Psychology, 41, 6 (1957), pp. 384–394.

Index

About the Authors

JOHN E. TROPMAN is Professor of Administration at the University of Michigan. His previous books include *Public Policy Opinion and the Elderly* (Greenwood Press, 1987), *Policy Management in the Human Services*, and *Meetings: How to Make Them Work for You*.

GERSH MORNINGSTAR is Managing Editor of *Central Florida Film and Entertainment Revue*.